M000307894

JUST LIKE FAMILY

ANIMALS IN CONTEXT
General Editor: Colin Jerolmack

Just Like Family

How Companion Animals Joined the Household

Andrea Laurent-Simpson

NEW YORK UNIVERSITY PRESS
New York

NEW YORK UNIVERSITY PRESS
New York
www.nyupress.org

© 2021 by New York University
All rights reserved

References to Internet websites (URLs) were accurate at the time of writing. Neither the author nor New York University Press is responsible for URLs that may have expired or changed since the manuscript was prepared.

Cataloging-in-Publication data is available from the publisher.

Library of Congress Cataloging-in-Publication Data
Names: Laurent-Simpson, Andrea, author.
Title: Just like family : how companion animals joined the household / Andrea Laurent-Simpson.
Description: New York : NYU Press, 2021. | Series: Animals in context | Includes bibliographical references and index.
Identifiers: LCCN 2020048476 | ISBN 9781479828852 (hardback) | ISBN 9781479852628 (paperback) | ISBN 9781479851300 (ebook) | ISBN 9781479875887 (ebook other)
Subjects: LCSH: Animal welfare. | Pet adoption. | Pets. | Human-animal relationships.
Classification: LCC HV4708 .L38 2021 | DDC 636.088/7—dc23
LC record available at https://lccn.loc.gov/2020048476

New York University Press books are printed on acid-free paper, and their binding materials are chosen for strength and durability. We strive to use environmentally responsible suppliers and materials to the greatest extent possible in publishing our books.

Manufactured in the United States of America

10 9 8 7 6 5 4 3 2 1

Also available as an ebook

For Mark, Aidan, Alex, Sam, Sadie,
and
Chewbacca Bear

CONTENTS

Introduction

This was the third time I had heard this, and from increasingly qualified specialists at that. Lymphoma with about thirty days left. I looked over at her big, brown, inquisitive eyes and marveled at how much we had shared over the past ten years. I had learned so much about myself from her. I knew she could comprehend everything that was being said in the exam room right now. Of course, I did not think she could understand words like "terminal," "chemotherapy," "vincristine," and "rescue drug," but I knew that she could sense the cocktail of gaping grief, denial, and hope in which I was currently floating. She inched closer to my side, using her moist snout to incessantly poke at my elbow—chow chow for "Move your arm out of the way. My chin should be there!" The gentle nuzzle that followed once I moved my arm said, "Is everything all right?"

"Stop," I said to the oncologist. "I'm not going to talk about options in front of her. Could one of the technicians take her out into the lobby?"—meaning it to be a question but clearly framing it as a demand.

She looked at me earnestly, pausing a moment, and then replied, "Yes, of course."

"I'm sorry, I know that seems ridiculous," I muttered, deflated. Chewbacca slowly stretched down off the bench, stopping characteristically to stare in suspicion at the tech who gently called her name. He jangled the leash by the exit, and after a bit of consideration, she cautiously accepted his suggestion.

"Of course not. You'd be surprised at how many clients say the exact same thing."

I watched Chewbacca, carefully but compliantly, follow the tech out of the room, her furry, red mane brushing across the door jamb as she pushed through the opening, ready to leave yet another veterinary exam room. In her ten years of life, she had been relatively healthy, only smelling the foreign but strangely familiar environment of a veterinary hospital for yearly exams and shots. But she and I had shared new territory over the past two weeks as I trudged from clinic to clinic searching for a different prognosis. I had refused to accept that the lumps in her neck indicated the diabolical spread of a terminal cancer.

In fact, I had been convinced that the first two veterinarians we visited (one our general practitioner, the other a private-practice veterinary oncologist in Dallas) were nothing but profit mongers seeking to saddle my husband and me with extensive, expensive treatments. Chewbacca could not be in stage 3 of a lymphoma diagnosis. She was eating and drinking well, loving and communicative, happy . . . *and* kissed me hello every morning. The only reason I had taken her to our family veterinarian had been because of those lumps. Sure, she had slowed down her activity in the past month, but she was ten years old, for goodness' sake. I was not going to allow some rapacious veterinarian to give my baby a potentially disastrous, debilitating chemo treatment just so he could line his pockets.

The protective mommy and the cautious consumer crashed together in a furious storm of denial, and before I knew it, I had wasted two weeks of her life. But now . . . now I was at the Texas A&M Veterinary Medical Teaching Hospital. There were no profit motives here. And the doctor with whom I was finally discussing alternative treatments was in the final year of her veterinary oncology residency. I had obviously let my sweet baby down. Now my husband and I had to do everything we could to maintain her quality of life in those last days—and to be ready to accept when the time came to let her go.

By the end of our meeting, I was reeling at the choices that had to be made, but as Chew Bear glared at me indignantly for having left her out in the waiting area, I felt strangely calm. As a trained researcher, knowledge has always made me feel empowered, and I left that veterinary hospital feeling like our family at least knew what we were in for. She would not be forever ripped from us in four weeks, and we would focus on experimental interventions and quality of life for all of us. I gently patted the back seat, asking her to jump in, and climbed into the driver's side, saying, "Let's go get you some ice cream."

It was in that instant that I realized the gravity of what I had been doing. How had I not seen it? And, more embarrassingly, who *else* had seen it? The intersubjectivity, or the shared meaning that we have with others, was palpable. Indeed, as a sociologist, I know that who we are, our perceived realities, is wrapped up in our interactions with one another, the meaning developed, and definitions forged in those interactions. But, up to that point, I had understood that perspective to be applicable to humans only, not animals.

In my case, we had always called Chewbacca "our baby," though I suspect now that my husband had adopted that particular identity pairing with her because I had. But our relationship went far deeper than a simple label could indicate, at least between a companion animal and her owners. She had really been like a young child to me, and I had eventually internalized what some scholars have called an idiosyncratic version of "parent" to her. I had adopted her before ever meeting my husband, and she had come screaming into my twenty-year-old undergraduate lifestyle with the middle-of-the-night screeching protests that first-time parents of human children report make them like zombies. However, unlike what first-time parents of human children are permitted to do, I promptly stuck the poor girl out on my tiny concrete patio each night, hoping that the neighbors would not wake up and that I would get to fall asleep. That had only made it worse for both of us (and countless neighbors, I am sure).

"Put her in the bed with you," my father had counseled. "She misses her littermates and her mommy. She'll feel your warmth, snuggle up with you, and love you for life if you do this for her now." Before I knew it, I was not only co-sleeping with Chewbacca but running home at lunch to let her out for play time, strolling the pet-supply aisle at Walmart for surprise stuffed animals and treats, and having "conversations" with her (and for her) over dinner about how both of our days had gone.

My Finnish future mother-in-law, who started calling me "Mommy" when she "spoke for" Chewbacca, extended that relationship to create something akin to grandmother. When we visited Farmor (Swedish for "father's mother"—a distinction that is missed in English because the language removes that relational element by simply using an all-encompassing "grandmother") for dinner, she would coddle Chew Bear, telling her how smart she was and what a beautiful girl she was. And then Famoo would look at me, patting that big, red, furry face by her side, and say, "Mommy, can't I just have one bite of your chicken?" or "Mommy, look how beautiful I am now that Famoo has given me a good brushing!" I, of course, would dotingly respond, eye to eye with that dog, as if she had spoken directly from her own two flews, saying, "Of course you are gorgeous, but only one piece of chicken. We don't want you to get sick!" This was usually followed by a good-natured scolding of Farmor for spoiling her.

An outsider looking in (or possibly anyone reading this right now) would have probably thought these interactions a bit ridiculous. But, looking back, Chewbacca was clearly a social actor in my mind, prancing around our negotiations with intentionality and nods to our shared history together.[1] My demands for obedience (which were inevitably negotiated into "requests" that she carefully considered before deciding to act) were met with measured acquiescence or firm denial, depending on her emotional state at the moment. If I suggested "going to the park," I could not open that car door fast enough for her. However, if I mentioned the veterinarian, she would sulk in defiance as far away from the back door as she could manage (I, in fact, learned very quickly *not* to mention the veterinarian at all). If it was time to bathe her and she did not agree, then I had to think of tantalizing distractions (like peanut butter or a favored squeaky toy) that would convince her otherwise. Indeed, those distractions were typically based on our history together and what had been successful in the past—much like her responses to my "requests" were capped at a certain level of my patience—a point that she intimately understood all too well. I knew her needs at the flick of a tail, the nudge of a nose, the intensity of a glance. And she interpreted my words, moods, and physical actions with the ease of a well-versed family member, layered in the shared intimate knowledge of one another that is so characteristic of primary groups like the family.

I was fiercely loyal, protective, and proud of her—and my husband bought into the relationship wholeheartedly. She traveled everywhere with us, and when she could not go where we went, she stayed at Famoo's house, spoiled with new toys, treats, and co-sleeping. Playing the game that couples in love play sometimes, I liked to ask my husband whom he would save from drowning in a lake first, Chew Bear or me. "You, of course!" he would proclaim, then turn the question on me.

"Well, I would save you both together." But he would playfully press for an answer, with me finally admitting, "Well, Chew Bear first. She'd be in more danger. And then I would go back for you!" Of course, he has never let me live that down (fortunately for all of us, we never had to find out!). She was my baby, and I was her Mommy—she depended on me. This would have been my job anyway in our child-centered culture. Period.

And so it had gone in our ten years together as a human-childfree family—allowing neighborhood children to play with her so that she was properly "socialized," asking for her opinion on dog beds at Pet Smart, bringing Famoo along to help on our move to Los Angeles by watching Chew Bear while we hunted for pet friendly housing, shirking my job responsibilities as a new teacher at my first job (and being sanctioned by my employer for doing so) so that my husband and I could desperately search for her when she disappeared from our new condominium patio for two days straight, interviewing and choosing new veterinarians carefully, researching vaccination schedules for her in her youth and doling out heartworm and flea medications religiously, and now seeking a way to keep her with us, battling lymphoma but without the perils and pain of chemotherapy.

But none of that had seemed unusual at all, to me at least. What struck me then, sitting in the car at Dairy Queen with Chew Bear (who had devoured a kid-sized ice cream cone in one fell swoop), was what I had asked the oncology resident to do as we spoke about treatments. I had asked her to take Chew Bear out of the room because I did not want her to suffer through a conversation that included discussion of how vincristine leakage from the IV could eat away the tissue around her paw and cause tremendous pain. I did not want her to listen to us discuss the expense of treatment as if we could place a price on her pain-free life. I did not want her to even conceive of the idea that I would consider euthanasia. And all of this was because I knew she understood. At minimum, she understood the gravity of the situation. She had been an extremely intelligent dog, and—deep down—I knew she understood that we were speaking about her death.

* * *

This book is about family—a particular kind of family, one that has gradually emerged in its current form as part and parcel of the diversification of the American family since the early 1970s. This book is about the American "multispecies" family. In it, I provide a sociological treatment of the development of this new form of family via analysis of original data collected over the course of four years. My data come from multiple sources, including thirty-five in-depth interviews with people who own dog(s), cat(s), or both and who hail from multiple types of family structures in the United States, including both voluntarily and involuntarily childless families, families with children under eighteen, and "empty nest" families. Over one hundred hours of veterinary-clinic observations provide insight on the kinds of commitments families make to their four-legged family members. Finally, an in-depth content analysis of advertisements geared toward companion-animal owners provides a macro-level examination of how the multispecies family has become firmly entrenched in American cultural expectations of who counts as family.[2]

The preceding story about my first multispecies family as a married, childfree (at least at the time) adult has remained a primary driver behind the collection of these data, the project, and, ultimately, the desire to write this book. Although Chewbacca passed away in 2005, ten months before the birth of my first son, her memory is alive and well, periodically bubbling to the surface of my lived experiences within my current multispecies family. Both of my children know her name and have heard countless stories about her. The little red cedar chest that we were given upon her cremation still holds a prime spot in the top drawer of my nightstand, its shiny brass plate a reminder of another family life from so long ago. And, up until a recent reorganization of our household, we still kept a few pictures of the three of us in the Grand Canyon together on display in our front entryway.

Such a long-term commitment to a dog, even well beyond her passing, is a testament to the fact that dogs and cats in multispecies families like the one I have described with Chew Bear are more than just pets. They are also more than just generalized family members. They are significant others, recognized social actors who, in concert with their humans, have the capability to transform family structures into distinct forms of family with unique requirements.

Both of my boys, well aware of my research trajectory in this regard, have opened their eyes to instances of this new form of family and become accustomed to pointing it out when observed. An example of their developing sense of qualitative research in the area came in the spring of 2019 while we were standing in the checkout lane of our local grocery store.

My nine-year-old had been perusing the magazine racks as we waited when he called out to me, "Mom! You've gotta see this! You just gotta see this!"

Initially, I resisted. "No, baby, we just need to get through the line. Piano lessons start in twenty minutes."

"But, Mom! You'll love this! It's about dogs!" His enthusiasm was sweet, but I had things to do, plus a meal to plan out that evening—and no intention of buying a magazine.

"I'm sure it's great. Why don't you take a look at it and tell me what you find when we get to the car?"

"Okay," he said, a bit disappointed. "I just thought you would like it. It says 'pet parenting' on it."

I immediately pressed pause on my resistance and turned toward him. He had already turned back to the rack when I caught him, saying, "That actually sounds pretty interesting. Can I see it?" A broad smile spread across his face, and he excitedly handed the magazine over to me. It was titled *The Essential Dog: Pet Parenting Reimagined* (see figure I.1). He had hit upon something that—even as I was writing this book—I had failed to notice. There, in the checkout lane, was a magazine targeted toward multispecies family consumers who had a parent-child identity pairing with their dog(s). I flipped through it, somehow surprised that such a thing existed. The perpetual line ahead of us began moving. I flipped faster, quickly snapped a photo of the cover, and asked my son to place it back on the rack from whence it came.

In the following months, I have started paying closer attention to magazine racks, with a sociological eye geared toward identifying other such offerings that might suggest that the "multispecies" family that I discuss in this book has increasingly become an acceptable mode of "doing family" in the United States. And I have found more publications to this end. For example, *The Ultimate Guide to the Animal Mind* promises to teach owners how to decode their pet's personality and learn the secret languages of cats and dogs. *USA Today* published *Pet Guide* with stories about food trucks that cater to our dogs, tips for bringing kitty home (similar to tips for bringing your human infant home), and other features that would help you discern whether your dog needs eyeglasses and how pet insurance works. *A Letter to My Dog: Moving Stories and Tender Notes* is a special issue

Figure I.1. Pet parenting reimagined

chock full (literally front to back, excluding the table of contents and the front and back covers) of letters from celebrities, children, athletes, soldiers, and so on to one (or many) of their closest family members, their dogs. These letters are accompanied by pictures of the dog(s) and/or their owners, often with intensely tender moments

depicted. Almost half of the letters written are signed with some v
sion of "Mom" or "Dad."

The multispecies family that I discuss in this book is not just alive and
well. It is thriving. This book is my effort as a sociological social psychologist to illuminate its prominence as a special type of family structure in which identities that are typically reserved for humans are now
intimately acknowledged in the animal companion. This book is also
my way of calling attention to its growing significance within American
culture.

A Sociology of the Multispecies Family

Sociology as a discipline has traditionally confined its study to human
society, investigating the origins and development of such; interaction
of various social structures; social problems that arise within these contexts; and human interaction, meaning making, and resultant behaviors.
The field has always been dominated by an anthropocentric viewpoint
(that is, that humans are the center of the universe and necessarily the
most important element to be considered). Only recently has sociology seen development of subdisciplines that attempt to examine the
entanglement of human society with nonhuman animals, science and
technology studies, and the environment. Much of this original exclusion of nonhuman animals (and other nonhuman entities) rested on
claims originating in the thought of the seventeenth-century philoso-
pher René Descartes. Descartes argued that nonhuman animals in
particular were mindless machines incapable of thought and feeling,
primarily because they were alingual (or without speech). Privileging
human language as exhibiting consciousness, intentionality, and soul,
the Cartesian orthodoxy would, carte blanche, nearly strike nonhuman
animals from social scientific research for the next few hundred years.
Indeed, the ability to communicate via spoken language would be used
as part of the epistemological foundation for anthropocentric knowledge production.

Scant exceptions to this claim on human exceptionalism and specific
to sociology arose in the first half of the twentieth century. For example, Max Weber, a classical theorist of sociology who used a social conflict perspective, noted that animals might be of use in a sociological

analysis of the "relations of men to animals, both domestic and wild. Thus, many animals 'understand' commands, anger, love, hostility, and react to them in ways . . . both consciously and meaningful and affected by experience."[3] However, Weber failed to produce much beyond this observation in his own theoretical work. Alternatively, Talcott Parsons, a contemporary theorist of sociology, argued that animals lacked mind-edness and were ruled by biological programming that disallowed for goal-oriented interactions characteristic of lingual humans.[4] Likewise, Émile Durkheim, a classical theorist of sociology in the structural func-tional tradition, used "homo duplex" to describe the inferior status of nonhuman animals. That is, human nature is twofold, with humans driven by instinct on the one hand but also guided by morality that has been produced within society. Nonhumans were different, he argued, incapable of moving beyond their own immoral, passionate individual-ism to create the social solidarity and social facts that are unique to the collective consciousness of human society.[5] As a microsociologist, Erv-ing Goffman engaged nonhuman animals as mere props or "expressive equipment" to be used in human interaction and performance.[6]

However, George Herbert Mead's work in the area is probably the most influential source of a complete elimination of the nonhuman animal from the purview of sociological thought.[7] Mead contended that nonhuman animals lack the symbolic nature of human language—leaving them devoid of the ability to negotiate meaning and only capable of instinctual stimulus response needed for survival.[8] Furthermore, he claimed that when people do perceive animals as minded, they are sim-ply engaging in anthropomorphism (assigning human-like qualities to nonhumans). As a result, Mead argued, "We, of course, tend to endow our domestic animals with personality, but as we get insight into their conditions we see there is no place for this sort of importation of the social process into the conduct of the individual. They do not have the mechanism for it—language. . . . We put personalities into the animals, but they do not belong to them; and ultimately we realize that those animals have no rights."[9]

Mead's sociological canon would later be coined as "symbolic inter-action" by his student Herbert Blumer because of its emphasis on the repeated use of linguistic symbols between individuals as they interact with one another. This repetition, and the interpretation of meaning that each actor engages in across the course of varying interactions, helps to produce and reproduce the meaning that shapes the social world while simultaneously shaping individual interaction. The replication of earlier social scientific beliefs regarding human exceptionalism became inherent in symbolic interactionism and would continue to influence the discipline toward anthropocentric analyses for several decades. Indeed, even today, an analysis of a range of Introduction to Sociology textbooks confirms that, even when animals are mentioned to the discipline's earliest students, it is to confirm the dichotomy present between human and nonhuman animal and highlight human exceptionalism in the process.[10]

The classic call for sociology to open its "minds" came from Clifton D. Bryant, an American sociologist who pointed out that nonhuman animals were inherent to human social life and thus could not simply be removed from a sociological analysis of society. Accusing sociologists of being "derelict in their failure to address the zoological component in human interaction and attendant social systems," Bryant demanded that the discipline acknowledge the influence of sentient animals on everything "human," including their presence in every facet of human culture and language, their involvement in social problems, their entanglement with work and crime, and (specific to this book) their presence as surrogate humans within the family sphere.[11] Raymond Murphy, a Canadian environmental sociologist, has since critiqued the discipline, lamenting the practice of sociology "as if nature did not matter." Indeed, creating a dualism between human and animal has "obscure[d] what we share, . . . and this too is crucial for understanding social action" and society.[12]

Both of these calls to action as well as the trailblazing work of multiple, contemporary sociologists working in human-animal interaction, identity theory, and family demography have been inspiring to my work and the book that I now find myself writing. The symbolic interactionist approach has been especially grounding for me as I tiptoe in the steps of scholars determined to break the paradigm from its anthropocentric stranglehold. This work includes stalwarts in the effort such as the American sociologist Clinton R. Sanders, whose counterarguments to traditional symbolic interaction have produced the foundational concept of "doing mind" for the companion animal.[13] Groundbreaking work on the sentience and agency of companion animals from another prominent American sociologist, Leslie Irvine, has driven me to assess how such recognition would promulgate the intimate familial bonds that are now characteristic of so many multispecies families today.[14] The ethnographic accounting of cat culture by the American sociologists Janet and Steven Alger has continually reminded me that these bonds are interspecies (and intraspecies) in nature and cannot simply be anthropocentrically analyzed as the result of human perception.[15]

Regarding foundational, interdisciplinary work on the multispecies family, I stand on the shoulders of the sociologist Adrian Franklin's sociohistorical treatment of human-animal relations ensconced in modernity and postmodernity in the West and the sociologist Nickie Charles's discourse regarding the potential for posthuman families steeped in multispecies kinship.[16] I build on the historian Katherine Grier's work on the sociohistorical evolution of pets within the American family and the psychologist Gail Melson's ideas about the intimate relationships developed between children and companion animals.[17] And I am influenced by the darker side of family exposed in Arnold Arluke's sociological investigation into animal cruelty on the family front and Clifton Flynn's examination of the impact of the companion animal on domestic-violence victims.[18]

Inspired by social psychological reformulations of traditional symbolic interaction (and determined to provide an avenue for the paradigm's extension to nonhuman animals), I tread tenaciously in the sociological shadows of Sheldon Stryker's structural symbolic interaction and his ensuing ideas about identity theory, George McCall and Jerry Simmons's work concerning counteridentities, Peter Burke and his development of identity verification and, later, collaborative extensions of that research with Jan Stets.[19]

Compelled by family demography to better understand the impact of the Industrial Revolution and consequent demographic transitions within society, I focus on the diversification of family within the United States and the resulting transformation of who becomes an acceptable definition of family and household structure. Indeed, in order for the multispecies family to come to fruition in its current form, major society-level, attitudinal shifts had to occur. These shifts meant moving from a focus on family subsistence to higher-level concerns with loving and belonging to, eventually, self-actualization and self-happiness. As a result, I adhere to the foundational ideas rooted in the European demographers Ron Lesthaeghe and Dirk van de Kaa's second demographic transition (SDT), in which they argue that extraordinarily low fertility rates and subsequent diversification of family structures in the Western hemisphere (and especially the United States) have been driven by the technological advancements of the Industrial Revolution.[20] In following these ideas, I am also tightly bound to the French demographer Phillipe Ariès's original contentions regarding the decline of fertility in the West as tightly intertwined with a society-wide ascension through Maslow's hierarchy of needs.[21] Indeed, I argue that the growth of the current multispecies family present in American culture today was similarly fueled by the same forces that produced increasingly diverse family structures in the United States, including the childfree family, single-parent family, LGBTQ family and stepfamily.

Likewise, more recent scholarship regarding the multispecies family has fed my expansion of the way in which the multispecies family fits concomitantly within diverse American family structures. Indeed, innovative work from Amy Blackstone, an American sociologist specializing in childfree families and gender; the American anthropologist Shelly Volsche, whose work focuses on kinship and family formation; and Dafna Shir-Vertesh, an Israeli anthropologist interested in human-animal interaction within the family, have all provided nice interdisciplinary backdrops with which to develop my own ideas.[22]

Why Do We Need This Book?

A scholar of critical race theory recently asked me what the point was in multispecies scholarship. "After all," he reasoned, "shouldn't we be more concerned with impoverished children, foster kids, and the historical oppression of families of color? I think these are far more important issues than some yuppie delusion that their dog is their kid. I mean, why are people doing this, anyway? Why don't they think about adopting a child if they care so much?" As an African American man, my colleague had had difficult times with dogs, in particular, in the poor southern community of his childhood. He recounted a time when he was a young boy and had been attacked by a White couple's German shepherd while walking down his neighborhood sidewalk. His experience is not unusual within the African American community,[23] and his questioning of my topic was certainly not the first time that I had heard some variation of this (nor would it be generally unfamiliar for human-animal interactionists in sociology).

However, this scholar's question drives home the need for more, mainstream family scholarship focused on the multispecies family. Indeed, why has this family type arisen? And what does it look like? What motivates one of my participants to read "The Pokey Little Puppy" to her dogs or another of my participants to drop $5,000 in veterinary expenditure on her adult daughter's dog "child"? Why might another of my participants, unable to conceive another child, bring a dog into the family fold, specifically to give their only daughter a sibling of sorts? Why do so many voluntarily childless families internalize a "parent-child" identity pairing with their companion animals when they argue that they do not currently want (or may never want) a child in the first place? When an *involuntarily* childless couple desperately wants a human child, why turn to companion animals for this connection instead of adopting a human child who is condemned to the foster system otherwise?

Regardless of the importance of these questions (and while scholarship from the human-animal interactionist perspective in sociology has been on the rise), core areas in the discipline, such as race and ethnicity, stratification, and family, have been hesitant to integrate the impact of the multispecies family from their own perspectives. Family sociology, in particular, has been "slow to rethink underlying categories of analysis . . . in the wake of significant changes in family experience. Assumptions about the kinds of family forms and household arrangements underlying family research have not yet expanded to meet new realities in American family life."[24] Certainly, the institutional coding of the Canadian sociologist Dorothy Smith's Standard North American Family, in which a married man, woman, and their children constitute our understanding of "family," continues to be the measuring stick by which nontraditional families are analyzed in family sociology.[25]

Dogs and cats are dominant animals in the American family landscape, with the percentage of families reporting a dog or cat present in the household ranging anywhere from 49 percent to 68 percent.[26] The most conservative findings regarding the multispecies family note that

85 percent of dog owners and 76 percent of cat owners in the United States think of these nonhuman animals as members of their human family.[27] The most generous findings argue the percentage is closer to 95 percent.[28] These numbers alone represent an astounding oversight of family form and function within *mainstream* sociological research regarding families in the United States. However, this is not unusual for scholarly literature focused on family types that are considered "nontraditional" (as opposed to the traditional, heterosexual, two-parent family).[29]

It is my hope that this book helps to explain why the presence of the multispecies family is an important domain of research, particularly for family scholars. I mean to do this in a way that makes it clear that dogs and cats within the American family have profound impacts on things like immediate and extended family member interactions, fertility considerations, socioemotional development of children and the parent-child relationship, family finance, the involvement of extended family members, family life course, and household structure itself.

I also demonstrate that the multispecies family in American society today—the one that has been born out of significant demographic and attitudinal changes inherent in the SDT and postmodern society—is clear and present at the macro-level of society across a variety of institutional contexts. We can see the significance of the multispecies family in the $90.5 billion that Americans spent on their companion animals in 2018.[30] Certainly, evidence of the impact of such financial expenditure is prolific within the advertising industry when advertisers and marketers target the parent-child relationship that is present for so many multispecies families in the United States.

A Word on Theoretical Position

Of course, as a social scientist, I am guided by theoretical premises. Whether that theory is inductive or deductive, theory is an essential part of how we make sense of our data. If it is inductive (or grounded theory), then we derive guidance on social behavior from what we see in our data. If it is deductive, then we start with preexisting theory as a means of guiding the entire project—from methodological design to analysis.

Sometimes the theory that we use is a hybrid of multiple theoretical positions—potentially causing unrest in those who remain pure in their allegiance to a specific position. This is the case for my work. I build on two different microsociological, theoretical platforms that are disparate because of their positions on nonhuman animal agency, cognition, and sense of self. The first of these, identity theory, considers the impact of social interaction on the development of particular identities that we use to form our understanding of self. Sheldon Stryker, a stalwart in American sociological social psychology, repeatedly, either directly or indirectly, reinforces the idea that cultural statuses (e.g., "parent," "child," "grandparent") with which people can identify themselves and others are specific to "persons" placed in that category.[31] The meanings that we attribute to each status as we interact with one another are derived from cultural expectations that have been set in place because of past social interaction between *human* social actors. That is, identity theory argues that the identities that we internalize as parts of our sense of self and the meanings that we attach to them are ultimately and solely unique to human interaction.

For some scholars, using identity theory in my work on human-to-*animal* interaction may be problematic because the perspective is predicated on human-to-*human* social interaction. However, I subscribe to identity theory here, arguing that one of the main reasons that we know that who counts as family has changed is the emergence of family-related identities counter to the companion animal. I base this argument on a hybrid of identity theory and human-animal interaction theory. First, I use Peter Burke and Jan Stets's contention that we are able to know that an identity has been internalized by a social actor by examining their behavior.[32] That is, if someone's actions match the cultural expectations of a particular status, then we know that the identity not only is being performed but has become part of self. For example, if my new puppy is crying incessantly at night and I choose to forgo my own sleep in order to help my puppy fall asleep, then my behavior may suggest the presence of the "parent" identity aligned with the American cultural standard that expects parents to engage in night care with their young children. If I do not forgo my sleep and instead place the puppy in his crate in the garage so that my sleep is not interrupted, then I am not adhering to the cultural expectation of "parent" in American culture, and the status of parent may not be present for me. Of course, one culturally expected behavior does not necessarily translate into convincing evidence of an identity. However, a range of consistently performed actions that represent "parent," "grandparent," or "sibling" (as I describe in this book) suggests otherwise.

Some symbolic interactionists may argue that, because my puppy cannot speak with me, no social interaction has taken place. Instead, privileged by my exceptional human access to the symbolic systems of language, I have simply applied a human-derived definition of "baby" to the puppy in the context of the family home, and I am pragmatically using that object (the puppy) as such. This is where creating a hybrid of two seemingly disparate theories comes in handy. Using Sanders's theoretical work on "doing mind" in human-animal interaction,[33] I argue that, by having a shared history with this puppy, I have developed a theory of mind for him, or an understanding of his intentions, desires, and emotions, because of our extensive interactions with each other. Furthermore, my acknowledgment of the puppy as sentient, communicative, and with personality leads me to engage with him as a social actor in much the same way that I might with an infant or newborn who cannot yet speak. Subscribing to both identity theory and the human-animal interactionist position regarding "doing mind" allows me to demonstrate not only the presence of particular familial identities formed in concert with the companion animal but also how they may have arisen absent of verbal communication between two social actors. As a result, I predicate the theoretical positioning in this book on a need for the extension of identity theory to include nonhuman animals as influential social actors. And I argue, as others have,[34] that omission of nonhuman-human animal interaction on the basis of human exceptionalism risks continuing an anthropocentric dualism in identity theory.

A Word about Words

George Orwell wrote in his essay "Politics and the English Language," "But if thought corrupts language, language can also corrupt thought."[35] While Orwell was referring to the use of language within politics to hide the truth, the quote is quite useful to assist in explaining how and why certain words are used in this book. Interdisciplinary scholars interested in human-animal interaction have argued that the ways in which we refer to nonhuman animals and how we subsequently construct the human role in relationship to them have dramatic implications for our thoughts, attitudes, and behaviors toward other species. The use of the terms "pet" and "owner" has become increasingly unacceptable for people who have developed "animal capital"—the recognition that nonhuman animals are sentient beings with agency who may be alingual but are individual social actors with a distinct selfhood.[36] The term "pet" conveys a much different meaning, one that reflects the dog or cat (or other species) as entertainment and pleasure for the human rather than as a unique social individual with whom to create long-lasting bonds. Likewise, "owner" overtly declares that the "pet" is a piece of property to be possessed—just as is a piece of furniture or a cinnamon roll.

Vehemently opposed to this framing of the nonhuman animal, many human-animal interaction scholars, animal ethics philosophers, animal rights activists, and others who have animal capital sewn into their relationships with the nonhuman animal have sought to limit the use of such phrasing. Instead, a growing movement is afoot in which non-anthropocentric terms are lobbied for that actively dispel the human-animal dichotomy. The argument goes that making this change helps humans to better grasp that "we are as vulnerable as other animals, and our knowledge is limited by our sensory mechanisms and ways of being situated socially and politically."[37]

Animal ethics scholars have lamented the proliferation of the term "pet" in our language, noting that "'pets' is surely a derogatory term with respect to both the animals concerned and their human caregivers. . . . The word 'owners' harks back to a previous age when animals were regarded as property, machines or things to be used without moral constraint. Likewise, 'he' or 'she' should be utilized in relation to individual animals rather than 'it.' The odd notion that animals are only a species and not individuals should not be perpetuated in our language."[38] And, indeed, we can point to a number of legislative efforts today to this end. For example, the state of Rhode Island; Boulder, Colorado; West Hollywood and Berkeley, California; along with fourteen other US cities all have passed legislation replacing the term "owner" with "guardian."[39] Multiple organizations have supported this move, including the Humane Society of the United States. In Defense of Animals, an organization dedicated to animal rights efforts, maintains "The Founder's Guardian Initiative," in which it seeks to "disavow the concept and accompanying language of animal ownership [to] reconstruct the social and legal relationships between human and nonhuman animals."[40]

However, other scholars argue that a change in language such as this is empty because referencing dogs, cats, and humans as "pets," "companions," or "guardians" is irrelevant. The fact of the matter is that, by law, they are still defined as property.[41] The American Veterinary Medical Association (AVMA) fervently opposes replacing "owner" with "guardian," noting that such changes may serve to worsen pets' lives. Pointing to the eventual question of animal as "ward" of the "guardian" means that the pet has achieved legal status with rights that have far-reaching implications. For example, new, species-inclusive wording may keep owners from transferring an animal to another party, prevent humane acts of euthanasia due to suffering, and affect privacy issues surrounding how veterinary and medical records can be shared with others.[42]

Scholars of human-animal interaction find themselves at odds on this issue as well. For example, James Serpell, a renowned professor of animal welfare, argues that such changes in language could lead to absurd extremes such as labeling the ornamental fish a companion animal.[43] Leslie Irvine has argued in *If You Tame Me: Understanding Our Connection with Animals* that companion animals have sentience and agency and should be treated as such (including rethinking the terminology that we use).[44] However, she made concessions to such terminology in her later book, *My Dog Always Eats First: Homeless People and Their Animals*, writing that this reversal from her earlier writing allowed her to better reflect how her participants "spoke for" their dogs and cats.

The debate surrounding these issues is a cogent one, especially when considering a push to make sociological inquiry less anthropocentric. As a result, I feel the need to explain my use of these words, including "pet," "companion animal," "owner," and "caretaker," in the context of this book. Some scholars have argued convincingly that humans "speak for" their pets regularly as a means of communicating their thoughts and feelings.[45] Indeed, this makes sense if a shared history with another sentient nonhuman allows the human actor precious insight into what the nonhuman's emotions and desires are via the interpretive process that Sanders terms "doing mind." These are important concepts as well because the process of "doing mind" and, thus, "speaking for" the animal allows a translation of the inner self of the dog or cat by those humans who know them the most intimately. This book is filled with narratives about just these types of relationships and how they complete the family sphere through shared experiences, knowledge, and lives together in kinship.

Earlier, I discussed a myriad of different scholars who have influenced my thought on this topic. But even more important to me here are the voices of the participants in my research who have shared with me, cried in front of me (and made me cry in front of them), and taken positions of social and emotional vulnerability, even as many of them were acutely aware of the potential for social judgment over their own human-animal relationships. Many have personally introduced me to their four-legged family members and allowed me to watch their interactions with their dogs and cats not only in an interview format (where it might be easier to "perform" the way that they think they should for me as a researcher) but also in the veterinary clinic environment (where most times their attention immediately goes to the veterinarian). The last thing I want to do in this book, using participant narratives as exemplary, is to make them feel ostracized.

I use the participants' words here and reflect the ways in which they narratively "speak for" their animals in the context of their shared histories with one another. Every person whom I interviewed thought of their dogs and cats as, *at least*, a general family member. The vast majority of narratives displayed the existence of more specific familial identities for the companion animal, such as "child," "grandchild," "sibling," and "baby." All thirty-five narratives were poignant, even when familial identity was more general in nature, and definitely demonstrated that words like "pet" and "owner"—as human-animal scholarship defines them—do not adequately capture the human-animal bond present within their multispecies families. Nevertheless, "companion" was used far less frequently than "pet," and the quantitative presence of "guardian" was overshadowed by the word "owner."

As a result, I use words such as "pet," "companion animal," "caretaker," and "owner" interchangeably to reflect participant narratives accurately. I also periodically use "child" and "parent" but only to describe the behavioral presence of such identities as they have been reported to me by participants or when I am relaying actual participants' words. Using these terms interchangeably also allows me technical freedom in my writing while providing the reader with a more smoothly flowing text.

Another issue regarding words should be addressed here as well. The people with whom I spoke or observed for the data contained in this book hailed from a variety of family structures (all multispecies in one way or another). This included traditional, two-parent families with young children present, both single-mother and single-father families, empty-nester families, stepfamilies, and singles.[46] I also spoke with families in which children were not present. These families in particular require clarification regarding the ways in which I discuss them throughout this book.

People with whom I spoke who did not have children fell into two distinct categories: those who had actively chosen not to have children (or, at minimum, to delay having children until later in their lives) and those who presently desired (or had desired, at some time in the past) having children but were unable to. Some of these participants straddled both categories. While they had initially been told by medical professionals at some point in their lives that they (or their partners) would never be able to have children, they wound up conceiving against all odds.

Scholarship regarding the terminology with which to identify people in these varying categories has had an evolving history.[47] Terminology, especially in the 1970s, saw "childless" and "childlessness" in frequent use by scholars, with an emphasis on deviance from the traditional family for those who actively chose not to conceive. However, this moniker conflated in an indiscernible manner both those who chose not to have children with those who wanted children but could not have them due to infertility or sterility. "Voluntarily childless" (people who had chosen not to have children) and "involuntarily childless" (people who wanted children but could not have them for one reason or another) as common descriptors began to emerge in the 1980s as a way of providing more precision to the categories with which researchers were investigating.

However, "childless," even with the word "voluntarily" in front of it, still anchored people without children as "less" than those who did have children. By the 2000s, the term "childfree" began to appear in the literature, reflecting the fast-paced growth of people who had chosen either to opt out completely from childbirth or to delay children until much later. Indeed, the percentage of childfree adults aged forty to forty-four in the United States doubled from 10 percent in 1976 to 20 percent in 2006.[48] Reflecting the increasingly frequent choice to delay childbirth (making one temporarily childfree), the mean age at first childbirth for women has steadily increased from 21.4 in 1970 to 26.9 in 2018.[49] These society-wide demographic changes have made it progressively necessary to distinguish between the varying experiences of the childfree and childless.

The people with whom I spoke in interviews rarely used any of this terminology. Most often, those who could not have children but wanted them simply stated that: "We couldn't have kids" or "We wanted kids so badly, but it just wasn't in the cards for us." One participant and her husband had not given up hope and were trying to adopt, but their options "seemed to be dulling by the day" because of their financial state. These were sometimes emotionally charged conversations that involved expressions of grief. One of my participants scolded herself for wanting to be validated as a family by society even though she and her husband could not have children, saying, "I get mad at myself because I don't need that [validation]." Others cried as they discussed their deep-seated desire for children and the ways in which their animals helped them derive a sense of family.

Likewise, people who had actively chosen not to have children were frank about it. "Children give me anxiety; I prefer not to be around them" or "I guess I have never had that strong of a desire to have kids." These conversations were also sometimes emotionally charged. One childfree person with whom I spoke was decidedly against treating her animal companion as a child in any way. She shared with me the pressure that she and her husband felt to "be normal" and "have children." But she became visibly upset as she described the pressure that she felt from others to "at least try to treat your dog like he's a baby."

These conversations are difficult to encapsulate with any terminology. But scholars are in the business of knowledge production, and to produce knowledge that can be widely accessed and applied by others, we must use similar terms. As a result, I have to choose some kind of terminology to distinguish between the different types of families without children present. "Childfree" is the most obvious, "honest-to-participant-narrative" choice based on my conversations with people who have chosen either to delay children or not to have children at all.

"Childless" is tougher. I do not like this term, as it still signifies that these families may be less than those who can or do have children. However, the term continues to be used in the literature today. "Involuntarily childless" is also still in use and at least signifies that the person has not chosen to be without children. Both fill me with trepidation, as they are connected to real people who are much more than their "childless" state. However, I use both here interchangeably as a means of precision and knowledge production. I have attempted to include bits and pieces of some of these narratives throughout the broader stories about the participants' multispecies families as a way to honor them and their experiences.

A Brief Summary of the Book

The ultimate goal of this book is to demonstrate how the multispecies family has developed in the context of increasing diversification of family structures within the United States. In doing so, I illuminate not only how this emergence is reflective of increasingly diverse family experiences within the United States but also how familial identities (such as "parent," "grandparent," and "sibling") have adjusted to include the family dog and/or cat as a specific category of family member, including "child," "grandchild," and "sibling." Chapter 1 examines how various historical, macro-level forces have driven the emergence of the multispecies family as it exists today. After reviewing existing literature on the sociohistorical impact of postmodernity and subsequent recognition of companion animals as sentient, agential beings, I argue that we cannot truly understand the multispecies family as a new family form without considering the influence of the Industrial Revolution and concomitant demographic transitions on the diversification of family structure within the United States.

Using identity theory, chapter 2 explores the ways in which traditional familial identities emerge within the childfree and involuntarily

childless multispecies family. These identities, and accompanying behaviors, demonstrate the multispecies family as a type of family structure, different from other, single-species families without children and
with increasing levels of macro-level support. Highlighting behavioral
expectations of the "parent" in American culture, like caregiving, socializing, and nurturing, I show how participants are parenting their animal
children in ways that are steadily transforming definitions of family as
well as who can legitimately claim the "family" label. I also use participants' behavior to show the unique repercussions that this family form
can have, compared to other single-species families without children,
for economic expenditure, work-family balance, and emotional support
within the multispecies family sphere.

In chapter 3, I demonstrate how both childless and childfree participants discussed the role that their own parents, partners, and sometimes
siblings played in verifying their "parent" identities. This confirmation
was important to the maintenance of these familial identities. Childfree
and childless people often feel scrutinized by society in general, even
as American women increasingly delay childbirth or even opt out of
having children entirely. Indeed, being without children is stigmatized.
Being without children while also parenting animal "kids" can feel more
stigmatized. This societal pushback is familiar to nontraditional families
in general, but we can see that justification for judgment from broader
society for my participants lies in the multispecies nature of their families. Consequently, support of the parent identity from significant others
was both meaningful and important for the people with whom I spoke. I
further explore how this support ultimately produces other identities in
the immediate and extended family, such as "parent," "partner," "grandparent," and "aunt" and "uncle."

Human-animal interaction scholars specializing in family have
known for a while now that companion animals appear to serve fun-
damentally different functions in the American family, depending on
household structure. For households with human children present, this
difference often rests on the utility of pets for the human child. In chapter 4, I develop extant literature to examine the types of identities that
are ascribed to pets when human children are part of the household
structure. For example, parents with children currently at home as well
as empty nesters provided narratives suggesting that their children were

apt to assign "brother," "sister," or "sibling" to the family animal companion. Alternatively, some parents shared that they had thought of the family dog or cat as a sibling for their only child.

I also utilize the sociologist Barrie Thorne's concept of "borderwork" in chapter 4 to explore the strict boundaries that parents draw between their human children and the family dog and cat.[50] While these boundaries remain intact throughout the children's childhood, they appear to blur a bit when children leave the nest. This results in the emergence of a "caretaker" identity for empty-nester participants in which some parental behavior emerges related to the companion animal but not in the intense manner with which it is present for childfree or childless families.

In chapter 5, I analyze macro-level evidence found in pet product advertisements to connect the multispecies family form to specific familial identities, like "parent" and "child," demonstrating how these new relationships are increasingly reproduced in mainstream American culture. I argue here that advertisers have increasingly designed ads that reflect the new pet status as family member in the United States, effectively producing and reproducing the companion animal as "family" with all of its attendant identities. I examine print ads for products such as companion-animal food and toys, obedience school, adoption, household cleaning products, shoes, and insurance to show how advertisers are negotiating companion animals as important family members in American society. In turn, these images provide macro-level reinforcement for micro-level interactions that have gradually developed new meanings for what constitutes "family," "parent," and "child."

In the conclusion, I suggest multiple future directions for scholarly inquiry. I also further discuss the relevant mainstream need for both sociology of family and identity scholars to begin to consider the impact of these relationships both on identities within the family and on family structure.

1

Has the American Family Gone to the Animals?

The New Multispecies Family

Without a doubt, American culture has embraced the companion animal as a legitimate family member, extending statuses such as "child," "sibling," and "grandchild" to the family dog and cat. In 2006, a public opinion poll administered by Pew Research Center confirmed this trend, noting that 85 percent of dog owners think of their canines as family while 78 percent of cat owners assign the same importance to their felines.[1] In 2011, the percentage of Harris Poll respondents feeling this way about their pets had reached 91 percent, and by 2015, it had hit an astounding 95 percent.[2]

The number of dog-owning households in the United States has dramatically increased, from thirty-four million in 1991 to forty-eight million in 2016, representing a 40 percent increase between the two time periods.[3] When people were asked if they planned on adding more dogs to their households in 2017, a resounding 8 percent of households (almost four million) responded yes. Compared to the 35 percent increase in American households overall since 1991, it is clear that the number containing dogs has continued to outpace growth in overall households over the past thirty years.[4]

Likewise, cat-owning households have seen a steady increase since 1991, albeit not as robust as the rise seen in dog ownership. In 1991, twenty-nine million American households contained at least one cat, compared to thirty-two million households in 2016, representing a 9 percent increase over the two time periods.[5] Of these households, 4 percent planned to acquire another cat in 2017.

On the surface, statistical changes in household ownership of dogs and cats over the past few decades only provide a descriptive measure of the presence of pets in the United States. However, there is a deeper story to be told here requiring qualitative contextualization to underscore the ways many of these households have been transformed by the relationships built between dogs, cats, and their humans. A major goal of this book is to tell that story. To that end, one of the objectives of this chapter is to provide a silhouette of these multispecies families by weaving together findings from my work, recent research on human-animal interaction, and broader macro-level evidence of the existence of this new, nontraditional family type. Accomplishing this contextualization is important to providing an overall picture of what the multispecies family really looks like today.

But this is only the beginning of the story. How Americans have finally come to a place in which the dog and cat are more than "just pets," more than "just family," and have now become children, grandchildren, and siblings for so many people requires a sociohistorical explanation. This accounting is another, equally important, aim of this chapter. Indeed, changes in who counts as family have occurred alongside massive demographic shifts that have occurred since the 1970s. These shifts have allowed for increasing diversification of the traditional nuclear family to progressively include nontraditional family structures, such as single-parent families, childfree families, grandparent families, LGBTQ families, stepfamilies, and now multispecies families. A final goal of this chapter is to use a demographic perspective to deepen both scholarly and general understanding of how the same historical processes that gave rise to other nontraditional family structures contributed to the unique rise of the multispecies family.

Contextualizing the American Multispecies Family

Mass-media outlets abound with stories about the new multispecies family. For example, in 2018, *AP News* described changes in California divorce laws that would broaden judges' purview over custody arrangements. These changes would address discrepancies in how judges handle custody disputes in divorce cases, giving them new latitude to decide on a particular kind of custody, namely, custody over the couple's dogs, cats, and other companion animals. Until 2018, pets in California divorce cases were treated like any other piece of community property, including bath towels, area rugs, and the living-room sofa. And while California law has not officially recognized these animals as different from family property, it has now allowed judges to make determinations about when, where, and how each partner will be able to spend time with their companion animals, on the basis of the quality of interactions that they had during the marriage and ownership of the pet.[6]

Other mass-media stories focus on the trauma experienced by multi-species families in the midst of natural disaster. News reports following the devastation of California's 2018 Camp Fire, the deadliest and costliest wildfire on record in the state, detailed the sheer agony of companion-animal owners as they were forced to abandon or otherwise lose their dogs and cats to the fast-moving fires. For example, shortly after the fire was contained, *The Today Show* ran a story about the Gaylords, a multispecies family that lost both of its Anatolian shepherds in the fire.[7] Andrea Gaylord, away from her home when the fire ravaged her neighborhood, had not been able to save her dogs and anguished over what had happened to them. Andrea was quoted as saying, "It was the worst feeling in the world. It's like you have to choose." Although a rescue organization found one of the shepherds and reunited him with Andrea, the fate of the other dog remained a mystery. When the second dog was finally found, it made national news. The dog, named Madison, had subsisted on food and water left by volunteers and remained at his burned-out home for a month, awaiting Andrea's return. Feeling immense relief, Andrea reveled, "It was like there is a higher power. It was like a sigh of relief." The Associated Press, the *Washington Post*, the *Los Angeles Times*, *USA Today*, *Fox News*, and *The Hill*, among other major outlets, ran the story. The nation was transfixed.

Still other news stories report on the impact of dogs and cats on major economic trends such as real-estate purchasing. A 2018 CNBC report exploring home-ownership trends among Millennials found that 89 percent of those who bought a home in 2018 also owned a pet.[8] But this is not the surprising part of the report, given that Generation X and Millennials now constitute the largest percentage of pet owners by generation in the United States.[9] Rather, it is what Millennial new home owners placed at the top of their home-buying priorities that may raise eyebrows. Of the 89 percent who closed on a new home, 79 percent noted that they would pass on a property that was perfect in every other way if it did not meet the needs of their pets—signaling a willingness to make major, life-impacting decisions with their pets in mind. Major

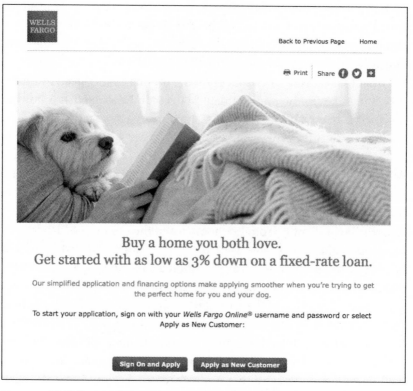

Figure 1.1. Wells Fargo website ad for customers who consider their companion animals when purchasing a home

home-loaning institutions have picked up on this trend. In October 2018, Wells Fargo Mortgage launched a new ad campaign (see figure 1.1), in which potential borrowers who owned dogs were reassured that Wells Fargo was the place to go as they search for the perfect home for both themselves and their furry family members.

With regard to social media, "pet influencers" have become a fast-growing, favorite form of advertising for social media users, especially Millennials and Generation Zers.[10] Companion-animal representation on social media has grown exponentially over the past several years, and for good reason. A recent 2016 Mars Petcare survey of American pet owners who used social media platforms including Facebook, Instagram, Twitter, and YouTube found that pet owners post an average of twice a week about their pets, with 33 percent admitting that they post similar amounts about their companion animals as they do their human family. Over 16 percent of pet owners noted that they had started a social media webpage for their pets. Related to other pets, 30 percent of pet owners reported following a "pet influencer" on social media.[11]

Grumpy Cat (aka Tadar Sauce) is arguably the most famous social media pet celebrity, known for her scowling glares at the camera. However, if we are talking big "pet influencer" bucks, Jiffpom—a fluffy, cream-colored, male Pomeranian—is arguably at the top, with approximately nine million followers on Instagram (see figure 1.2).[12] Jiffpom is an excellent example of how the love that Americans have for companion animals impacts not only what their interests are on the internet but also the kind of "animal involved" advertising used by marketers to sway consumer attention toward their products. For example, with sponsors such as Target and Banana Republic, Jiffpom earned an average of $17,500 per sponsored post on Instagram in 2017 and may well have topped $30,000 per sponsored post in 2018.[13]

Then, there is the spending. Annual expenditures on animal kin have reflected these increasingly important bonds, with purchases of pet products and services breeching $90.5 billion in 2018.[14] Furthermore, during the Great Recession, Americans experiencing the worst economic downturn since the Great Depression were forced to cut back on luxury-item spending, eating out, alcohol and cigarette usage, and

Figure 1.2. Jiffpom advertising the children's movie *The Secret Life of Pets* via Twitter

even some medical services. Yet, American devotion to the family pet produced an astonishing 28 percent increase in spending during this time frame.[15] In 2018, multispecies families splurged on pet health insurance, well-appointed boarding facilities, birthday parties, elaborate pet supplies like the Wi-Fi-enabled Furbo Dog Camera treat dispenser, and an array of increasingly elaborate pet-food options. In fact, with $30 billion spent on food and treats alone in 2018, research on consumer pet-food preferences has found that human-food preferences that are perceived as related to better health (think gluten free, organic, and fresh food) are translating into similar preferences for pet food and treat purchasing.[16]

Veterinary care is hot on the heels of the pet-food industry, with multispecies families spending $18 billion in 2018, and not just on basics such as annual exams and vaccinations (average costs ranging between $100 and $300 for dogs and $90 to $200 for cats) or dental cleanings (averaging $70 to $400 for dogs). More expensive services, such as diagnostic procedures (allergy testing, for example, runs from $200 to $300 on average) and higher-level veterinary interventions meant to extend the lives of companion animals represent a 6 percent increase over spending at the veterinarian in 2017.[17] With medical and veterinary innovation and intervention, American dogs and cats are living increasingly longer lives anyway[18]—reflecting the same aging trend that appears in human populations living in postindustrial societies.

A sampling of these interventions can include chemotherapy (average cost of $6,000 to $10,000 for dogs) or radiation treatment (average cost of $5,000 to $7,000) for cancer, removal of bladder stones, hip replacement (average cost close to $6,000), cranial cruciate ligament tear (similar to an ACL tear in humans, averaging from $1,000 to $4,000 by surgery type), and expensive treatment of chronic health conditions such as canine and feline diabetes (averaging $75 to $200 per month for treatment), and feline kidney disease (average annual cost $650).[19] The APPA notes that, as multispecies families increasingly work to absolve their companion animals of chronic pain and illness, veterinary expenditures increased by 5.8 percent in 2019 over veterinary spending in 2018.[20] Given that 35 percent of the pet-owning population is composed of Millennials (finally surpassing Baby Boomers at 32 percent of the pet-owning population), it comes as no surprise that this generation is seen by the veterinary industry as a driving force behind increasing annual veterinary expenditures.

Institutional examples of this new type of family, the multispecies family, go on and on. Pet trusts designed to ensure that the family companion animal is cared for in the way that benefactors wish have been developed, and a substantial percentage of dog and cat owners (37 percent and 39 percent, respectively) have named a caretaker in their wills.[21] An emerging movement that includes dogs and cats in food-stamp calculations is slowly gathering steam to ensure that underprivileged families do not have to surrender their beloved nonhuman family members because they cannot financially sustain them.[22] The growing "doggy day care" trend offers services beyond luxurious overnight boarding facilities for dogs and cats to offer workers who are out of the home for long periods of time each day access to in-house day care for dogs.[23] Genetic preservation of the beloved animal's DNA for cloning upon death or some other later date (at a cost of $50,000 for dogs and $25,000 for cats) is rapidly gaining momentum as pet-cloning services work to get the cost down and veterinarians begin learning how to incorporate the process into their practices.[24]

From Lively Commodity to Consumer to Data Collection

It is evident that the cultural fabric of the United States is steadily transforming, in macro- and microstructural ways, who counts as family today. Indeed, major social institutions display the results of widespread, group-level patterns that increasingly acknowledge "personhood" and family membership in the companion animal. In the process, this social recognition of sentience and agency in dogs and cats has culminated in the kinds of institutional shifts discussed in the preceding section, including kinship, economy, media, law, government, and science.

These macro-level changes related to human-pet relationships have become sustained enough within the American family itself that major, nationally representative data sets based on large-scale survey methodologies have been developed to explore them. Of course, the most obvious of these data-collection efforts are market- and industry-based analyses of consumer research behavior. The information kingpins in this kind of research are composed of professional associations such as the American Veterinary Medical Association (AVMA) and the American Pet Products Association (APPA). Since 1981, the AVMA has collected long-term consumer and market trends data in five-year increments, with special emphasis on veterinary services and pet-ownership demographics. The APPA has followed pet product and service trends biennially since 1988 to inform its members about developments in pet ownership, care, and product purchasing across an array of common companion animals.

To be sure, consumer market research like this seems a no-brainer for industries working to sell their products and services to consumers. Donna Haraway, an American women's studies scholar known for her work in science and technology, ecofeminism, and human-animal studies, has noted that, in the system of capitalism, the dog (and cat, for that matter) is a lively commodity, who gains value in the economy precisely because he is a living, breathing, organism.[25] For example, the sale of purebred puppies (selectively bred by people to choose for human-desired traits specific to the breed) who come with extensive pedigrees, painstakingly tracked lineages, and kennel-club registrations as a means of increasing their economic value can be items for consumption, with price tags that indicate status for those who purchase them. Indeed, these puppies often produce market values running into thousands of dollars.[26]

The pedigree-sporting cat is no different. The Scottish fold, a breed of cat that originated with a particular genetic mutation involving an ear tightly folded to the head and creating an owl-like appearance, can run owners anywhere from $1,000 to $2,000. Depending on pedigree and potential show record, the extremely affectionate ragdoll can cost upward of $2,000 if the buyer is inclined to show their kitten in competition. The popularity and prevalence of the Siamese cat means that she carries a lower price tag, in the range of $600.

New, designer breeds of dogs have also flooded the market in ways that exemplify lively commodification of the companion animal. Labradoodles (a cross between a poodle and a Labrador retriever), puggles (the combination of a pug and a beagle), and the zuchon (selectively bred between a bichon frise and a shih tzu) all command high price tags. Historically, elite segments of society would have looked down on these same animals—had they existed at the time—as undesirable "mutts" or "mixed breeds" only appropriate for the poor. Today, however, they fetch high dollar from those who desire such crossbreeding and can afford it. Hybrid cats (different from crossbreed dogs because they are cross-*species*—think your household cat bred with a wild feline) have become increasingly popular in the "lively trade" of companion animals, too. From the most expensive Savannah cat (a cross of the domestic household cat and an African serval) to the Bengal (a housecat bred with an Asian leopard cat), hybrid cats can also run into the thousands of dollars to purchase.

But the multispecies family has also transformed the dog and cat into consumer as well—much like their human counterparts—with desires, tastes, diets, and steeply priced health needs. Indeed, the American pet, in the eyes of their human family members, has gained the right to a multitude of goods and services that have historically belonged only to humans. Organic and raw pet foods now available on the average grocery store aisle, posh doggy day cares, and increasingly extensive veterinary treatments and medications (often evolving from human medicine) are but a few examples of the ways in which companion animals are often commodities *and* consumers in one fell swoop. Both the AVMA and APPA have tapped into the companion animal (and their human proxies) as consumer and actively collect market data rife with valuable consumption trends. Manufacturers, advertising firms, and service providers (such as veterinarians, groomers, and day-care businesses) all benefit from this information in a way that allows them not only to create higher profit margins but also to repeatedly reproduce and reinforce the dog and cat as important economic consumers within the family sphere (even as they are also lively commodities themselves).

Dogs, and Cats, and Kin

Beyond the pet products and services industry, large-scale national data programs concerned with sociological, attitudinal, and housing trends have also begun to recognize the influence of the multispecies family on social behavior and attitudes. For example, in 2018, the General Social Survey, a survey maintained by the National Opinion Research Center at the University of Chicago and funded by the National Science Foundation, finally began asking survey respondents a battery of questions regarding pet ownership.[27] The American Housing Survey, a highly comprehensive survey of American households sponsored by the US Department of Housing and Urban Development and administered by the US Census Bureau, asked a question in both 2013 and 2017 (and will do so again in 2020) about pet ownership to gather data on the need for help evacuating pets during natural disasters.[28] This movement toward unbiased (at least regarding market outcomes), nationally representative, large-scale, scientific data collection on the multispecies family promises high-quality data to social scientists and policy makers working to understand these relationships.

Using a myriad of methods, human-animal interaction scholars have examined these relatively recent relationships and found scholarly evidence to support the notion that companion animals are increasingly considered family and kin, with the intimate bonds and identities requisite for such an acknowledgment.[29] In many cases, the family animal is considered the "glue" that provides cohesion within the family, while family ties are often strengthened when an animal like a dog is introduced.[30] And more people in the United States define pets as family (51 percent) than they do same-sex couples without children (32 percent).[31]

Research shows that the companion animal impacts mate selection, as well. For example, potential dating partners are vetted, in part, based on how well they interact with one's pets (though women appear to do this significantly more than do men).[32] Perhaps this is because adult dog owners (mean age = 47.95) are more likely to look to their dogs for support than to any other family member (including siblings, parents, children, and best friends) except romantic partners.[33]

Within the family, dogs (and cats) are often treated as surrogate children of sorts, complete with holiday celebrations (see figure 1.3) and home-cooked meals, and this is especially the case for childfree and childless people.[34] Many examples of this arose throughout my time researching for this book. Hannah, a childfree interview participant in my research, spoke of sharing her Thanksgiving dinner with her dachshund (see figure 1.4), "partly for fun but partly to include her": "My friend and I thought it was funny to have Sam partake in the meal, but it also just seemed right to do it for my baby."

Of course, recent research suggests that the trend for people without children to "parent" their pets is on the rise. In one study with

Figure 1.3. Sarah's daughter, Makenzie, and granddog, Kuper, ready for Halloween night in themed costumes

a sample composed of 90 percent women, almost 40 percent of respondents labeled themselves as "parent" of their companion animals, while other research has found that some childfree women in Sweden prefer to take on the role of "pet parent" rather than raise human children at all.[35] In research on "interspecies parenting," the American sociologists Nicole Owens and Liz Grauerholz found that over three-quarters of their childfree participants thought of themselves as parents to their dogs or cats. Indeed, the authors note that, in a society that culturally requires the presence of children in order to define a unit as "family," pet parenting may well be an innovative means of achieving this distinction.[36] Some temporarily childfree families choose to "raise" pets as training for future human children, thinking of their dog or cat in childlike terms.[37] Childfree couples may engage in cost-benefit analyses regarding having human children versus companion animals as "children," while some childfree women may choose to "mother" a companion animal rather than a human child in

Figure 1.4. Thanksgiving dinner, prepared especially for Sam (Hannah's beagle)

order to grow professionally or even to avoid contributing to human population overgrowth.[38]

However, as is the case with family in general, there is a dark side to these tightly bonded relationships for women who are victims of intimate-partner violence. Clifton Flynn, a sociologist widely known for his work on human-animal interaction and family violence, has examined the companion animal as a surrogate child for female victims of domestic violence. His research, and that of other family violence scholars, has shown that the relationship between an abused woman and her companion animal is so salient that it can contribute to women staying in abusive relationships to protect their animal "children."[39] This is attributed to a variety of reasons including fear that if the woman leaves her violent partner and is also forced to leave the animal, the partner will intentionally harm the pet. Alternatively, if the woman leaves the domicile and takes her animal with her, the violence may continue afterward, aimed at either her or the animal or both. Indeed, reasoning such as this is quite similar to that expressed by mothers with human children who are trapped in abusive situations.[40]

I observed this dynamic firsthand one day in the veterinary clinic when a young, childfree woman brought in her three-year-old, adopted rottweiler, Lucy, because the dog refused to drink water. As the woman wrapped her arm around Lucy's broad, sheeny black shoulders, she shared smartphone footage with us that she had filmed the night before of Lucy's raspy cough. Lovingly running her nails back and forth across the dog's chest, Lucy's self-described mommy laughed softly, explaining, "I'm a protective mom. I also keep this file on her!" Lucy coughed one hard time, slobber flying from her flews and landing on the neatly organized, though very thick, manila folder.

"Oh, babe! We're trying to get you better. I'm sorry we missed our big walk this morning." Her deeply focused attention on Lucy continued like this for the entire appointment as she answered the veterinarian's questions and watched him listen to the dog's lungs and heart. When the vet tech left the three of us alone in the exam room to run blood tests, I asked Lucy's owner if she had any human children. "Nope. Lucy's my baby. Aren't you, girl? It has been raining so much. . . . I'm so sorry we haven't been able to get to the park." She paused briefly, burying her face into Lucy's dark coat, and I thought for a moment that she was going to cry. Lucy leaned into her, providing a sloppy but lovely kiss.

After a few moments, Lucy's owner straightened back up, a few strands of dirty blond hair now loose and messy in her face. She looked at me—determined. "I'm in the middle of a divorce." There was a brief pause, a bolstering, then a watershed. "He strangled me twice. Now he wants Lucy. But he's not getting this girl. She's mine. She's my baby. He only wants her because she's my baby. He's using her as leverage. He's fighting. But she's mine." Then she was quiet. A deep but content grumble came from Lucy, who had now placed her thick, square muzzle against her mom's chest. I stared at Lucy's owner, not sure what to say but silently cursing myself for this failure.

The vet tech walked back in then, saving us both and quickly dispersing the thick awkwardness hanging in the room. After he provided instructions on Lucy's treatment, Lucy's mom gathered up her bag and the copiously filled manila folder. Without a word, she smiled sheepishly at me and turned to exit to the reception area. But on the way out, she stopped and turned to me, saying one last thing: "She's my only child." And with that, they were gone.

For families in which human children are present, children overwhelmingly consider pets as part of the family and appear to use the same parameters for defining what family is to label their dogs and cats as such.[41] Companion animals are frequently dubbed by children as siblings, with some research finding that, overall, early adolescents view their relationships with their pets as more satisfying than those that they have with their siblings.[42] Compared to their human sibling relationships, children also have similar rates of reported emotional disclosure with their pets, with girls reporting higher levels of disclosure to their pets than boys do.[43] This pattern of disclosure appears to extend into young adulthood, with dog owners in particular more likely to turn to their dogs than to their fathers and brothers and just as likely to access their sisters for support.[44]

"Only" children are more tightly bonded with their animal companions, and both they and the youngest child (in a family with multiple children) relate to the family pet as a younger sibling in need of care and nurturing.[45] The presence of a pet may well encourage more opportunities to engage in play and caretaking than having an actual baby sibling does—with this kind of nurturing behavior taking place five times more often than with a baby sibling. In fact, it is quite possible that this kind of relationship may well increase the likelihood for later nurturing toward humans.[46]

Examples of such relationships between children and the family pet were present throughout my fieldwork at the veterinary clinic as well as in interviews with people who had human children. In an admittedly endearing encounter at the clinic, a mother and her pig-tailed, four-year-old daughter engaged in a friendly debate about whether they had forgotten to celebrate their shih tzu Brady's birthday. The mother believed that the dog's birthday had passed a few days before, on June 14; the girl believed the date to be a month later, on July 14. With Buddy's shaking, white mass of curly fur wrapped apprehensively around the mother's shoulder, the little girl rose to her knees and stretched from her spot on the vinyl bench, touching her nose to Buddy's. "Your birthday's in July, Buddy," she stated, deepening her voice and doing her best to sound authoritative.

Mom answered, "Baby, I promise that he was born in June. Remember we got him when you were in Vacation Bible School?"

This prompted a revelation for the little girl, who, instantly concerned about Buddy's feelings, urgently jumped down from the exam-room bench and exclaimed, "We missed it! We can't miss it." Directing her attention up to Buddy, who had relaxed his grip on the mother's shoulders as she stroked his hind quarters, the girl promised him an immediate celebration that afternoon, complete with his favorite snack—Cheerios.

Pet to Person to Family

The multispecies family, and its varying intimate human-animal connections, has been around for hundreds, if not thousands, of years, especially for dogs. When scholars examine these human-animal relationships specific to the United States, Americans appear to have begun depicting pets as children, friends, and companions as early as the eighteenth century. James Serpell, an anthrozoologist known for his research on companion-animal behavior and welfare, has defined these human-pet relationships as focusing on social rather than utilitarian outcomes.[47] Serpell argues that the emergence of pets was originally rooted in a transition from animals who had jobs, such as hunting, herding, and guarding, to animals who served very little function other than to provide entertainment and companionship for their owners.[48]

Other scholars have further refined Serpell's definition of the pet.[49] In addition to family amusement, pets are also distinguished from other types of human-animal relationships because they are named, live inside the human home, and are never eaten. However, for the 85 percent of dog owners and 76 percent of cat owners in the United States who label their pets as actual family members, these relationships go well beyond the varying definitions of "pet."[50] A clear historical shift has occurred, especially in the latter half of the twentieth century, in which people have increasingly elevated their dogs and cats to more salient positions in the family unit, with assigned personhood and familial identities.

Much of the groundwork for this shift was laid earlier in US history, alongside industrialization and urbanization. Urbanization—the movement of vast numbers of people and families from rural to centralized, urban areas that promised jobs—marked a major transition for the American family *and* the omnipresence of work animals in daily life. Indeed, the last vestiges of purposeful contact with animals in urban areas were eradicated with the introduction of the automobile as a replacement for the draught horse.[51] In the late nineteenth century, middle-class mothers began viewing the pet as one way to symbolize a "domestic ethic of kindness" in which children were instilled with lessons of caring and responsibility toward their animals.[52] Burial of pets in animal cemeteries emerged during this time as well, with the first cemetery appearing in 1899 in Hartsdale, New York, revealing inchoate trends toward the incorporation of dogs and cats as family members.[53]

This growing interest in pets as a part of the family, especially for the middle class, became apparent in economic contexts emerging in the late nineteenth and twentieth centuries as well, with the advent of specific consumer products marketed toward American consumers and their pets. For example, the rapid growth of singing canaries as pets during the mid-nineteenth century led to increased availability of bird cages, toys, and treats for purchase. The idea of pet furniture and gifts for pets debuted for American consumers in the late nineteenth and early twentieth centuries. Ralston Purina introduced the first commercially available dog food in the 1920s and sold it through feed stores, while cat litter was not developed until after World War II. And the advent of dog toys as we know them today came later, during the 1950s.[54]

In Comes the Modern Multispecies Family

The Australian sociologist Adrian Franklin explains in his foundational work, *Animals and Modern Culture*, that the 1960s and 1970s brought in a range of features that were new to society and that would characterize a "postmodern" period in the United States and other industrialized societies while also paving the way to the multispecies family today. Ontological security, self-reflexivity, and misanthropy became part and parcel for families in the 1970s who were dealing with growing economic instability that flew in the face of the work and wage security that were present in the robust postwar US economy. The household unit in the United States underwent dramatic changes in response to the counter-cultural movements of the 1960s, which insisted that the progress of human society no longer take precedence over ecology and the environment. Society-wide demands were made to limit environmental and exploitative policies of the era. Divorce rates doubled between the 1960s and the 1980s.[55] Birth rates decreased dramatically with increased access to contraceptives and as increasing numbers of women chose to delay childbirth, pursue higher education, and/or develop their careers.[56]

First, Franklin argues that ontological security, or a sense of stability in our everyday lives, was dramatically decreased in this turbulent sociopolitical environment.[57] He notes that that the destruction of social and familial ties, born in postmodern society through increasing divorce rates, decreasing birth rates, and increased cohabitation, alongside decreasing rates of marriage starting in the 1970s, created a sense of unease and anxiety in the family sphere.[58] Other factors also contributed to this tumultuous period in American family life. Post–World War II saw social and economic demands for young people to move away from their families and communities, on which they had formerly leaned for support. For boys, obtaining work was no longer a function of simply following in your father's footsteps to a factory job. Accompanying significant recession during the 1970s, the decline of the manufacturing industry in the United States meant that young people would have to find different careers to support their own families, and these jobs were almost always somewhere other than their hometown.[59]

Stephanie Coontz, a sociologist who has spent her career examining the sociohistorical development of the American family, notes that women at the time were encouraged to place their aging parents in nursing homes rather than move them into their own homes. This would allow American mothers to focus solely on their nuclear families—further dismantling the support that extended family had traditionally injected into the young family unit. Spousal choice had traditionally occurred in the communities in which one had grown up and with advice from family members. However, physical movement out of childhood localities also meant that young people no longer had the security of familial support in choosing partners.[60] Lost in such rapid familial change, people actively searched for some semblance of stability and security in their daily lives. Ultimately, pets became surrogates for love and companionship because they provided enduring social ties, loyalty, and mutual dependency that were no longer as accessible in the extended family as they had been in the past.

Second, as the sense of insecurity became stronger, there also arose a sense of self-reflexivity with regard to a need for a moral identity.[61] The early twentieth-century attitude that framed nonhuman animals as unimportant and disposable in the face of technological advance became obsolete. Books like *Silent Spring* by Rachel Carson warned of

The two changes set by 60's & 70's

environmental degradation wreaked by modernity and its pursuit of human progress.[62] Paul Erlich's *The Population Bomb* reckoned an impending global population explosion that would result in mass human starvation.[63] Postmodern narratives that foretold the decline of humanity cast massive anxiety across much of American society as people grappled with their own contributions, indirect or not, to the destruction of nature and the future of humanity. Providing shelter, food, attention, and toys for a dog or cat felt like an accessible way to feel morally redeemed for past social ills that had been cast on the animal world.[64]

Third, misanthropic sentiment rooted in the pursuit of human progress at all costs began to arise as a burgeoning number of people dealt with the idea that human society had polluted and overfished the oceans, endangered the world's rain forests, and ultimately co-opted the wild for human development.[65] The risk of loss of entire species due to societal sprawl and technological development became a major social problem, encompassing the animals who were now dependent on human morality and responsibility for survival.[66]

Economic uncertainty, familial instability, and moral confusion defied a sense of social stability and made people nostalgic for the postwar golden era of prosperity. Indeed, people developed a self-reflexive desire to find moral balance and goodness in themselves while also searching for a way to rectify the ills that had been perpetrated against nature by human progress. Pets fit quite nicely as a solution to this struggle and laid the foundation for the emergence of a modern multispecies family—one in which particular species of animals would no longer be simple workers for human progress, nor would they be the entertaining "pets" of the early twentieth century.[67] The animals who would heal the moral wounds of modernity would eventually be acknowledged as actual family members, afforded luxuries that only the surpluses of industrialization could have produced and the emotional ills of postmodernity could have spawned.

Animal Agency and Sentience

Following closely on the heels of Franklin's sociohistorical analysis, the American sociologist and human-animal interactionist Leslie Irvine has argued in her book *If You Tame Me: Understanding Our Connection with Animals* that there is a dimension to be added to Franklin's ideas.[68] Focusing on interspecies intersubjectivity, Irvine conceptualizes a new kind of "capital" that has had a clear impact on the inclusion of the dog and cat as family. Like the French sociologist Pierre Bourdieu's "cultural capital," in which knowledge, tastes, and habits provide access to the upper strata within society, Irvine argues that "animal capital" implies the presence of resources that facilitate impactful, nonexploitative relationships with animals. These resources include a deep knowledge about what particular behaviors in the animal mean, concern over the animal's physical well-being, understanding of past lived experiences in the animal's history, and personality characteristics. As a result, a deep respect for the animal as sentient, thoughtful, and communicative develops alongside the understanding that the animal is an active participant in their relationship with their human. This acknowledgment of sentience and agency is concurrent with a human willingness to navigate through difficult situations that occur during the course of one's relationship with the animal.

Such a relationship was on full display one day during one of my clinic observations. An elderly, White gentleman brought his nine-year-old, blind, type 2 diabetic labradoodle named Matilda into the veterinarian for an annual checkup. The man spoke to Matilda throughout the exam, alternating between loving reassurance that she was safe to playfully teasing her about her love for American cheese slices. He was adoring, stroking her loose, golden curls as he might his granddaughter, as he shared with me their early-morning routine. "The only bad thing about her is she wakes me up at four in the morning to play. I don't mind, though. I give her her insulin at five a.m. and feed her, and then we just sit together for a bit. Right, girl?"

Conscious efforts like those of Matilda's human have resulted in the treatment of companion animals as intersubjective selves (social actors capable of recognizing both self and others as unique social actors, leading to shared agreements with others about interaction). Irvine notes that there are two requisites for this kind of relationship to occur.[69] The first of these includes both a human and an animal capacity for the development of a core self that is apparent in nonverbal behavior.[70] The nonverbal behavior of both dogs and cats reflects this capacity via four features that are very similar to those of the nonverbal human infant: a sense of (1) agency, (2) coherence, (3) affectivity, and (4) self-history. However, the capacity for the emergence of a core self is only that—a capacity. Second, social interaction with other actors is required for a sense of self to develop.

Irvine explains that agency encompasses animal awareness of desire. An example of agency in dogs can be found in training a dog to exhibit self-control by sitting on command and staying, even when a tantalizing squirrel beckons for a good chase. Coherence is characteristic of the knowledge that one is a "single, bounded, physical entity."[71] Previous work on shelter cat communities provides an excellent example of coherence in cats: the formation of friendships among feline residents who recognize and act on differences that they perceive in other shelter cats.[72] Affectivity, the third feature of a subjective selfhood, is apparent in the emotional states that both dogs and cats exhibit to their owners. When someone says that their dog is jealous of the attention that another animal or child is receiving, this is the recognition of emotional affect in the dog (and another good example of coherence, for that matter).

Finally, self-history is developed via a memory of significant social interactions that allows for the development of lasting relationships with other actors. A perfect example of the influence of self-history can be found in Sadie, my female German short-haired pointer. Sadie is a fanatic for chasing balls, whether they have been thrown for her or she has batted them away herself. Frequently, a ball menacingly disappears beneath a piece of furniture just out of reach of both her long snout and her never-ending front paws. This, of course, causes almost immediate whining as she realizes the dire consequences of this "inconvenience" for her. If, after trying on her own for a bit, she determines that she cannot reach the ball, she barks repeatedly at me to come save the day by moving furniture. This is part of her own self-history (and a shared history that has developed between the two of us): if *she* cannot retrieve the ball on her own, she can just get me to do it for her. Reminiscent of a toddler crying for help with a dropped toy, this example reveals the power of self-history in operation "across the other dimensions of the core self," including coherence (she sees her "self" as distinctly different from mine), agency (the self-willed act of calling for help), and affectivity (she immediately exhibits frustration by whining when the ball goes under the couch because she remembers that it will be difficult to retrieve).

Demographic Perspectives

The importance of these newly recognized—and accepted—dimensions of selfhood in the companion animal have no doubt played a very large role in the growing desire of American pet owners to access their own animal capital and work diligently to understand the desires and intentions of their beloved family animals. Irvine's perspective also helps us better understand how it is that pet-product corporations today are being advised to treat companion animals as consumers in and of themselves—with command over their humans' spending patterns and the power to fund a $95 billion pet-product industry.[73] Together, both Franklin and Irvine go a long way toward explaining how dogs and cats shifted from pets to family members in a postmodern American society. However, neither account explains how the family transformed from the heteronormative, human-centered, child-focused endeavor characteristic of Franklin's "modern" society to a postmodern structure that eventually became so diverse in its composition that, culturally, the very meaning of family in the United States became one that could include not only humans but also dogs and cats: the multispecies family.

That is, both Franklin and Irvine offer human-animal interactionists a significantly viable way to understand the sociohistorical and cultural transformation of the dog and cat from family pet to family member. But this is only one side of the story. Indeed, shifting values that ultimately focused on misanthropy, self-reflexivity, ontological security, and an ultimate recognition of the pet as emotional and thoughtful provide a medium by which the companion animal can achieve personhood and family status. But achieving family status does not a new, legitimate family form make. Instead, I argue here that other major institutional and cultural shifts affecting who could legitimately claim the label of "family" must have also occurred to see the emergence of the multispecies family.

The widespread appearance of increasingly diverse types of family in the 1970s—and their subsequent growing social acceptance—was a prerequisite for the emergence of the multispecies family. The same demographic processes that have enabled stepfamilies, single-parent families, intergenerational families, and LGBT families to newly lay claim to the culturally approved, legitimate status of "family" in the United States over the past several decades have also ushered in the foundation for the emergence of the multispecies family—complete with familial identities that have historically been reserved for humans.[74] And this provides the other side of the story with which to fully understand how who counts as family in the United States today has changed so much that people can treat their dogs and cats like full-fledged members of the family.

The postmodern multispecies family is a far cry from the nuclear, pet-owning family that dominated American society pre-1970s.[75] Dogs and cats were considered entertainment for and property of the family during this time, though consumer spending on the family pet simultaneously began to ramp up within the middle class.[76] This increase in consumer attention occurred as the animal welfare movement, protesting the poor treatment of captured strays, began to gain traction in the nineteenth century.[77] However, neither modernization, with its emphasis on human progress and increases in the standard of living for all people, nor American cultural prescriptions for "family" at the time would have allowed the pet to take on a culturally relevant, familial position within the American household.

The ideological code present even in postmodern cultural prescriptions surrounding "family" is one that Dorothy Smith, a Canadian sociologist concerned with feminist theory and family studies, refers to as the Standard North American Family (SNAF).[78] SNAF dictates a normative family as a legally married, heterosexual couple with children in which the man is the primary breadwinner and the woman is the primary domestic laborer and child caretaker in the household. SNAF as a concept is ubiquitous in American culture as the ideal family type, even in a society that has increasingly practiced far more diverse ways of "doing family" since the 1970s. As a result, the concept is the "objective" measuring rod against which all other diverse family forms in the United States are checked.

Many scholars argue that the historical imprint of the SNAF continues to be encoded within an array of institutions. For example, the US Census Bureau defines a family as "two or more people (one of whom is the householder) related by birth, marriage, or adoption and residing together."[79] Same-sex couples, who found new freedom to demand marriage licenses across all fifty states secured by the Supreme Court's *Obergefell v. Hodges* ruling in 2015, still struggle against legal obstacles that block them from adopting.[80] And partners in a cohabiting relationship (couples who are not married but live together in an intimate relationship) cannot receive each other's Social Security benefits—nor can they receive veteran and military spousal benefits. Indeed, family sociologists argue that the SNAF excludes a diverse array of family arrangements increasingly present within postmodern America, including single-parent families, foster families, childfree couples, LGBTQ families, grandparents raising grandchildren on their own, cohabiting partnerships, or even families in which a baby is carried by a surrogate, conceived via sperm and egg donation, and raised by biologically unrelated parents.[81]

This increasing family diversity now includes the multispecies family, in which the dog or cat is labeled as an actual family member (e.g., child, sibling, grandchild) and is treated as a person would be. In this context, people have tight, intimate bonds with the dog or cat that are strongly reminiscent of the kinds of bonds that family researchers see between human family members. However, opening the door for pets to be included as family within the American middle class required a major shift in taken-for-granted assumptions about the SNAF. This was certainly the case as individuals began moving from a concern over the role one played within the family to a postmodern value system in which an individual's feelings and needs take precedence over that of children and spouses.[82]

Changes in cultural perspective yielded multiple modifications to the SNAF, which represented 88 percent of US family structures in 1960.[83] These included a decrease in marriage rates and a concomitant increase in cohabiting couples; a rise in divorce rates (though these have stabilized since the 1980s); childbirth as acceptable outside of marriage; an increase in childfree families; and a continued increase in age at both first marriage and first childbirth. As in the United Kingdom (a similarly industrialized, sovereign state), these nontraditional, familial arrangements would have been stigmatized by the dominant culture present during the modernization period in the United States. However, today, they have become part and parcel of the diversity present in American familial composition.[84]

Demographic changes in household structure like this are deeply entrenched in cultural shifts induced by the Industrial Revolution in which

American society initially emphasized obtaining material security (e.g., shelter, adequate food, and clean water) over all else. However, when these basic needs were widely fulfilled through modernization, people began focusing more on fulfilling nonmaterial needs (e.g., self-fulfillment, freedom of expression, autonomy, and self-realization).[85] Individual concerns moved from survival to a desire to optimize personal growth and happiness throughout life.[86] As a result, more liberal ideas about reproductive freedom, gender equality, sexuality, cohabiting, child rearing outside marriage, or even having a child at all have arisen as catalysts to transform family structure.[87] Fulfillment of nonmaterial needs as a priority also introduced the potential for individuals and society to work toward feeling in control of and stable in their family lives. In relation to the multispecies family, these new, self-focused values materialized in a postmodern climate in which thoughtful care for the nonhuman animal, pets in particular, provided a sense of renewed stability. Indeed, a focus on nonmaterial needs made it much easier to adopt a dog or cat into the family fold as a *true* member of the family—one that could potentially bring self-fulfillment, love, and loyalty just as another human might.

Impact of Demographic Transition

How these changes came about is a focus of family demographers interested in historical transitions in household structure. Using the model of demographic transition (DT), demographers depict historical changes in family and household structure during the modern period by pointing to a society-wide decrease in mortality rates that occurred alongside very high fertility rates. Because people were no longer dying as early as they once did and women continued to give birth to large numbers of children, population numbers increased across society, and families remained large in size.[88] A decrease in fertility rates followed later as normative prescriptions for large families begin to give way to the realization that children were surviving at much-higher rates, that they were no longer needed as labor in a society building surplus via industrial capacity, and that the cost of having so many children was too great, socially and economically.[89] The long-accepted driver behind these dramatic changes is the Industrial Revolution, which brought with it an increased, sustained standard of living, increased production of food, and control of infectious diseases via antibiotics, vaccinations, and innovations in sanitation (all of which drastically reduced infant, child, and adult mortality).

Across this transition, the household structure changed radically, with low mortality leading to more interaction between generations (for example, grandparents, parents, and children), the average number of children per family dropping precipitously, and women spending less time actively parenting in adulthood (because they were living longer and having fewer children to parent in the first place).[90] The cultural emphasis regarding childbearing changed from large to small families that were actively built using varying modes of contraception.[91] Demographers believed that the outcome of this transition would be a balance in population growth in which fertility rates would settle at replacement value for the population (just enough children born to replace current population).[92]

Cultural shifts toward affection within the family yielded an era of "king-child" in which "seeing that one's children [got] ahead in a climate of social mobility was the deep motivation behind birth control"—especially for the middle class.[93] That is, parents worked to organize the family toward material investment in children, which, in turn, encouraged fewer births so that greater investment in each child could be made.[94] A pronatal emphasis on the parent-child relationship (and especially mother-child) in this environment would have posed a major obstacle to the emergence of the multispecies family. Nickie Charles, a British sociologist who examines kinship across species boundaries, confirms this idea in her findings regarding generational differences in the perception of childhood family pets in the United Kingdom. Indeed, participants in her research who had been children in the 1940s and '50s most often remembered the animals of their childhood as workers who provided sources of food and labor to the family (and, occasionally, as pets).[95]

However, the "king-child with parents" era transformed into the "king-couple with child" era, as fertility rates dropped even more dramatically between 1955 and 1970.[96] Rather than intensely focus on the development of the child, self-fulfillment and realization became the new emphasis for adults. What was culturally acceptable for who "counted" as family began to change. It is this shift from child to the happiness of individuals within the couple that would have been a prerequisite for the family pet to transition to family member, opening the door to the development of the multispecies family.[97] Again, Charles's work in the United Kingdom is informative here as a parallel to the United States. She highlights study participants born in the 1970s and later as remembering the family dog or cat as a family member, sibling, or even child.[98] Moving these kinds of identities to the nonhuman animal could not have happened if the *human* child had remained the central focus of family—especially for those who chose to label their dogs and cats with familial identities.

These changes were partially attributable to better socioeconomic outcomes for families as well as rising female employment in the United States.[99] However, scholars also note that the culture-wide shift toward higher-order and nonmaterial needs greatly contributed to new diversity in American family structure. Indeed, Andrew Cherlin, an American family demographer interested in sociohistorical changes in family life, argues that economic prosperity emanating from a booming post–World War II economy provided adults with more time and money to work on self-satisfaction. He argues that the current state of family life in the United States emphasizes that the individual is "almost required to . . . continually monitor your sense of self and . . . how well your inner life fits with your married (or cohabiting) life. . . . For according to the cultural model of individualism, a relationship that no longer fits your needs is inauthentic and hollow."[100]

"Pure Relationships" and the Multispecies Family

Anthony Giddens, a British sociologist who studies the development of modern society, argues that "pre-existing [social] patterns and habits" that were focused on the family and found in traditional societies began to erode during the postmodern period.[101] Intimate relationships became marked by uncertainty that Giddens says was brought on by rapid social change, producing a sense of individual instability. This uncertainty created a distrust in authority structures and an increased sense of risk, particularly for relationships. As a result, "the individual is continually obliged to negotiate life-style options. Moreover . . . such

choices are not just 'external' or marginal aspects of the individual's attitudes, but define who the individual 'is.' In other words, life-style choices
are constitutive of the reflexive narrative of the self."[102] This internal
reflexivity produces constant negotiation and renegotiation with the
self about the state of the external world and one's secure place in it.
As a result, the individual is continually working on the self to obtain
happiness and self-satisfaction, self-expression, and autonomy. This
uncertainty ultimately led to a search for loyal, long-lasting relationships, opening the door to newly emerging human-animal relationships
within the family unit.

Giddens argues that the rise in self-reflexivity is key to understanding what he calls the "pure relationship."[103] The pure relationship has
no structural basis, such as social tradition, with which to maintain
the intimate relationships that individuals develop with one another.
The cultural requisites that once dictated how relationships should be
formed, such as for survival (before the Industrial Revolution) or romantic love culminating in affectionate marriage, family formation, and
partners for life, have disappeared in postmodernity as individuals work
to understand and support the self rather than others.

With constant self-evaluation and reflexivity, the personal relationships that are now developed are based on equality of sexes and self-
disclosure with one another. Appreciation of one another and mutual
trust and affection become the foundation on which the pure relationship rests—*not* social demands about how and why the relationship
should progress. *Two* actors enter this relationship "for its own sake, for
what can be derived by each person from a sustained association with
another; and which is continued only in so far as it is thought by both
parties to deliver enough satisfaction for each individual to stay within
it."[104] That is, just as external social demands do not dictate how or why
the pure relationship forms, these imperatives also do not frame how or
why the relationship ends.[105]

This individual pursuit of self-satisfaction means that one has an
array of choices about how to structure family life. One might cohabit
forever; marry and stay married; get married, end the marriage, and
then cohabit. One may have a human child while cohabiting or while
married. One may be a never-married single parent, a divorced parent,
a custodial parent, or a noncustodial parent. In fact, one may choose

never to be a parent at all.[106] And, as has been noted by human-animal interaction scholars, one may choose even to "parent" nonhuman animals.[107] The most consistent trend apparent is that, while marriage and having children were intimately wedded during the first demographic transition, the two no longer have to occur hand in hand and couples no longer have to have children to be considered family.[108] Marriage is not a cultural requirement for childbearing anymore, nor is it required to be considered a family in the United States.[109] The most important obligation for family life is to oneself—not to one's partner or to one's children, if children are born at all.[110]

As a result, Americans now largely accept many kinds of living arrangements as "family," with no one family form dominantly accepted over all others anymore. As Brian Powell, an American sociologist interested in atypical family arrangements in the United States, and his colleagues have found, the vast majority of Americans now agree that both single-mother and single-father households count as family (with 96 percent and 95 percent agreeing, respectively). Childfree and childless heterosexual couples also earned the label of "family" in the study (92 percent), and 83 percent agreed that cohabiting couples with children should also be thought of as a family (if they did not have children, the number drops drastically, to 40 percent). Albeit a much lower percentage, 66 percent also agreed that a lesbian couple with children constitute a family (with 64 percent agreeing for a gay couple with children). Regarding cats and dogs, 51 percent of respondents agreed that pets should count as family members.[111]

In my fieldwork, one of the most obvious, aggregate indicators that so many people think of their companion animals as family was fully displayed in the lobby of the veterinary clinic where I conducted observations. Each of the two-and-a-half-inch photo albums, one wrapped in a forest-green vinyl and the other in a burgundy faux leather (and both too full to close completely), were unassuming at first. I had already traversed, observed, wandered, and chatted with clients and their humans in the bustling lobby across the entirety of a week before I noticed them lying together, covered in a thin layer of various pieces of fur, at the end of the large aquarium positioned right at the entrance to the clinic. Curious, I had opened the burgundy photo album first, expecting to find old magazine clippings about animal care or perhaps even photographs of past patients. Instead what I found was greeting card after greeting card sent from families that had used the clinic's services—easily over one hundred between the two albums.

When I spoke with the veterinarian who had compiled the albums, I was astonished to find out that she was not finished. Indeed, she led me to a back, dimly lit office crowded with the office manager's desk, several mismatched chairs, and a couple of old filing cabinets overflowing with charts. She pointed above a long card table stacked with dusty files and veterinary textbooks to a wall file brimming with even more cards. "I really want to find the time to put all of those in albums too. They mean a lot—to us and the families."

Sometimes, the messages contained in each card were upbeat and witty: "Thanks so much for your time and effort. Cleo is back on track and on the prowl! Sincerely, The Thompsons." Other times the cards were deeply emotional, tinged with grief: "Our Clyde was our baby through the end. Even though we still hurt for him we are so thankful to have had your staff provide him relief and kindness in his final days. So grateful to you, Amanda and Rick." Still other cards had pictures of the entire family—humans and animals perfectly posed together—jovially wishing the clinic "Merry Christmas" or "Happy Pawlidays!" The one thing that all of these cards had in common was that the health and well-being of these animals mattered far more than it had for the pet that characterized the first two-thirds of the twentieth century in the United States. In fact, just as the 51 percent of respondents had indicated in the research of Brian Powell and his associates, these animals were not pets at all. They were family—family that mattered enough to feel deeply appreciative to others for having helped.

Pets as Family . . . Until They Are Not

Mary was a thirty-year-old single mother who had volunteered to speak with me about her multispecies family of four: Mary; her two-year-old daughter, Marcy; her seven-year-old dog, Devon; and her five-year-old cat.[112] Mary and I sat quietly that hot summer day chatting in the cramped graduate-student office that I shared with four other doctoral students. A small personal fan rattled on another student's desk, working relentlessly to cool the space that had been abandoned by all but the two of us at that lunchtime hour. Mary had begun her interview in a confidant manner, discussing her multispecies family with much detail and attention. But now she had slumped down in her chair, her hands clasped tightly in her lap. She had just shared that, before she had Marcy, everything in her life had revolved around Devon. At one point, pre-Marcy, she had had two cats, one of whom had been a heavily spoiled favorite but had since passed away. As Mary lamented all of the changes to her multispecies family that had occurred after Marcy was born, I asked her why she thought so much had changed.

Quietly and with slight tears in her eyes, she offered,

> Well, I guess because I have Marcy, . . . I feel like there are too many things that I worry about. And Devon just went way back on the back burner. And the cat just went way back. So I am getting more annoyed with that cat. Like, "Oh my gosh, I have to feed her *again* . . ." It would be better if she wanted to cuddle every once in a while, . . . but if I try to get her for more than a second in my lap, she won't do it. It's really annoying because there is too much going on in the house.

"Do you resent them [Devon and the cat] at all?" I asked. Her response was firm, defiant:

> The cat. And I resent her even more because I miss River [her other cat who had passed away] so much. Why did he have to pass away? [*Crying harder now*] It makes me so mad. Sometimes I just wish she would pass away, too. It's just . . . My house is so cluttered. You should see it—it's horrible. That stupid cat. I had both of them at one point. I was so concerned about having a place for them to climb and play. So I had two cat towers. There is no room for all of that stuff now. I have one left now, and there is no room.

She paused to absorb everything that had just furiously escaped her mind into our tiny, restricted space. After a moment, she continued, "Yeah. I resent her. That damn cat. But I love her, and I would never give her up."

* * *

While the dog or cat is key in the composition of the multispecies family, that positioning can be fleeting in ways that do not apply to human family members (or at least are short-lived in ways that are far more immediate and permanent than is possible with a human family member—short of disowning one's family). Scholars who have studied the close bonds between companion animals and people have noted that assignment of human identity is not always predicated on a permanent familial status. Rather, that status is liminal in nature, with some owners opting to think of their animals as "just pets."[113] Other families may become multispecies in nature by proffering human identities to their animals for the time being—until something changes, such as the addition of a new human baby, or pet behavior emerges that is determined to be too destructive or irritating.[114] Still others may not think of their dogs and cats as family members at all. Indeed, millions of dogs and cats are relegated to animal shelters each year because they do *not* measure up to human expectations of "family member."[115]

It may well be that the multispecies family is a unique reflection of the pure relationship about which Giddens writes. Indeed, the multispecies family, especially among childfree and childless families, is built not on cultural prescriptions of the SNAF but rather on intimate, emotionally intense bonds that are marked by deep trust and communication between people and their dogs and cats. Self-disclosure and commitment characterize these human-animal relationships. The bonds present are sustained by loyalty, personal love, shared histories, and meaningful communication and characterized by deep levels of trust. They are permanent in nature—until they are not, because, just as people in a pure relationship may be seeking self-satisfaction in their bonds to one another, so too may be people within the multispecies family. When the situation changes, as with Mary, when something better or more fulfilling comes along that is better suited to satisfying the inner self, the human-animal relationship may dissolve because the internal impetus for its existence (self-attainment or satisfaction) no longer holds.

Examples of such a process are evident in research on childfree, multispecies, Israeli families in which the introduction of a human child means almost immediate demotion of the companion animal from "person" status to "animal" status.[116] It is also evident when the multispecies family parent is no longer satisfied with the behavior of their dog or cat. Destruction of property, aggression, or other negatively perceived behavior can potentially upset the fragile, internally defined bonds of the pure relationship between some people and their companion animals. No longer satisfied, one may well decide to terminate the relationship because it has become aggravating and stressful.[117] The animal is then removed from the family and, at best, relinquished to another family member, friend, or no-kill shelter—the ultimate example of the temporary nature of this unique pure relationship.

The veterinary clinic in which I completed my fieldwork was well aware of the "downgrading" that pets can experience within the family unit. Alicia, a veterinarian with whom I spoke, shared with me that aggravated owners periodically came into the clinic wanting to surrender or, worse yet, euthanize their pets when they failed to live up to human expectations that were beyond the natural behavior of the animal. She recollected a particular time when an owner came in with a new mixed-breed puppy, excited to bring him into her home, calling him her "baby boy," and coddling him after he received his vaccinations. However, as the dog entered adolescence, he began repeatedly "marking" his territory by urinating on various pieces of furniture around her home (a behavior that is common in intact male dogs). Alicia recalled, "When she first came in about his peeing everywhere, I explained to her that the behavior was natural and she should consider neutering him to make it stop. I remember her going, 'Nope, I'm not doing that.' I suggested going back to potty training, positive rewards for going outside, things like that. But she came back months later to have him euthanized because she couldn't deal anymore." Alicia explained that when owners come in requesting euthanasia for reasons like this, the whole staff works very hard to convince the owner to surrender their animal to the clinic. If they are successful, then the clinic has space to keep an animal whom they can then try to place. There is even a built-in crate in the lobby, positioned close to the clinic exit, where potential adopters can view surrendered, abandoned, or stray dogs and cats looking for a new home. This is what the clinic staff eventually convinced the woman to do with the dog who had begun his time with her as a beloved family member but ultimately became perceived as a nuisance in need of removal from the household.

Still other people may bring pets into their families for more extrinsic reasons. Scholars have noted that the proliferation of designer dogs (and hybrid cats) is rife with moral and ethical dilemmas regarding the exploitation of animals. The term "designer dogs" references a genetic crossing of two breeds to produce an animal with specific human-desired traits. The labradoodle is a classic example of just such a dog. Originally bred to select for the hypoallergenic coat of a poodle, the labradoodle has become one of the most popular crossbreeds in the United States. Teacup dogs, like the tiny teacup Yorkie, are the result of dog breeders taking the runts of litters and breeding them together to produce the smallest dog possible. Human-animal scholars argue that purchases of such animals highlight conspicuous consumption associated with consumers who want to obviously convey status to others in the same way that an expensive purse or watch might.[118] And celebrities such as Paris Hilton, who often sports one of her tiny dogs in a designer purse, or Kendall Jenner, who is commonly seen posing with her Doberman pinscher for paparazzi, have served to fuel the purchase of particular types of dogs in the hope of conveying status.

The explosion in popularity of designer dogs, and the desire of many owners to have a pet with a particular set of personality characteristics and physical features, means that animals are bred repeatedly to emphasize those exact features (or created from a combination of genetic traits from across breeds or species). However, doing so can have disastrous results, as bad recessive genes are replicated and concentrated as well. This is especially the case if the health of the animal is not at the forefront of the breeder's mind. For example, both purebred and designer dogs often come from puppy mills, where the main focus is profit over animal health.[119] However, buyers, eager to replicate what they see as the perfect companion or even fashion accessory, are often surprised at the host of health problems that come from chronic over- and in-breeding by unscrupulous profiteers who seek to maximize profit margins. Saddled with unexpected bills related to crippling arthritis, hip dysplasia, chronic respiratory issues, heart defects, a plethora of allergies, unpredictable behavior problems, and lifelong pharmaceutical interventions, to name a few, many people eventually surrender their animals to shelters.[120]

* * *

The multispecies family that has emerged in postmodern American society has received limited attention from family researchers within sociology.[121] In keeping with the anthropocentric approach of sociology as a discipline, this may be due to the nonhuman nature of pets.

However, it is quite certainly the case that the multispecies family can traverse all other family forms, moving across singlehood, marriage, parenthood, divorce, stepfamilies, and widowed families. Indeed, although American households with human children under the age of eighteen have the highest rate of pet ownership, there are hefty numbers of singles, childless and childfree families, empty nesters, and cohabitating couples who also have pets and consider them family.[122] And, as other scholarship has noted, the family dog has begun to appear more frequently in divorce court as couples fight over who will retain "custody" of their animal child, with "such cases . . . so common now that they hardly warrant mention [anymore]."[123] Furthermore, the determinations in pet dog and cat custody cases are increasingly reflecting rulings present in child-custody cases, with decisions about "dog support," visitation schedules, and police warrants that enforce those schedules.[124] Institutional changes such as these, which mirror widespread cultural change, indicate that the multispecies family should be part and parcel of the call for family research to more closely reflect the lived experiences of Americans today.

2

"She Loves to Be Read To"

Parents without Children and Their Animal Kids

I first met Jody via email.[1] Her message revealed that she was forty-four years old, married, and had, for a long time, thought that she "could not have humans, so [they] were going with dogs." She fit the parameters of the study nicely, so I immediately messaged back that I would be quite grateful for her contribution and set up a time to meet. She then sent me the memoirs that she had written for two of her family's dogs, noting that she thought I "might like seeing this." She shared in that message that she had written these because she "was just so overwhelmed by Sally and Newton's deaths . . . because they were younger when they died."

The first memoir was about Sally and was fifty-eight pages long and had twenty-five chapters. Jody had written incredible amounts of detail about Sally, a golden retriever mix that had lived for about eight years. Her writing reached far back into their history together, starting with how she and her husband had come to adopt Sally near an air base at which her husband was stationed. She recounted Sally's fears and separation anxiety, love for frisbee and basketball, sleeping habits, health issues, and dental milestones. She carefully recorded Sally's extraordinary intelligence, her affinity for singing and music, her involvement in relationships with "Grandma" and "Grandpa" as well as "Uncle John" and closed the memoir with a gut-wrenching chapter describing Sally's last few days alive. As I read all of this, I realized long before I met with Jody that she thought of Sally and Newton as her children and interacted with them accordingly.

* * *

One of the main objectives of this book is to provide empirical evidence demonstrative of the existence of a new and unique family structure, replete with all of the identities that confirm the existence of familial relations. These identities include statuses such as parent, child, grand-parent, and sibling and are, when present in interaction, cultural signposts that signify a family unit is afoot. Because I am arguing that the multispecies family of today should be considered a newly diversi-fied, nontraditional family structure worthy of research, it is incumbent on me to provide evidence that shows why these families should be con-sidered as such.

For example, one may ask why we should consider a family with pets as its own separate structure, distinct from other structures such as the two-parent family, the single-parent family, or the family without children present. To answer this, I employ identity theory to demon-strate that the multispecies family is a separate type of family structure in which identities that are normally assigned to humans are instead assigned to dogs and cats. The multispecies family creates new, nontra-ditional definitions of family that ultimately impact how family can be done. As these behaviors become more widespread, macro-level forces found in digital media, the economy, and corporate policy emerge to support gradually changing definitions of family to include the multi-species family without children present.

The performances of these new definitions also have unique reper-cussions for the ways in which the multispecies family engages in an array of activity typically associated with broadly accepted functions of family. These include economic expenditure, work-family balance, emo-tional support, caregiving, and socialization. Each of these activities is distinctly altered within the multispecies family precisely because of the intimate connections formed between dogs, cats, and other, significant family members. The presence of these identities, the unique behavior that arises because of them, and macro-level reinforcement are how we know that the multispecies family constitutes a new type of diversified structure worthy of separate study.

Using an Identity Lens

While there are three types of identity (role, group, and person) cur-rently discussed in the identity literature, this book is hinged on role identity.[2] In this capacity, identity theory posits that *statuses*, or posi-tions within society, such as parent, student, or cashier, are connected to cultural expectations that have developed across the course of repeated and patterned interaction between social actors and groups. These statuses are "relatively stable, morphological components of social structure," organized and embedded within social structure, and changing gradually as meaning and use evolve across history.[3] The set of cultural expectations and behaviors that are associated with a particular status are termed *role*. When a person internalizes those cultural expectations as part of the meanings of self, an *identity* is formed, recognized by other social actors, and negotiated and enacted within particular social situations that require its performance.[4]

Role identities are important because they "give the very meaning to our daily routine . . . [and] largely determine our interpretations of the situations, events, and other people that we encounter."[5] This information is an important component of any social interaction, but the conglomeration of role identities in the family sphere can tell us much about how family relationships are structured. For example, the role identities present in the multispecies family help us understand how the dog or cat functions as a member of the family. The roles, or cultural expectations for behavior that are attached to those role identities, tell us much more than "My dog is like my family." When someone consistently behaves as we would expect a parent to behave, doing night checks on a new puppy, intensively researching health information about the puppy, and vetting local day-care options or pet sitters to be used while the owner is at work, that behavior is indicative of a relationship that is far more detailed than the vague qualifier "she's like family." Rather, such performances allude to the presence of a parent identity because this is how American culture would direct a parent (especially one in the middle class) to behave. And because we expect parental behavior to occur in the presence of one's child, these actions also make it apparent that the puppy is perceived as something more akin to a child than a pet.[6]

Likewise, when an adult child's parent offers to babysit the cat during a vacation week, takes the cat to veterinarian appointments, and offers to help pay for expensive medical treatments, that behavior suggests the presence of a grandparent identity. Such behavior also means that the cat is perceived as more of a grandchild than a family pet. This is not to say that if these human-animal identities are not present within the relationship, then the animal companion is not thought of as family. But multispecies family members who have internalized specific identities like "parent," "child," "sibling," or "grandparent" counter to the dog or cat have created more intense relationships that further refine the multispecies family as a familial structure in its own right.

While identity pairings like "parent-child" or "grandparent-grandchild" have been conceptualized by identity theorists as exclusive to human interaction, other scholars have stressed the importance of using sociological analyses to examine human-to-animal interaction in certain contexts.[7] Indeed, multiple human-animal researchers have recently used an interactionist perspective to explore mindedness and the perception of such in human-animal relationships.[8] These arguments pit themselves squarely against the stance of George Herbert Mead, the founding father of traditional symbolic interactionism, who argued that nonhuman animals are incapable of thought, mind, and meaningful interaction because they lack the language required to do these things, which is unique to humans.[9] Instead, human-animal interactionists argue that lingual capabilities are not a prerequisite for significant, symbolic interaction between species. This argument is rooted in the idea that animals have personhood and a self that exists regardless of linguistic capabilities.

Following this vein, it has been argued that mindedness and a sense of self are sufficient for symbolic exchange that is created through shared experiences and knowing of one another. Clinton R. Sanders, a prominent human-animal interactionist at the University of Connecticut, has argued that "doing mind" as an interaction process is far more integral to human-animal relationships than is language.[10] He contends that this process occurs when a theory of mind is constructed by human caretakers for the animal, allowing them an understanding of the animal's thoughts, emotions, desires, and intentions. Citing research on nonverbal humans such as Alzheimer's patients, physically or mentally disabled persons unable to speak, and infants, Sanders pointedly notes that spoken language is not a prerequisite for the creation of the rich, interactional worlds shared between these people and their caretakers.[11] Instead, he argues that through shared experience, a theory of mind arises "in those who interact with alingual others devise[d] in understanding and constructing their interactions, . . . allow[ing] them to understand the thinking, emotions, preferences, desires, and intentions of the other."[12]

In the case of human-animal interaction, caretakers also develop a meaning structure attributable to both the animal and extensive, ongoing human-animal interaction. The development of this meaning occurs in much the same way that it would for an alingual human other, such as the infant or the Alzheimer's patient. It is the historical, shared, long-known, and intimate experiences between these actors (human or not) that enables this to occur.

In the opening of this chapter, Jody's memoirs for both Sally and Newton provide us with a written diary of the importance of such history to the continued existence of her multispecies family, even after each dog's death. While increasing research points to the similarities in the grieving process between human loss and companion-animal loss, Jody actually shares her grief by revisiting all of their lives together. Each chapter melds together human and dog as a reflection of multispecies love and familial dedication. Her writing is a testament to the parent-child relationship, especially in the ways in which Jody knew her dogs as family but also in the ways in which her dogs knew her.

For example, Jody wrote that she had "come down with vertigo really bad": "I could not move without getting sick. I finally crawled down the stairs for something to eat. Then I crawled back upstairs. Sally knew this was not normal. She laid beside me and would lick my cheek every 20 minutes or so. She would not stop until I moved. I guess she was just checking to make sure I was okay. . . . I really think that she knew that I was not well." Sally knew Jody intimately from their time together and was able to adjust her behavior according to the illness that Jody was enduring at the time. More importantly, all of this was done without the benefit of spoken language (at least the kind of spoken language with which humans are labeled as superior to other animals). Instead, their history together directed not only Jody's memory of this event in her family but also Sally's response in real time based on her own past understanding of normal behavior for Jody.

As is evident in these memoirs, a human understanding of the companion animal's emotions, desires, intentions, and preferences, and the knowledge generated by it, enables the person to give a voice to animal action. Research has shown that this voice is used to convey companion animals' thought to other human actors, such as the veterinarian, who are not privy to the same understanding present between the animal companion and their human. The owner speaks as the animal, sharing information about the ailing pet and effectively introducing the pet as a legitimate social agent.[13] Indeed, in my own observations within the veterinary clinic environment, I have watched veterinarians wholeheartedly accept this human-animal relationship and begin talking directly to the animal. Likewise, veterinarians in my observations have time and again directly addressed the animal patient by name and as an accepted, minded, family member in the interaction, both with the human client and face-to-face in verbal and bodily interaction with the patient.

For example, one of the veterinarians in the clinic in which I made these observations made it a habit to sit down on the floor with his larger canine patients. When I asked him why he did this instead of having a vet technician hoist the dog up onto the exam table (which periodically happened anyway), he shared that sitting on the floor with the dog enabled him to gain his patient's trust. Additionally, and in much the same way that my pediatrician explains to my son what a shot is for or how long a throat swab might take, this particular veterinarian often explained to the patient why he moved his hands across the dog's chest, hips, spine, or other areas in need of examination. He did this regardless of where he examined the animal (on the table or floor) and regardless of species (both dogs and cats). He also provided time markers to the patient, such as "just one more minute, buddy" and verbal empathy like "I know you are tired of me poking at you, babe."

Other research has focused on human *perception* of the companion animal as a minded social actor. For example, one such approach argues that the possibility of interspecies intersubjectivity is irrelevant because "interaction" only requires the perception that other actors are purposely engaging in interaction.[14] Neither refuting nor completely supporting the idea of interspecies intersubjectivity, Colin Jerolmack, an environmental sociologist with research interests in human-animal interaction, has considered how human-animal play can be coordinated via human perception "as if" the animal is human, pointing the sociological significance of human action toward the companion animal as a minded actor.[15] He notes that human behavior is altered in interaction with the animal precisely because of the "projection of human qualities onto the animal . . . whether dogs are 'really' playing or not."[16]

For example, when I grab a tug toy that my dog is chewing on and proceed to pull on it roughly, I interpret this as play. When he growls at me and yanks back, tightening his grip, I assume that he understands that I want to play and shares the same goal. Jerolmack argues that we have no way of knowing if my dog and I agree that we are playing with each other (in fact, the dog may be growling to make me go away), *but* the fact that I interpret it as such and base that on past history with the dog is sociologically significant.

Regardless of whether these relationships develop between people and their dogs and cats due to interspecies intersubjectivity or human perception, enough interaction like this between people and their animals eventually creates new patterns of familial behavior that involves the companion animal. These patterns have become widespread enough in the United States in the past few decades that dogs and cats have become accepted as family members in a way that now reflects the multispecies family. And changing cultural expectations for familial identities like "parent" to include the dog and cat signal the increasing importance of these interactions to both identity theory and scholarship concerning the American family.[17]

Both childfree and childless participants in my research demonstrated behaviors that were clearly parental in nature—illuminating the multispecies family without children as uniquely different from childfree or childless families that do *not* have companion animals.[18] To be clear, none of my participants claimed that taking care of their companion animals was the same as raising a human child. Instead, they shared day-to-day life experiences with their animals that produced and reproduced the parent-child identity pairing in ways that the human counterpart was often unaware of. For example, Jody was surprised when a new acquaintance needed clarification that Sally was a dog and not a human child, and Jed, a childless male participant, admitted that, while he had not wanted to think of his two dachshunds as "children," his actual behavior "obviously indicated otherwise."

Parent Identity and the Multispecies Family

Research on role identity has shown that behavior consistent with the expectations of a certain identity confirms the presence of that identity.[19]

My participants' narratives indicate the presence of a parent identity, meaning that they have internalized the cultural expectations associated with being a parent but idiosyncratically related to an animal rather than a human child.[20] The status of parent in the United States is an important one for most people, and the transition to that status is a highly significant role transition during the life course.[21] In fact, the expectation that both male and female adults in the United States eventually become parents, whether that be through birth, adoption, stepparenting, or foster parenting, is strong enough that people who are childfree may be perceived as deviant.[22] Prior research has noted this pressure as particularly intense for women who are perceived as childfree as well as for women with only one child and comes particularly from both their own parents and medical professionals.[23] Internalizing the parent identity is especially salient for women, who are socialized as children to become mothers as adults—performing "mother" can help a woman to feel as if she has satisfied social expectations.[24]

This mandate to have children, especially for women, finds its place in the pronatalist tendencies of American culture as a means of slowing the decline of fertility rates while also bolstering the "family values" social and political movements.[25] Indeed, Nancy Russo, the feminist psychologist who coined the term "motherhood mandate," has pointed out that the expectation to bear children and enact the mother identity is inseparable from femininity.[26] These expectations lead those who opt out of having children to have vastly different experiences from those who ultimately do have and raise children.[27] Particularly, those who choose to delay or opt out of childbirth are viewed as especially nonnormative compared to those with at least two human children. However, those individuals and couples who are perceived as delaying are not judged as harshly as those who are seen as permanently opting out.[28] Likewise, those who are viewed as involuntarily childless, while still judged for not having children, are judged less harshly than those who are seen as having actively chosen not to have children.[29]

Differences are also apparent in the experience of childfree households, childless households, and households with children present with regard to the ways in which companion animals are perceived. For example, young singles and couples who have chosen to delay or opt out of childbirth often raise companion animals as a means of nurturing another living being, setting limits, and expressing affection.[30] Furthermore, young childfree couples can appear to treat their companion animals as if they are surrogate children.[31] Women, in particular, without children in the household are more likely to develop mothering bonds with their pets than are women with human children present.[32]

Prior work on the cultural expectations regarding parenthood in the United States has shown that there are multiple culturally valued domains relevant to this status. These expectations encompass behaviors such as caregiving; promoting development and socialization; breadwinning; the establishment of a parental relationship with the child; giving love, support, and nurturance; and responsibility and commitment.[33] Mothers, in particular, are expected to engage in "intensive mothering." This includes being child-centered, providing nurturance, socialization, both physical and emotional nourishment, and large financial investment.[34] Christina Bobel, a feminist theories scholar, details this expectation further by acknowledging the cultural ideal of mother in the United States as subscribing to attachment parenting, organic feeding, co-sleeping, and "baby wearing" (when the mother uses a sling-type carrier to hold her baby close to her body).[35] The mother status also requires protection, training, and nurturing of children regardless of social location or culture.[36]

The expectations for both the parent and mother status were clearly on display in participant narratives via themes like caregiving, parent-child relationships, socialization, discipline, and modifying life paths for their animal children.[37] And each of these themes provides increasing evidence for the existence of one type of the multispecies family, one without human children, that clearly displays parent-child identity pairings. These pairings would have, in the past, only characterized families in which human children were present. However, the diversification of who counts as family, alongside the increasing number of people who do not have human children, has enabled a flourishing of the parent-child relationship that marks this kind of multispecies family.

Caregiving

Among the participants in my study, caregiving was a key component of parental behavior and was present throughout all of their narratives, on a basic level. Regular feeding and basic veterinary care were always present, as was consideration for acceptable care while the family vacationed, for a variety of reasons. For example, Julie, a childfree female, reported being quite concerned about Chance, her schnauzer mix, with regard to making travel arrangements. Specifically, she empathized with the stress and strain of being boarded. "I can only imagine being in a totally different environment that you are not used to. It's very stressful. It's stressful for me when I when I am visiting one place that's not my home, . . . and he's never gone long periods of time without us [her and her partner]. So . . . I just think it would be too stressful for him."

"Doing mind" for Julie was an ever-present activity concerning Chance's comfort levels, and throughout the interview, she reported repeatedly making decisions with regard to perceptions of his sentience. Empathy over how one's animal feels about being left to live outside was also prominent across interviews. When participants were asked where their animals lived, inside or outside, a common theme was that their companion animals lived inside. They often cited the extreme heat typical of Texas weather or the "comfort" of the animal child.

Shay, a childfree participant, likened leaving an animal outside to being abusive. "We only take her outside to go to the bathroom and go on walks and play. That's it. But she lives inside, she sleeps inside . . . because it's too hot. It's animal abuse to let a dog sleep outside. I can't stand it. I mean, you know what, what's even worse to me is seeing . . . dogs outside panicking, you know, especially without water."

These basic caregiving themes were common across all narratives (for all interview participants) and demonstrated a basic level of "doing mind" for the animal child, in which the owner actively interpreted "desires" of the animal. This was not surprising given that all participants identified their animals as members of the family rather than as property, as the family pet was characterized throughout the first two-thirds of the twentieth century. But it highlights a basic component of symbolic interaction in which the actor makes determinations about their own future behavior on the basis of the perception of the other actor's intentions.

IN-DEPTH HEALTH CARE AND VETERINARY RELATIONSHIPS

Participants without human children were particularly concerned for their animals' health, beyond basics such as routine veterinary care. This concern appeared in several different forms including large financial expenditures on critical care, carefully researched medical options, and patient advocacy. Maeve, a childfree female in her early thirties, worked very hard to ensure that her puppy, Cavan, was not exposed to bacterial or viral infections that could give him life-threatening illnesses, much like the parent of a newborn human child might do. She explained how she protected his health for the first several months of his life with her. "He can't really be out yet. We bundle him up, everything. He doesn't touch anything. We pick up our shoes. Any guests that comes to our house gets hosed down by just everything. 'Wash your hands. Take off your shoes.' Hose you down before you'd be able to touch Cavan. Basically, we don't really have people over, because . . . just to avoid that [danger]."

For people without human children who were dealing with serious animal injury or chronic illness, willingness to spend much-larger amounts of money to get their animal children healthy, much like a parent would do for a human child, was a frequent subtheme. This kind of experience was often quite painful for participants, both emotionally and financially. However, euthanasia was never viewed as an option simply for alleviation of financial strain. Becky, a childless female, recounted how she and her husband took out a loan to cure their dachshund "baby" of partial paralysis.

> They said she had a calcified back injury. Basically, they said there is a microsurgeon that does back surgeries. . . . They said, "You can take her over [to surgery], or we have to put her down. . . ." And so what are we doing? We are not going to put our baby down. We took her, . . . and they said it's gonna be a bit over three thousand dollars. . . . They had CareCredit available for veterinary situations. . . . We went for the three thousand dollars to save her. Because we weren't gonna . . . most people would be like, "That is just a dog." Like, it is *not* just a dog! If a person has a head injury, you won't sit there and say, "Hey, Mom, I'm sorry if you broke your leg. We are putting you down," you know [*laughs*]. . . . They are like little kids. You cannot sit there and say, "We cannot afford [it]."

Wrenn, an involuntarily childless female, empathized with her animal children, reporting that, regardless of the cost, she would do whatever it took to ensure that her babies got what they needed. Explaining that three of her four rescue "babies" had recently been diagnosed with expensive-to-treat ailments, including diabetes requiring "daily insulin shots," a thyroid disorder, and seizures of unknown origin, Wrenn questioned, "What is wrong? Were these dogs brought into our lives because we were able to [financially] provide the medical care they need? We have the means to give them the love that they need?" She spoke of the first animal child whom she and her husband had brought into their family. "He just instantly became our baby. . . . He was very spoiled. I remember as he was aging, he had to have this really high-dollar stuff to go in his food. And I remember somebody said to me, 'You would spend that on your dog?' And I remember not even stopping to think. . . . And I said. 'Well, if your child needed it, would you buy it? He's *my* child, and he needs it, and he's going to have it. If I have to take a second job, he's going to get it.'"

The majority of participants without children were very well read on their animal children's health situation, knowledge of which is also culturally and institutionally expected for the adequate care of human children. This kind of knowledge armed animal parents with the confidence to engage in patient advocacy. Wrenn spoke of the veterinary decision to increase a phenobarbital dose for her "baby" with seizures: "I Googled it and researched it [endlessly], which I knew I shouldn't do because I am constantly driving the vet crazy with, 'You gotta check his liver.'"

Careful, studied care of animal "babies" and associated patient advocacy were common as well. Indeed, animal parents were not willing to compromise their animals' health because of perceived inadequate veterinary care.

Shay, a childfree female, noted that her animal child, Mia, was prone to vomiting, and she was irritated with one veterinarian in particular, who insisted on regularly administering an antinausea medication that was particularly painful. "It really, really stinks, and most of them [vet patients] cry when they get it because it hurts so much. And I am like, 'Why does she need it?' Just make sure she is not dehydrated, and she will be fine." Shay became so irritated with the vet who would not acknowledge her questions that she finally chose to see a different vet in the practice, who listened to her concerns and agreed to try alternative treatments.

Julie, a childfree female, described her discomfort with further entrusting her schnauzer-mix "baby" to a veterinarian who had misdiagnosed an invasive lipoma located on the dog's back leg.

> I don't even feel comfortable. . . . Even the vet I took into for his leg, I'm not even comfortable with that anymore. So we have to find a different vet to take him into. Because while grooming him, . . . I found that they had left part of a suture knot in his leg from the surgery. And I had to remove it, and I was so upset that I had to remove it! I was already skeptical about this . . . because even within the same clinic, we got two different diagnoses, . . . two different [pieces of advice] about his leg and about how they advised us to go on his surgery for his leg.

PHYSICAL AND EMOTIONAL PROTECTION

Just as protection of human children is a primary function of the parent, protection of the animal child emerged as another prominent subtheme of caregiving.[38] Over two-thirds of participants without human children were very concerned about protecting their animal children, ranging from protection from physical attacks to defense against emotional attacks such as teasing or harassment from others to protecting their babies from psychological trauma.

Jed, who had chronic mobility problems from a decade-old leg injury, was willing to risk his own physical safety in order to protect his dachshund, Wilma. While he had been adamant that he did not think of the dog as a child because he and his partner both wanted human children so badly (Jed's partner had been diagnosed with infertility), Jed later explained, "[Wilma had] taken on that role [even though] I didn't intend for [her] to." When asked what made him feel like that, he said, "I guess the way I react to things with them would be the best indicator that it's kind of turned into that because we are very protective of them, . . . like you would be of kids. . . . It's gone beyond just taking care and looking out for a pet." He recounted a particularly poignant experience in which he willingly used his own body to protect his aging dachshund:

We live in not the greatest place right now, but there's a lot of stray dogs that come by. Of course, Wilma's always on a leash. She never gets off her leash when we're outside because we don't want to lose track of her. I had taken her out. This is when I'm in the condition I'm in right now, which is hard for me to move or get around, and I was standing on our deck. She had run down the steps, and here comes a dog this way. The dog just started heading for Wilma, and so I got upset and started yelling and just took off down the stairs. I could have injured myself, but just without thinking, I'm going to protect her. . . . I don't think I've made it down those steps that fast in a long time. I ran down. I grabbed her and was yelling at the people and the other dog. "You need to have your dog on a leash!" I didn't know if the dog was going to attack her. The dog's much bigger than she is, obviously much younger. I don't know. You just run down, protect. I didn't really give a thought that I could fall down these steps. I could be attacked by the dog myself. I don't know these people coming. They could be whatever. They could be angry or a hothead. You never know how people can react, but I didn't take any of that into account. I just wanted to protect the dog, protect Wilma.

This kind of willingness to provide protection in the face of one's own safety was repeated throughout other interviews. Hannah discussed her experience of "terrifying" fear when her animal child disappeared from her sight on a camping trip. She suddenly heard high-pitched screams from her dachshund, Sam, as she was attacked by another, larger dog.

I heard Sam crying and squeal out in pain. . . . Not being able to get to her, . . . not being able to get *to* her, was really upsetting. . . . [I was] feeling really worried and wanting to know she was safe and really wanting to get her into a safe place. I wanted to run to her, and I couldn't. I mean, I physically could not run. . . . With the biting, I just remember feeling so helpless because I could not get to her, could not make the other dogs stop. . . . I think she was a little bit freaked out but not as much as I was. Like, I was far more upset by the entire situation.

Hannah's helplessness, worry, and fear at not being able to keep Sam from physical harm show that her concern is parental in nature, even as she also reported being worried that Sam may have hurt someone else.

Of course, noting that she was far more "freaked out" than Sam is also reminiscent of a parent reporting greater levels of concern over a traumatic event than a human child expresses.

Physical protection also appeared in the form of preventative measures. Beth, a childfree participant, had fashioned a carabiner through a seatbelt in her vehicle to create a "car seat" for her animal child, a male cat named Owen. She explained her rationale for doing this: "To me that's what it is. It's like a baby seat back there. Because if I have to slam on the brakes, I don't want him sliding. . . . If we were rolling around . . . or flying or something . . . It is bad enough with the seatbelt on a human. He can't be just back there rolling around."

Still other evidence of concern over physical safety appeared in participants who had dogs with seizure disorders. Kathy remembered, "[When] Rom would seizure, my husband and I would lay in a circle around her, . . . with seizures, sometimes for an hour and a half." Likewise, Wrenn and her husband had a very detailed plan in place for the safety of their husky/shepherd mix:

> Mostly what we are doing is keeping him from hitting his head on anything. We love on him. We talk to him really calmly and tell him, "Luke, you're going to . . . be okay." We're also telling everybody else [their other three animal children] that it is going to be okay. [Bob] is usually on one side of Luke, and I am usually on the other side to keep him safe. . . . So we are mainly trying to get him padded and comfort him so that when he does come out of the seizure, we are the first people that he sees that he is okay.

The hour and a half that Kathy and her spouse (both working professionals) invested in keeping a seizing Rom safe or the extensive lengths that Wrenn went to for Luke highlight a relationship that is far more than that of a pet owner and animal. Rather, these are people with a substantive identity connected to their animal children, willing to stop their lives for the safety of their multispecies family. The disposition to invest so much in protecting the animal child suggests behavior that is not only seen in parents of human children but also culturally expected. Participants without human children were able to provide instances of exactly this cultural expectation, highlighting their performances as parent.

Figure 2.1. Wrenn and Luke in recovery from his seizure

Many participants also reported engaging in emotional protection against teasing and bullying of the animal, as well as past traumatic experiences, another parental behavior that is written into American cultural scripts regarding the parent identity. Emma, a childfree female in her twenties who worked as a speech-therapy professional, shared that "if dogs could have autism, Brady would have autism, [being] very skittish, . . . jumping at the click of a remote, and wanting to go to the door and outside." She had had repeated discussions with her husband about his intentionally making Brady "freak out" by "throwing a soccer ball or hitting the remote on his chest every once in a while." She explained why this irritated her: "He likes to annoy Brady. He thinks it's funny, and I am not thinking it's funny. I am thinking he's really scared and it is *not okay*." She also reported reprimanding her husband for yelling at Brady: "He is just wanting some attention. Like, if you will just . . . tell him you love him, he will go lay down and be happy."

In another instance of "doing mind," in this case by interpreting teasing as hurting her dog's feelings, Lynn, a childfree participant, was furious with her friends for making fun of Roger's chronic, asthmatic cough, remembering the last episode of teasing: "The last girl I think I made feel really bad. But I'm like [*irritated voice*], 'I don't make fun of you or your kid or anything like that.' I mean he can't help it [*defensively*]. He's sick." Lynn had been quite transparent that she viewed her dog as a child and made no qualms about standing up for Roger when needed.

Reminiscent of an "adoptive mother," Wrenn also spoke of psychologically protecting her animal children from traumatic memories as best as she could, noting, "I have a philosophy that all of my babies have been on the streets at some point. And I just set my goal to make sure that they don't ever have to think about that or fear that again. I want them to know that they are safe and protected and loved. Because I just feel like they had such a rough start."

These reports of physical, emotional, and psychological protection were laced with poignant accounts of people defending their animal children without concern about their own physical safety, social rebukes, or loss of time. Furthermore, the extensive lengths that Wrenn went to for Luke's comfort highlight a relationship marked by the perception of both animal mindedness and parental behavior. Likewise, Jed's willingness to sacrifice his own safety and Beth's proactive "seatbelting" reflect the cultural expectation of American parents to protect their children.

NIGHT CARE

Just as in-depth health care and protection are key elements of caregiving for children, the bevy of sleep-training literature makes it clear that, culturally, American parents are expected to interrupt their own sleep for the young child's sleep training or illness.[39] Over half of the animal parents in this research reported a variety of disturbances in sleep for their young or ailing animal children. Julie remembered sleepless nights teaching Chance to fall asleep as a pup:

We, much like couples who just had a baby, kind of alternate nights. . . .
We would do that with him. There were times when [her partner] couldn't
get Chance to sleep. He tried everything—giving him food, taking him
outside to use the bathroom—but he still wouldn't fall asleep. I used to
take him to the couch out in the living room, and I would sleep on the
edge of the couch, and he would sleep on the inside of the couch, and I
would just rub his belly until he went to sleep. And it worked!

Julie acknowledges here the similarity in her and her partner's efforts to
that of a newborn child's parents, and their reported behavior is indicative of a commitment to a parent identity that they both share and even
support in each other.

In line with another sleep-training strategy used by parents with
human infants and toddlers, Michelle, a thirty-something, childfree participant, spoke of allowing her bulldog to "bark it out." While Michelle
did not appear to parent Champ, per se, she reported that she thought
her husband, Nick, was far more likely to think of Champ in ways similar to that of a young child. When I asked her why she thought this, she
provided an anecdote: "In the last eight or ten weeks, Champ has started
barking at night . . . because the neighbors and their kids moved in, and
they have two more dogs. . . . Their dogs are out at night, and we think
this is disturbing Champ. He just starts barking, and we are not getting
any sleep at all. My solution is we let him just bark it out. That's what we
did when he was a puppy."

Caught off guard, I asked her, "Did you just say 'bark it out'?" She
answered,

Yeah, bark it out, cry it out. Eventually he would just know that we are not
going to come and that he has to stay in his crate. Well, we just couldn't
take it anymore. We got him a bark collar, and it's like I had to tell Nick
all about the research and that this is not a cruel thing, and we got him
one of those high-powered things. . . . The first few nights he would still
bark through it. So I tightened it up one night. At 5:30, when I got up, I
was like, "Oh, *sweet*, he slept through the night, and this is great." I go in
the living room, and there is Nick and Champ at 5:30 in the morning, and
they slept in the chair all night because he was worried how tight the bark
collar was. And that made him [Nick] uncomfortable. I said, "Hey, honey,

he is a dog, all right?" We checked it, he has lots of skin, he is fine. So the next night we just let him sleep through the night with his bark collar, and he was fine. It just took Nick that time to be convinced that it's all right. We are adults, we managed the risk, the dog is gonna be all right.

Both Michelle and Nick engaged in "sleep training" of sorts in this example. However, there was a clear distinction between Champ as a "dog" in Michelle's eyes and Nick's parental behavior. Nick, worried about the health implications of a shock collar for Champ, sat up in a chair throughout the night with a wary eye toward the outcome. His concern for Champ both clearly outweighed any desire for his own comfort throughout the night and also demonstrated behavior characteristic of intensive parenting.

Other participants discussed different nighttime scenarios as they struggled with sleep deprivation out of concern for their animal children. Wrenn discussed Jasper's first several weeks of adapting to their home as an "adoptive child" but being scared to be inside the house. One night, she said to him, "Jake, at this house babies don't sleep outside. You need to come inside the house": "And he . . . wagged his little tail and climbed into my hands. But for about the first three months, I literally had to rock him to sleep at night, so that he can relax and go to sleep. So I would literally stand in our bedroom, just like a human child, and I would basically rock and pat him until he would relax and go to sleep, and then I would let him down in his little bed that we had. And then he would sleep all night." This was typical of Wrenn's behavior with all four of her animal children. She actively worked to make her animal children feel welcomed as *her* children, noting that the dogs "ruled their home."

Lynn shared that she was up often in the middle of the night out of concern for Roger's chronic asthma. When asked why she stayed up at night with him, she explained, "I have to . . . because he's usually coughing, and I can't sleep through that. . . . I get really worried about him. I just don't know if he is going to be okay. I usually wind up giving him a breathing treatment or something which has steroids which wakes him up. . . . I try to do everything in my power that I can do. Sometimes we [herself and Roger] wind up calling the emergency vet."

The in-depth health care, protective behaviors, and night care engaged in by participants without children reveal an adherence to the

Figure 2.2. Wrenn with Annabelle, shortly before Annabelle's death

cultural definition of how a parent in the United States should behave, regardless of the species of the child. As Sanders has also found, participants constructed meaning for the mental states of the animal child.[40] However, "doing mind" as a means of translating the animal child's emotions, desires, and needs was not the end game in these interactions. More potently, the act of placing oneself in the "paws" of their dog or cat led to the formation of a salient parent identity that strengthened the bond of their multispecies family.

At the macro-level, we can see these parent-child relationships reproduced and reinforced by veterinarian newsletters geared toward people who parent their pets, with a special focus on younger generations who are increasingly thinking of themselves as a parent to their pets. *Veterinary Practice News*, an industry publication focused on industry news and products, encourages veterinarians to approach their human clients as pet parents to animal children. Emphasizing the need to build trust with Millennials, who strongly scrutinize veterinarian reputations and services, the industry reinforces the existence of the multispecies family without children by reporting on ways in which these parent-child relationships require unique treatment within the clinic environment.[41]

Parental Relationship with Animal Child

Participants without human children overwhelmingly described experiences during which an identifiable parent-child relationship had emerged. While both those with human children and those without often described their animal as a "child," "kid," or "baby," only the group without human children substantively described experiences in which an identifiable parent-child relationship had emerged with the companion animal. Fourteen participants without children provided considerable depictions of a parent-child relationship between themselves and their animals.

For example, Becky described a relationship with one of her dachshunds, Sasha, that decidedly depicted a parent-child relationship between the two of them. "If you could have a five-year-old child ever, she is the one. She wants to be your shadow everywhere. . . . She is like a little shadow. She's kind of like the five-year-old little girl. She loves stories. That sounds crazy. We read stories to them. Like 'The Pokey Little Puppy' books [*laughs*]. But when we read stories to them, she would look up at every word." But it was not just the kinds of things that Becky did with Sasha or the similarity in Sasha's personality to a human child that painted a vivid picture of the mother-child pairing. It was the way that Becky described their relationship.

> She is part of your everyday life. And there is a bond, . . . not much different than a human bond. I'd rather enjoy spending time with her than some of the people I know [*laughs*]. You have an *unconditional love*. And part of it too [is] like the way you hold them. . . . It kind of feels like holding a baby, 'cause I have her little head up here [*motioning toward her shoulder*] and hold her little feet underneath here, you know. It's kinda like holding a human baby in a way. . . . You get the hormonal attachment there, maternal instincts kick in, you are protective, and all that.

Scholars have described the parent-child relationship as marked by internal boundary maintenance in which the parent works to draw "clear hierarchical difference between themselves and their children."[42] Just as parents with human children might, participants provided examples of boundary maintenance. Emma, a childfree participant, described the hierarchy in her family as a collectivity, saying, "They are just our babies. They are younger than us. They listen to us. So, collectively, we are like their parents. And they are like our children." Beth also thought of her relationship as one containing a parent-child boundary. When asked if she thought of herself as Owen's mom, she replied, "Oh yeah. And he is my little boy. . . . I call him 'little boy' and 'mama's little boy.' . . . He definitely is. I care about him. I take care of his health. I am always worried about if he is okay, if he is going to be all right."

After asking Jed if he felt like his two animals fulfilled anything for him and his spouse as children in the family, he answered, quietly crying, "I think they do. I think truthfully they probably fulfill the role of children because . . . I don't consciously think about it like that, I guess, because I set out not to purposely—because we want [human] children. . . . Whether we wanted them to or not, or whether we identify them like that or not, they really do."

This delineation and definition of boundaries between the parent and animal child extended beyond the participants' own private experiences too. Jody, who had originally been told by her doctors that she could not have children, described how her dialogues with other people concerning her dog, Sally, were so marked by this boundary that other humans sometimes misunderstood the relationship. "Oh, she was my daughter. I talked about her so much that when . . . I had a new employee start and I was just talking about Sally, and somebody said to her, 'Just to keep you straight, Sally is a dog, not a human.' And that is when I realized I must be talking about her like she is a kid."

Life Modification for the Animal Child

Life modification for the animal child inductively emerged, as something that I had not originally expected, in interviews with both childfree and childless participants. Over half of participants spoke of making major life decisions about work and family while taking the welfare of their animal child into serious consideration. For some, this meant career changes, while for others, it meant changes in relationships with other significant human actors. Hannah, a childfree participant, spoke of a program that she had been doing called "Seven Habits of Highly Effective People" that had created a new direction in the lives of her and her dog, Sam, together.

> I think the more I do like things like Seven Habits, . . . I start to question where you're putting your time and attention. The more things add to my life, the more time I stop spending with her, and I don't want to do that. I want to find more ways to be around her. And I think it is probably—our emotional bond has grown over time. Part of it is that I enjoy being around her, and I would love to be more around her. I think another part of it is knowing that there are huge chunks of parts of the day where she is just existing, right. And that's all there is to it. I mean, there's no interaction. There is not really anything for her to do. . . . I mean I am at this place, and I'm not spending time with her. It just seems silly to have her.

Indeed, research has found that spending more time with one's child is imperative to "good" parenting, even in the face of a full-time job or career. Rectifying the strain that naturally emerges from the competing demands of being a parent and being an employee or professional is actually indicative of work-family balance.[43] Hannah found herself making career changes and plans that would allow her to spend more time with her child, prioritizing the quality of relationship with Sam in a way that impacted time spent on her career.

Hannah was not alone. Beth spoke of choosing to return to college for both her and her cat Owen's future. "I feel like I am preparing for the future. And if Owen is in that future, then he is affected by my future. And I even surprised myself the day that I said [to Owen], 'Mommy is going to make a better life for both of us.' And I thought, 'Gosh, where did that come from?'" Beth later paralleled her motivations to that of a single mom as she sought a way to describe why she had said this to Owen. "I see even in myself identifying with single moms who want to go back to school to create a better life for their kids." This kind of identification with other single mothers struggling to return to school makes it clear that Beth thinks of herself as a parent. It was the enactment of this identity as she discussed motivations for returning to school that prompted her to tell Owen she was going to make a better life for them both.

Life modification for the animal child on a personal level was also present in participant reports. This typically involved cutting off or altering other human relationships because of the animal child. Four participants noted that the human-animal relationship had prompted them to reconsider a growing relationship with an opposite-sex partner. Hannah is one example:

> I was dating this guy, and he was great, but he doesn't like dogs. So I was like, "All right, we're dating, but this isn't going to be long term, you know?" And so we had a very nice time together, and that was great, but, like, we're never gonna go on vacations where my dog's gonna chase his cats and . . . So it was like, she kind of helped to keep the relationship casual, which is probably good [*laughs*]. . . . But that is one thing I never thought would happen either, that somehow she would . . . which I guess it's kind of if you have a human kid, it's the same thing. You wanna make sure they like your kid.

Beth, who had met and married a man with adult children after Owen came into her life, found out shortly after she and her new husband made their first move together that he might want her to give away Owen and another cat she had at the time. She was incensed.

> That was a tense moment, where I thought, "What do you . . . ?" We have known each other for a long time. . . . He knows what I am about. And I thought, "I can't even believe you are suggesting that." And we worked out an arrangement with the house in Colorado that [the cats] had the whole bottom level. . . . But for me to go there without my cats, that would have been a deal breaker [*quietly pausing*]. . . . Because I feel like—first of all—these cats were here before you were. So I am going to pull the rank card. And I am not going without these cats. My husband has three grown sons. Are you just going to forget about your

kids? Because [*pausing*] . . . that sounds totally crazy coming out of my mouth, . . . but if you are not going to forget about your kids, I am *not* going to forget about my cats.

Beth was adamant that her animal children were not simply pets to be given away. Instead, she reported feeling committed to them as if they were her children, paralleling her parent-child relationship with them to that of her husband's own biological children.

Other participants were willing to alter their lifestyles for the sake of their animal children. Wrenn recounted how, fresh out of college, her husband had gotten a job in another state, where they could not find a place to live that would allow their first animal child, Jared, as a resident. After having a serious conversation about living arrangements for their family of three, Wrenn and Bob made the decision to live apart, with her staying in Texas with her family, while he moved on to his job. The arrangement would only be in place until Bob could secure a suitable home for them, but they agreed it was better for Jared that he have Wrenn in his life rather than being left behind with Wrenn's parents while a new home was secured.

Still others made it clear that the emotional and physical well-being of their animals took partial precedence over other significant family members. Julie, her partner, and Chance had lived for several years in close proximity to her tightly knit family in Massachusetts, visiting often. However, they moved to Texas when they both began graduate school. Julie explained why they had not gone home to visit her family since the move: "We really haven't been home to visit together. And it's not the easiest to take him on a plane: . . . put him in a crate and board him with the luggage. And Chance just is not used to being in the kennel. I'm not riding in a kennel, and my baby is not riding in a kennel." When asked directly if Chance was the reason they had not been home for a visit, she said, "I am going to go yes. Because I would not feel comfortable . . . boarding him. . . . I would want to take him." Enacting the parent identity, and prioritizing her animal child over other significant familial relations, Julie chose to stay in Texas for the welfare of Chance, maintaining contact with her family long distance.

The willingness to make major occupational changes or to alter personal relationships for the animal child is important to consider alongside the claim that the multispecies family has emerged as a new, nontraditional family structure. For example, an entire industry has cropped up to support animal parents who, striving for work-family balance in their multispecies family, require products and services to help them do just that. For example, Camp Bow Wow, a dog-services franchise, provides doggy day care, overnight boarding, and in-home pet care. Webcams are kept on-site so that moms and dads can check on their family members throughout the day.[44] For owners who decide to leave their pets at home during the day, the Furbo Dog Camera is a full HD Wi-Fi pet camera that allows people and their pets to "speak" to each other. Treats are dispensed on the owner's command, and the system alerts the user if their dog begins barking, allowing for check-ins to make sure everyone is safe at home.

Corporate policy has also begun to shift to address the needs of multispecies families that parent their animals. For example, Brew Dog, based in Ohio, offers employees "pawternity" leave, allowing them to take one week of paid time off when they bring a new dog into the family. Bark, parent company to the online BarkBox, provides extensive support to employees who are new pet parents while also allowing them to bring their dogs to work with them.[45] And, combining both service and corporate policy, Dogtopia, a doggy day care franchise, is now partnering with other corporations to provide employees with on-site, company-subsidized dog day care.[46] Growing demand for products, services, and corporate policy such as these examples accurately reflects the narratives of the childfree and childless people with whom I spoke. These examples also show structural reinforcement from formal organizations for the multispecies family as a distinct family structure in need of unique solutions.

Socialization

Most of the people with whom I spoke who did not have human children made it abundantly clear that they understood that their animals would not develop morally, academically, or otherwise in the way that a human child would. However, almost two-thirds of participants in this category reported engaging in some form of socialization activities with their pets that is generally regarded in the United States as requisite in the promotion of early childhood development.[47]

PLAYDATES

Over a third of participants without human children discussed socializing their own animals with other animals and their families via playdates and trips to the dog park. One participant discussed slumber parties. These activities were interpreted as modes of socialization both because the participants often referred to them as such and because the playdate and slumber party can be key elements of peer play interaction important to the social development of children.

Playdates involve parental facilitation of meetings between young children in which they can play together. Playdates assist in the practice of social skills involved in peer play interactions.[48] The practice is widespread enough among parents in the United States that playdate applications and websites such as Playdate Planet have been developed to help parents of human children navigate their children's social calendars. A quick search on Google indicates that application designers realize that multispecies families that parent their dogs need playdate matching for dogs as well. As a result, a variety of "matchmaking" apps have become available, depending on what one's dog needs in a playdate match.[49]

This same type of socialization emerged in several interviews, reinforcing the idea that parental activity that is common to people who are raising children has also come to be expected of those who are parenting especially dogs in the multispecies family. Shay preferred playdates rather than dog parks for socializing Mia because she did not feel that Mia was old enough or confident enough to navigate dog parks. Shay described her process for setting up playdates: "I will seriously text up my friends who have puppies and be like, 'Hey, do you wanna come over and let our dogs play?' She [Mia] had one on Saturday. And she loves them. . . . She will completely tire herself out. . . . I love it!" Shay also noted that several of her friends did not have human children but had dogs. As a result, the group had begun to have their "puppy playdates together," increasing both her own and Mia's social activity with the group.

While Julie did not speak about playdates per se, she worked to socialize her animal child in other ways. She and her partner enjoyed

Figure 2.3. Maeve's "boys," Luke (*left*) and Cavan (*right*), at their birthday party, where both canine and human friends were in attendance

taking Chance to the dog park on a regular basis, especially when regional weather had permitted it:

> We liked to take him to Wiggly Field. . . . It's nice because it's gated, and you can let your dog run free with other dogs, . . . just because he needs time to play and be off the leash and go socialize with other dogs. . . . He should have that time. . . . And we would see more usual faces, and that was nice. So that way, if he liked playing with a particular dog and

he made friends, we could go there every evening and see the same dogs and the same people.

Julie and her partner worked hard to get Chance to the dog park each evening. And if they did not make it to the dog park, then they would simply take a bike ride together, pulling Chance behind Julie's bicycle with a baby bike trailer that they had purchased for Chance.

Jody socialized her animal child, Sally, with other humans, noting that she would send Sally on slumber parties with a close human friend of the family. Jody said that Sally had "claimed" this friend as hers and was very jealous of others when he was around. After Jody and her husband added another dog to the family, the friend would pick up Sally on Saturdays for a slumber party at his house. This was done as a way for Sally to have independent time with the friend away from the newest dog member of her own household. Jody noted, "He had a big queen bed, and she would sleep there with him. And she would just go have a slumber party." When Jody was asked why she did this, she said, "Because Sally wanted to, and he wanted to have a dog, and she just thought it was great. And so we would just let her go off. And she would come back . . . in such a good mood." Not only does this explanation suggest that socializing Sally in such a manner was good for her, but it also indicates the importance that this family placed on Sally having both human and dog friends.

Participants spoke about not only experiences socializing their animal children but also regrets for not having socialized them well enough. Kathy explained,

> We spent a lot of money! We had a trainer who came up to our home, and when you are doing one-to-one training for weeks, it is expensive. All that training, and we really did not socialize Rom enough. He could not be around other children. And when I had my relatives over, I had to put Rom in another room. . . . And there were some neighbor children who would throw things and tease Rom. And that was the saddest thing. And that was the big thing. The next dog that we had we promised we would take it to parades and schools and people and every chance we got when April [a subsequent dog] was little.

For Kathy, getting their next dog out and around others as a puppy became important because she wanted to be able to include her in activities with others. When she spoke of this particular facet of Rom's life, she was clearly bothered by it, and this was evident in her promise to get their next dog out around "other children."

Playdate activity only emerged in interviews with participants who had multispecies families without young children, with one exception. Amanda, a mother of three human children, noted that she had done puppy playdates in the past with a neighbor. However, that neighbor was childfree and had pursued Amanda for the interaction out of concern that her own single dog was becoming depressed. When Amanda was asked if she would have done playdates with her own dogs were this neighbor not involved, she said, "I don't think so. . . . It was not like I would say, 'Hey, can we have a playdate?' No." So even this one exception was linked to a childfree neighbor who, according to Amanda, treated her own dog as if he were a human child.

The macro-level emergence of applications and services meant to ease pet parents' needs for socialization are a good example of the emergence of broader social support for these multispecies families. However, other examples abound as well. Advice on how to plan the perfect dog playdate is common when searching online, with advice offered such as dog-proofing ahead of time, planning the guest list, and being prepared with the right supplies for the most successful outcome.[50] But such advice is not limited to dogs. The socialization of kittens is also encouraged, with similar advice tailored to the species, including starting playdates off at a young age, finding a neutral territory that neither cat feels possessive of, and watching the body language of all involved so that mom or dad can step in immediately if need be.[51]

DISCIPLINE

Discipline is also an expected role related to the parent identity and used as a means of socializing children about both appropriate and inappropriate behavior across a plethora of contexts. Indeed, multiple culturally accepted forms of discipline exist within the United States, including corporal punishment (spanking), time-outs, and crying it out (usually in time-out). Spanking is highly normative, with the vast majority of parents engaging in its practice and large swaths of society supporting the method.[52] Other, noncorporal modes of punishment are also viewed favorably within the United States. Time-outs, in which children are removed from the social situation to sit by themselves for an assigned period of time, are another form of discipline used with children, with 42 percent of parents reporting that they engage in the practice.[53] The removal of privileges also appears to be a prominent parental technique of correcting misbehavior, with 41 percent of parents noting use of it with their children.[54]

Likewise, a third of participants discussed in this chapter reported the necessity of engaging a variety of disciplinary techniques in line with those used by parents of human children, sometimes revealing characteristics of particular parenting styles examined in classic, well-researched child development literature.[55] Corporal punishment, time-out, or removal of privileges appeared in one way or another throughout these narratives as a way of socializing dogs about their "parents'" behavioral expectations, in both private and public contexts.

For example, one of several reasons that Emma provided for why she thinks of her two dogs as her kids concerned discipline and corporal punishment. When I asked her directly if she thought of her dogs as her children, she promptly answered with an example about Sasha, her 120-pound Rhodesian ridgeback: "Yeah, we have to use a belt for Sasha because he is so big, and he likes to get into everything, and if you spank him, it hurts you more than him because he is so big. So, whenever he's getting into too much, all we do is pick up [the belt], and as soon as he hears the jingle, he runs back."

Lynn also discussed her use of corporal punishment on Roger and her immediate rejection of the practice, revealing deep guilt about her one-time practice of the technique. Sharing her permissive style of parenting with Roger, she noted, "Nothing is ever his fault. It's always my fault. He never gets into trouble. I never discipline him. . . . Like, if he gets into the trash, I shouldn't have left it down on the ground. And my friend will be like, 'Lynn, he's a dog.' And I'm like, 'I don't care. He's my baby. . . . I love him, and I don't want to discipline him!'"

I pushed a bit more, asking, "Do you ever discipline him?"

"He's gotten into trouble once or twice, but not very often."

"When he got into trouble, what did you do to discipline him?"

"Depending on what happened. I don't remember what he did to get in trouble. I usually yell, 'No! No! No!' And he just looks at me like, 'What??! I'm so cute!' He knows he's cute and can get away with it. [There was] a spanking. But I just felt like . . . [*momentary silence and then speaking to Roger*] 'I'm so sorry! I'll never do it again!'" And with that, she craned her head in toward Roger, who had been patiently propped up on her shoulder like an infant during this part of the interview, and reminded him, "And I haven't. Have I, baby?"

Revealing a more authoritative style of parenting, Maeve offered a different take on her discipline style for her two Chinese shar-peis, Cavan and Luke. Cavan, a puppy when we completed this interview, was still integrating into Maeve and Josh's (her fiancé) current multispecies home. Luke, an older male sometimes short on patience with Cavan's high-energy, youthful vivaciousness, had been correcting Cavan's indiscretions by biting him as they played. Maeve explained how she and Josh had handled this "sibling rivalry": "They get a time-out. Because they are playing aggressively, and we tell them not to, . . . then it's a time-out. Cavan goes to the crate, and Luke goes to the hallway with the baby gate, so ten minutes. Nobody talks, no contact, you do what you got to, but that's it. After ten minutes, we let them out again as if nothing happened."

Reflecting the arguments that couples often have regarding discipline of human children, four participants' narratives reflected disagreement with their partners regarding discipline styles. Maeve offered the most comprehensive discussion of such disagreement, sharing that her fiancé handled discipline "differently" in their household. For example, while she might be willing to overlook one of "the boys" jumping up on her, Josh pushed her to "be a lot stricter." She also understood that being too easy on her dog children was not best in the long run, because "you don't want the dogs to grow up and not be disciplined and fight some kid or some other dog, and then they have to be put down."

But Maeve also struggled emotionally with Josh's style of discipline. Discussing how she and Josh had negotiated disputes about disciplining their dog children, Maeve offered, "It's just been ups and downs a little bit as in terms of discipline. He's [Josh] very disciplined and forceful, in a sense that sometimes I will just take Luke to the room and say, 'Let's just go to bed.'" When I asked, "Why do you do that?"

she answered, "Because I can't watch it." When I asked, "Is he aggressive with them, or does he spank them?" she said,

> No, there's never anything hands on. Nothing. For example, if Cavan is trying to jump, we step towards him with our body language to corner him and then say, "Shhh." But it's just the fact that [Josh] will do the "Shh . . ." and then sort of like a little nip with [his] hands on their skin, even though they have several folds. He would do that multiple times, but it's just the way of cornering him that makes me feel sad, because it's like, "How long are you going to corner him? He's just a puppy." Then I just have to leave.

Demands from people like Maeve and her husband for more knowledge about how to appropriately socialize, discipline, and train dogs and cats are on the rise. At the macro-level, book publishers have noticed this need and begun to produce an array of offerings for those who are parenting pets. The *New York Times* recently published an article titled "New Self-Help Books for Pet Parents," detailing key texts for reading, such as *Modern Dog Parenting: Raising Your Dog or Puppy to Be a Loving Member of Your Family* and *The Trainable Cat: A Practical Guide to Making Your Life Happier for You and Your Cat.*[56] A sampling of other titles, such as *Being a Super Pet Parent: Everything You Need to Know to Foster a Long, Loving Relationship with Your Dog* and *How to Behave So Your Dog Behaves*, reveal a market working to answer the needs of pet parents, especially those without children, who are seeking ways to ensure the success of their multispecies families.[57] This is an important contribution to the families themselves, but the increasing presence of publications like these also serves to accomplish something on a broader scale: the reproduction of the multispecies family as an acknowledged family structure with socialization needs that are unique compared to other types of family.

* * *

These themes clearly demonstrate the ways in which participants are behaving as "parents" to their dogs and cats in the culturally defined sense of the word. These acts reflect parenting within the family in ways that would be unsurprising in the context of the traditional parent-child relationships that defined "family" throughout the twentieth century. However, the presence of these relationships in the context of human-animal interaction makes them simultaneously unique to and indicative of the diversified nature of family structure in the United States today. Like the widespread emergence of single-mother or LGBTQ families, the multispecies family without children maintains distinct differences compared to the diminishing two-parent, heterosexual family with children of the past.

The most obvious of these differences is the absence of human children. Today, being without children would not preclude being acknowledged as a family. Indeed, if a man and woman are married without children, 92 percent of Americans regard them as a family.[58] While attitudes would not have trended this way before the 1960s, the diversification of family structure inherent in the second demographic transition has changed that.

However, the multispecies families that I discuss in this chapter bring to light even further diversification of the now culturally accepted family without children. These families are different from their single-species, childfree and childless counterparts because of the emergence of a parent-child relationship that owes its existence to the intimate relationships developed with their dogs and cats. They are unique in that they straddle both family structures—one in which the parent-child identity pairing exists because human children are present and the other in which such identities do not exist because human children are not present. The multispecies family without children is a hybrid of the two.

While people who are engaged in this type of family are clear that they know their dogs and cats are not children, they obviously treat them and think of them in ways that approximate that very relationship. In doing so, they experience the parent-child relationship inherent in families with children while not actually ever having children present in their immediate family. Their behavior also signals to others that they are engaged in the culturally expected practice of parenting (albeit it in an idiosyncratic manner), creating an emotional barrier against critics who would judge them precisely because they are not parents.

As people without children increasingly "do" this new kind of family, similar in form and fashion to families who are parenting young children, the resulting patterned behavior related to dogs and cats is captured in cultural conceptualizations of "family." We know this to be the case when demands for new federal policy arise to address multispecies family issues, such as the movement that seeks to expand the federal food-stamp program, Supplemental Nutrition Assistance Program, to pet-food purchases.[59] While the movement has not yet been successful, other nonprofit programs have been developed to answer the need, including STARelief Pet Food Pantry in Connecticut, which provides temporary pet-food assistance to those who financially qualify.[60]

Finally, the desire to demonstrate parental behavior within these multispecies families may well be the result of cultural mandates that measure ultimate adulthood via such activity.[61] However, the desire to feel acknowledged as a family may be felt even more deeply by those multispecies families that are also childless, compared to those that are childfree. For example, Wrenn spoke of "feeling validated as a family" because of her and her husband's relationship with their "babies." She reported having struggled for years with the fact that she and her husband could not have children, concerned that the world would question them as an *authentic* family. But her multispecies family and the intense bonds that she formed with her dogs are what ultimately allowed her to "show the world" that they were all family too—just like other families, except multispecies.

3

"Phil's Calling Grandma"

Supporting Family Identities

About halfway through the time that I spent engaged in fieldwork at the veterinarian's office, a vet tech came into the sick-bay area looking for me. I had been engaged in a conversation with one of the veterinarians about an eight-month-old terrier puppy who had contracted canine parvovirus, a highly contagious and deadly gastrointestinal virus. The damage from the virus can be greatly mitigated with proper vaccination, but, otherwise, it can have a mortality rate of over 90 percent, especially for young dogs. Days before, her owners had frantically rushed her to the clinic because she had been alternating between vomiting and bloody diarrhea throughout the day. But today, isolated from all other animals in the heavily disinfected sick bay, she was, surprisingly, in recovery. The veterinarian staff had provided constant care for her, nursing her throughout the night, providing her with intravenous fluids, antibiotics, and electrolytes in a bid to support her immune system as it fought off the virus. They had been successful, and Cleo was now resting in her sanitized, metal crate, her silky brown head too weak to pick up but her eyes alert and focused on us as we spoke.

The vet tech approached us quickly, motioning for me to follow him to a client whom he thought I would find interesting.[1] "This woman is *crazy*," he had informed me. "I think she is going to be great for your work!" While the sociologist in me shied away from the classification "crazy" to characterize a potential participant, I was admittedly curious. So I followed him away from the cold, patient-filled, stainless-steel sick-bay crates, through a heavy metal door that separated us from the cacophonic lobby filled with an array of different small animals, and then back through an old wooden, brown door that opened to a quiet, timeworn exam room only used in case of patient overflow.

When I entered the room, I found an older woman wearing a pair of tattered glasses framed by frazzled salt-and-peppery hair. She stood adjacent to, yet tightly against, the wire-mesh crate door that provided protection from the outside world for her aging calico cat. The cat had been diagnosed with stage 2 chronic kidney disease (a malady that is actually quite common in cats as they age). As we sat in the exam room together, she shared that she had adopted Carmella in the aftermath of Hurricane Katrina in New Orleans. Carmella was in on this particular visit because her owner had recently noticed that one of her teeth was missing. Now, she lounged calmly in the homemade wooden carrier in which her owner had transported her, peering out with golden eyes, curious about what was going on. As we waited for a different vet technician to arrive for a pre-exam check, Carmella's owner pulled out several sheets of newspaper, meticulously opening each page to its fullest extent and carefully lining the exam table with it. I watched quietly as she worked. I can only imagine that she felt conspicuous completing this activity in my presence, as she explained, "Because of her kidney disease, I am very careful with her. The paper protects Carma from all of the gross germs running around here." She gently pat Carmella on the head, murmuring, "We can't have you getting sicker, can we?"

The clinic was slammed with patients that morning, and the veterinary staff had seemed to move in a blur—running as fast as they could from patient to patient, room to room, drawing blood, giving vaccinations, running heartworm tests, examining clinic calls that could result in life-altering decisions no pet owner wants to make. When the vet technician finally entered the room to gather pre-exam data on Carmella, we had been waiting for close to an hour. Before the door to the back hallway had time to close behind the tech, Carmella's owner immediately advocated for her cat, asking, "Can I get you to wash your hands before you touch her?"

The vet tech, seemingly caught off guard by her request, paused for a brief moment. "Yeah, sure. No problem." He proceeded over to the small sink in the corner, nestled next to three jars stuffed to the brim with fluffy white cotton balls; crispy, brown, bone-shaped treats; and dum-dum suckers, and turned on the small faucet. It was only after he had washed his hands that the owner, offering no explanation to him, pulled Carmella from her temporary abode, gently placing her on the paper-lined table.

"We clean our rooms after each patient so that you don't have to worry about it," he offered as he stared at the exam table, unsure of what to make of her preparations. But, if he wanted an explanation, there was none forthcoming. The owner, stroking the cat's back repeatedly, simply provided loving reassurance to her, softly singing, "Carmella, Carmella, lovely, lovely Carmella."

* * *

In late 2019, a simple search for "crazy pet parents" on Google returned about ninety-seven million hits. On the first query page alone, there were ardent opponents to the idea, with links such as "Having Pets Instead of Kids Should Be Considered a Psychiatric Disorder," "Pet Parents Are NOT Moms," and "Sorry 'Pet Parents,' but Your Animals Are Not Your Children." However, there were also a plethora of supporters, indignantly defending the status: "Here's Why Pet Parents Are REAL PARENTS," "Dig Deeper before Mocking 'Crazy' Pet Parents," "Are You a 'Crazy Pet Parent'? Welcome to the Club."

The staunch posturing on Google reveals a society increasingly polarized by the way the family is defined and who *really* counts as a parent—or a child, for that matter—in American culture. As has been the case with single mothers by choice and gay and lesbian adoptive families that do not match up with the traditional ideals of Smith's Standard North American Family, performing the parent identity without human children present and in the context of nonhuman animals challenges widespread social norms that govern the definition of a legitimate family and parent(s).[2] Assigning a human identity like "child" to a companion animal is a blurring of the human-animal boundary that is worthy of a psychiatric disorder diagnosis (according to Google anyway). It is an act that is considered abnormal by a society wrapped up in the anthropocentric belief that humans are vastly superior to nonhuman animals.[3] But behaving as a parent would with a child is also symptomatic of the ways in which family has changed and diversified in the United States since the 1970s.

Erving Goffman, a social psychologist ubiquitously cited for his close, qualitative treatments of face-to-face interaction, used the term "stigma" to conceptualize behaviors that other actors—and society—perceive as unnatural and aberrant in those persons who engage in such expression. Actors who are stigmatized like this have been "disqualified from full social acceptance" and are expected by society either to alter their behaviors to fit in or to justify their actions.[4] In the United States, choosing to be childfree is a stigma in and of itself; choosing to be a pet parent is considered "crazy" outside of the pet-parent community.[5] Indeed, being intensely bonded with one's companion animal is met with memes like "crazy cat lady."

My research confirmed that performing as a "parent" without human children present would be a discreditable identity (an identity that, while not visible, could be discredited) and certainly viewed as an "unnatural passion."[6] For example, Lynn, the very first interview participant in my study, was a childfree female who proudly "parented" her Pomeranian Roger "as much as many would care for their kids." She had brought Roger with her to our interview, and he was a beautiful, shiny-black, snorty boy who clearly loved to be in Lynn's arms at all times. She mentioned in her interview that she thought Roger was better than human children. That peaked my curiosity. I asked, "What makes Roger a better option than kids?" She responded, "I know this is bad, but it is the truth. Since children give me anxiety, I see children as a burden. I see the life that I have with Roger or any other pet is superior over what people have with their children. I know that every person out there with children says that you don't know love until you have had a child. However, to me, a pet that is considered my all, as a child would be, is all I need to be complete." She tentatively paused and then said, "I hope this makes sense. Don't think bad about me because of my views. I know my views are not traditional, but they are how I see things, and to me, I see pretty clear." She was unmistakably worried about what I would think of her perception of her animal child. She qualified her statement twice by letting me know that she understood I would think she was a bad person but that this was just the way it was for her.

In stigma-management research, Lynn's verbal qualifiers are considered a classic technique for managing the judgment that is received from others for the performance of a disreputable identity. Lynn was justifying her "parent" identity by using self-fulfillment (as in "a pet that is considered my all, as a child would be, is all I need to be complete") as a reason for the identity's continued existence.[7] Indeed, from a stigma-management perspective, none of this was surprising. Lynn's excusing tactics (e.g., "I know this is bad, but . . .") and normalizing statements about her behavior (e.g., "Since children give me anxiety, I see children as a burden") allowed her to save face in our meeting while managing the stigma associated with her childfree parent identity. However, I wondered something else after that very first interview. Would any of my participants reveal that they felt supported in their roles as parents without children in a multispecies family (rather than just generally stigmatized)? And would that support prove meaningful to the ever-growing presence of multispecies families in the Untied States?

* * *

One of the main goals of this book is to empirically demonstrate how the multispecies family has developed as a form of diversified family structure in the United States, similar to other nontraditional families and increasingly accepted as such. Indeed, successfully making this argument is an important scholarly step toward two goals. First, recognizing these families as a legitimate familial structure bolstered by significant external support highlights how these relationships have moved from the "crazy cat lady" meme to the broader acceptance necessary to restructure cultural definitions of who family can be defined as. Second, arguing that the multispecies family is similar to, but also distinct from, other types of nontraditional families unveils the unique nature of this family structure. It also illuminates similar struggles, such as stigma, that other nontraditional families endure. Accordingly, I argue here that the stigma associated with the childfree multispecies family in which the dog or cat is treated as if they are a young child, is characteristic of the kind of pushback that any diversification of the traditional American family form has always received.

For example, families headed by teen mothers have been judged as both the cause and consequence of deep poverty, with some policy makers arguing that teen mothers seek to collect welfare so that they can stay at home and avoid working.[8] Gay marriage has been so historically stigmatized as an assault on the Standard North American Family that, up until the *Obergefell v. Hodges* US Supreme Court ruling in 2015, same-sex marriages were not recognized at the federal level, nor were states required to recognize any such union. Indeed, the Defense of Marriage Act, passed by Congress in 1996, legally codified the SNAF standard by defining marriage as only between a man and a woman. By the same token, childfree and (and childless, to some degree) multispecies families have been accused of contributing to a decline of the American family—first, by not having children and, second, by masquerading as parents to pets. Another criticism leveled at these same families is that they are contributing to a decline of fertility rates in the United States, endangering economic stability for generations to come, because they have replaced the need to nurture children by nurturing a dog or cat instead.[9]

Of course, having children in the United States is a moral imperative, even though one in five women (aged forty to forty-four) in 2006 and one in six women in 2016 have never given birth.[10] Childfree women, as well as men (though to a lesser extent), are met with staunch resistance from broader society as well as from their own families about not having children.[11] Indeed, Kristin Park, an American sociologist interested in women's lives, has noted that the stigma associated with not having children may actually be stronger in the past thirty to forty years than it was in the 1960s and 1970s.[12] Further, men and women who are childless because they experience infertility report feeling guilty and inadequate—emotions related to a sense of failure surrounding relationship development with their partners and meeting social expectations of such.[13]

Increasing numbers of men and women are choosing to delay or even opt out of childbirth, with the childfree movement standing firmly in the path of a pronatalist society that judges them for not having children.[14] In response, US culture continues to overwhelmingly assign "family" status only to those units that have borne children (or are at least in the process of doing so). With so much judgment being passed around traditional, middle-class family structure, it makes sense that families without children, especially those that internalize a parent-child relationship with their animals, are predisposed to the same kind of stigma. The second demographic transition has produced visibly different, and increasingly diversified, modes of family structure across increasing swaths of the US population. With growing cohabitation rates, decreasing marital rates, increasing divorce rates into the 1980s, and dropping fertility rates, each of these ever-evolving modes of "doing family" has been stigmatized in the name of the "American family" and, thus, family values.

Some scholars have noted that, in many ways, these particular couples and their multispecies families have been forged in response to this pronatalist imperative.[15] That is, as a protective barrier against the stigma of not having children in American society, many childfree and childless families and individuals have engaged in the building of their own multispecies families—treating their dogs and cats as surrogate children of sorts in an effort both to shut down criticism and to achieve legitimate family status. The level of concern from participants in my research over feeling judged for these relationships confirms this dynamic.

Childfree and childless participants repeatedly reinforced the idea that there is an additional stigma associated with intensive parenting of a companion animal.[16] The acknowledgment of a stigmatized identity was apparent in almost three-quarters of the interviews—indicated by some version of the same verbal qualifier: "People would say I am crazy for doing this, but . . ." or "You are going to think I'm nuts when I tell you this . . ." or "People might say 'it's just a dog,' but . . ." were all deliberate ways used by childfree and childless participants to acknowledge the violation of social norms for their behavior. One participant even sanctioned *herself* for her relationship with her dog, telling herself to "quit being stupid." The stigma was present as well in several interviews with participants who had both human children and companion animals present in the household, via statements like, "I could never be one of those people crazy about their dogs" or "It's definitely not my child like some weirdos out there."

Of course, social support, especially from those individuals who are the most important to the stigmatized person, is integral in creating a social environment in which the stigmatized identity can be performed and verified as legitimate. Indeed, the successful and continued performance of a role identity such as parent can rest very heavily on the support, or verification, that an actor receives from significant others.[17] This is especially so when an identity is stigmatized, as is the case for actors who choose to interact with their dogs or cats in ways that are reminiscent of a parent and a young child. Indeed, achieving a "favorable identity" in interaction with others is the foremost consideration of actors as they choose which of their identities they will enact in any given situation.[18]

That is, if an actor chooses to enact an identity that is neither acknowledged nor perceived favorably by significant others, then future performances of that identity could create unpleasant emotions for the actor. This negative experience leads the actor to do one of three things: reconsider their own interpretation of the identity, attempt to resituate other actors' perception of the performance, or abandon the identity completely.[19] Thus, the question of external support for the idiosyncratic parent-child identity pairing related to a pet highlights the importance of other, significant actors in successful enactment of these components of self.

The influence of other important, human actors is apparent in something as simple as Lynn's recounting a friendly argument that she and her mother have each time they discuss Roger, her Pomeranian. When I asked Lynn, "What does your mom call [him]? Just 'the dog'?" she promptly responded, laughing, "God, *no!* . . . She always says, 'How's my baby?' And I'm like, 'Mom, he's *my* baby!' . . . Every time I talk to her, she calls him her baby, . . . [but] if she is talking to somebody [else], . . . she is like, 'This is my grandbaby' or 'This is my grandson.' Actually, my ex-husband's mom does too." Indeed, this friendly disagreement between Lynn and her mother reinforces for Lynn not only that Roger should be accorded familial status (e.g., "How's my baby?" and "Mom, he's *my* baby!") but also that he should be afforded specific familial statuses such as "son" and "grandson." Both of these actions reinforce for Lynn that it is appropriate for her to internalize the parent-child identity pairing with Roger. Furthermore, both actions provide inarguable, clearcut support from Lynn's mother, who, acting as a doting grandmother might, playfully vies with Lynn for ultimate control over who gets to call Roger "baby."

This external support is also important for identifying the emergence of the multispecies family, in any form, as one that is gaining legitimacy as an acceptable form of family in American culture. As identity theory tells us, cultural expectations of what is acceptable behavior for any status only changes gradually. Those changes can only take place in the presence of repeated and patterned reproduction of new behavior across increasing numbers of groups. In this case, identifying external support that comes from one's partner, parents, siblings, and others is about showing that these patterns are increasingly spreading across diverse familial groupings and identities. Illuminating these relationships here lets us see that the multispecies family without children has unique characteristics that are supported and reproduced by other, immediate and extended family actors. This fabric of familial relationships only exists by virtue of the human-animal relationship.

Most importantly, this network of extended multispecies, familial identities helps to create and sustain the multispecies family without children as a new and acceptable form of diversified family structure. This occurs in similar ways to the emergence of other rapidly growing modes of "doing family," like the single-parent family or the LGBTQ family. Indeed, these diversified family structures have also relied greatly on external support from others to thrust their legitimacy as "family" into the cultural framework of society.

Identity Theory and External Support

A key component of identity theory is the importance of other actors for the existence of identity in self. Charles Horton Cooley, a classic stalwart in American symbolic interactionist theory, constructs the looking-glass self as a reflected appraisal—how one's knowledge of self comes from the *perception* of others' judgment of self.[20] In turn, these reflected appraisals allow the person to develop a self-concept that influences his or her behavior.[21] The enactment of identity is situational, dependent on the acknowledgment of other actors in that social space and place. Once a person has assessed any number of identities appropriate to enact in a given situation, the most favorable identity for that context is chosen.[22] Indeed, identity is only "established when others place [the actor] as a social object by assigning . . . the same words of identity that he appropriates for himself or announces."[23] As a result, successfully performing a particular identity only occurs if everyone in that situation agrees on its enactment.[24]

However, performance of the identity outside of situations that only involve the person and companion animal requires positive support from a team of other human actors for two reasons. First of all, acknowledgment and support from other significant actors, those who are important to the pet owner, allow one to situate the parent identity in additional social contexts that are not limited to just the owner and companion animal. Second, the support of other actors is key to both self-verification (where the person's actions replicate the cultural expectations of the status) and the positive affect that is related to performance of, in this case, the parent identity.[25] Commitment to an identity is produced when an actor works to maintain one's "perceived self-in-situation" with that of identity expectations within the culture. If an actor's reflected appraisals, gathered from other social actors, do not bear this out, then the actor works to behave in the ways that culture dictates one should when performing in a particular status.

Rewards and praise from other significant actors play a particularly important part in strengthening the positive feelings associated with identity verification.[26] An actor who is not successful risks feeling badly about him- or herself and may even completely abandon the identity to avoid future negative feelings.[27] Thus, identifying external support for any identity is germane to its resilience for an actor who views the identity as particularly important to one's self perception.[28] I assume here that external support of human-animal identity pairings such as the animal "parent" is paramount to the continued existence and enactment of that role identity.[29]

External Support for the Childless Parent and Its Value

Role identity requires external support, *among other factors*, to become increasingly salient and verified for its performance in particular contexts.[30] While I had expected participants with animal children to feel marginalized, I had not expected discussion of external support for the identity, though the identity literature has reiterated its importance for identity hierarchy and verification. Nor had I expected to encounter reports of the importance associated with such external support even though human-animal research has noted that people may speak of themselves as "grandparent" of a family companion animal, possibly suggesting an acceptance of an adult child as "parent" of an animal.[31]

As a result, comments in which participants labeled their own family members in relation to the animal "child" (e.g., grandparent-granddog; mother-father; uncle/aunt-niece/nephew) prompted me to consider whether participants without children (but who still internalized a parent identity) received any kind of external support for their behavior.

Indeed, almost two-thirds of participants recounted intense support from three different groups of people: their own parents, their partners, and, in one case, their adult siblings. This confirmed that other social actors might also access social role schemas typically reserved for human children and congruent with "grandparent," "coparent," or "aunt." Participants also clearly valued this support, using it to verify their own role identities, the validity of their relationship with the companion animal, and the overall multispecies family structure within which they lived. Additionally, empty nesters with pet-owning, adult children who were currently childfree provided further evidence that the multispecies family can produce new identities within the extended family structure that would not otherwise exist.

Grandparents Verifying Parents

Scholarship on grandparenthood makes it clear that explaining exactly what characteristics go along with the "grandparent" identity is challenging.[32] Indeed, the role that the "grandparent" should play has been called ambiguous in American culture, with a "diversity of roles into which grandparents are thrust, increased role confusion, [and the] idiosyncratic manner in which grandparents are forced to define their roles in today's society."[33] Much of this ambiguity surrounds issues such as the impact of parental divorce and remarriage on grandparent-grandchild relationships and the ever-evolving age at which one transitions to grandparent. However, based on an array of scholarship, it appears that behaviors such as financial help, emotional support, and domestic help given to both the adult child and the grandchild provide a reasonable basis for the purposes of this chapter.

In keeping with the literature on the increased grandparenting of fictive kin, well over half of the childless or childfree participants in my study reported some experience of their own parents identifying their animal "child" as a "grandchild" or "granddog."[34] Jody recounted how her mother labeled her golden retriever mix, Sally, as a "grandchild from the beginning." However, such emotional support did not stop at superficial labels. Jody elaborated by explaining how her mother had "pictures of [Sally] up around the house": "as many of her as she did of us kids sometimes, . . . [and] with her friends, she talked about her quite a bit."

Figure 3.1. Grandparents touting their love for their granddogs

The friendly arguments that I discussed earlier between Lynn and her mother over whose "baby" Roger *really* is provide an obvious indicator that Lynn's mother is willing to provide emotional support for both Lynn's internalized parent identity and Roger as a grandchild. However, Lynn's narrative makes it apparent that her mother is deeply vested in maintaining this multispecies relationship for Lynn while also engaging in grandparent-like domestic support of both Lynn and Roger. For example, Lynn remembered when her aging, asthmatic baby, Roger, had suddenly stopped eating and walking around on his own. She recalled her terror:

> I had just moved to North Texas, and I didn't know many people, and my family is like an hour away. . . . I thought he was dying, and I had to find

a vet immediately. He didn't wanna walk, he didn't wanna eat, he was just laying there. I was just scared out of my mind, . . . and the doctor says it's allergies. I was like, "Oh my gosh, what is wrong with my dog?" And my mom came and stayed that day with us for a week just to make sure he got all of his medicines on time and just to make sure he was okay.

When I asked, "As a result of that, she came and stayed with you?" she answered, "Yep. Yeah. And now every time I take him to the vet, she is like, 'Is he okay??! Is he okay??!' She . . . just knows he is a part of my family, and he is just like . . . my kid. He is my child."

Indeed, Lynn's mother made a habit of repeatedly showing emotional support for Lynn and Roger that was reflective of a grandparent identity, even going so far at one point as to lie to restaurant management concerning Roger's status as a service dog so that Roger could accompany them to dinner.

Lynn explained,

Well, my mom lied about him going to On the Border and sit[ting] on the patio. . . . This other family was like, "Oh, that's so disgusting. You shouldn't have brought him in here. . . ." And so they [the restaurant] weren't going to let us eat on the patio. And so my mom . . . [long pause] lied . . . [pause] and said he was a service dog [laughs], which is probably a big lie. She could have probably gotten in trouble for that. And so the manager comes running after us and says, "Oh, he's a service dog? Let me go talk to the other family."

Actions such as these both provide support to Lynn's labeling of her Pomeranian as her child and suggest that Lynn's mother has developed an identity within the group as a protective grandmother. Both actions are important to verifying for Lynn that her animal "parent" identity and the role performances associated with it are acceptable, thus increasing Lynn's commitment to the identity across a variety of social situations that involve more actors than just Lynn and Roger.

The importance of this kind of emotional support was evident when Julie explained how other family members think of Chance, her schnauzer-mix animal "child." She shared with me, "I think that they recognize that [my partner] and I have a very close attachment to

Chance. I think that they understand that Chance is not just our dog. He really is like our baby. He is our family. . . . There are some family members that think, 'All right, you're taking it too far. . . . It's a little bit ridiculous.' But there are family members who really get it. . . . My dad really gets it." When asked what she meant when she said her father really "gets it," Julie explained that he had included Chance in a cultural tradition reserved just for human family members:

> I think my dad treats him a little differently, like he is my baby. I think it's pretty common for Hispanic families [to give] everybody in the family . . . a nickname. And you have a nickname that is specific to your personality. It identifies something about you. My name is terrible. It sounds like a very ugly name. My nickname is Molonca. And in Spanish that means . . . "the baby corn." That's what it's called in Spanish, according to my dad. And the reason he calls me Baby Corn is because I had only one growth spurt in my entire life, so I was always very small compared to the other kids who were my age. So that's what he calls me. And Chance he calls Wolf Boy in Spanish because he says Chance looks like the wolf boys in Mexico, you know . . . the ones who have hair all over their faces? So my dad says, "Oh, you look like wolf boy!" So he calls him Wolf Boy in Spanish.

For Julie, this inclusion of Chance in a cultural tradition reserved for human family members signifies a "working agreement" between her, her father, and Chance. According to McCall and Simmons, a working agreement exists "when the cognitive processes of one person, with respect to social identities, are not in gross conflict with the expressive processes of the other person."[35] In Julie's case, a working agreement acknowledging Julie's parent identity and Chance's child identity exists in their interactions with her father. Julie recognizes his use of the nickname as evidence that he emotionally supports her identity:

> I appreciate it because . . . everybody has nicknames, but they are not meant to be derogatory in any way. They're actually meant to be endearing. . . . I think it means a lot, because it really is something that is specific to you. It is unique. And so it kind of means a lot. None of the other dogs that my mom has—two poodles and . . .—they don't have

nicknames, and Chance has a nickname though. I think that it's a big deal, I think. It's a big deal if Chance has a nickname but the other dogs don't.

Julie sees the nickname as an identifier, unique to a specific personality in Chance. Furthermore, she perceives the fact that none of the other family dogs have this support as a privilege (that is, her and Chance's identities in interaction both with each other and with her father). Her father's support reinforces her actions as a parent, even as other family members sanction it as "a little bit ridiculous." Ultimately, the positive feelings that she has as she enacts the parent identity make her feel like it is acceptable to perform "parent" in the presence of her family, especially when her father is involved. Furthermore, her father's verification of the identity increases her commitment to the parent identity across social situations outside of just her interactions with Chance.

Shay also discussed this recognition that the animal child is treated differently from other companion animals in the extended family. Her narrative highlighted emotional support from "Grandmomma" in a way that both reflected "grandparent" while also making Shay feel emotionally supported in her childfree role *and* as a parent to Mia, her nine-month-old husky. After Shay told me that Mia knows her (Shay's) mother by "Grandmomma," she went on to explain that her mother also calls Mia "her grandpuppy": "because she knows she is not gonna get kids from me." Shay and her husband visit her mother's home far more often than they visit his family because Mia is treated both lovingly and differently than other dogs in the home. Shay explained, "She gets special treatment over at Grandmomma's house. 'Cause the other dogs have to stay in the kitchen. Mia gets to go upstairs and all around." She warmly went on to label this individualized treatment of Mia as "favoritism!"

The identities of animal parent and grandparent were immediately negotiated between Wrenn and her mother and father when she and her husband adopted their first animal child, a canine mix named Phil. Emotional support of the "parents" and the "grandchild" was conveyed immediately via relevant familial labels. "As soon as we got Phil, . . . they were just instantly like, 'Phil's our granddog'—even then, that many years ago. They had always looked at it like that. Phil wanted to call and see how Grandma and Grandpa were doing. . . . They have always loved our dogs. They have always been welcomed in their home. They feed them whatever they want, just like grandkids, . . . to the point that I'm like, 'Don't give them any more bread! We're going to get in the truck and drive four hours!'"

Like Lynn's mother, the grandparent identity for Wrenn's parents went well beyond basic activities like gift giving and spoiling (though this is often the extent of American grandparent-grandchild relationships today anyway) to include the strong intergenerational domestic support present in some families. Wrenn's parents were both willing to invest time and effort in the supervision of their granddogs when Wrenn and her husband went out at night or traveled out of town. I asked Wrenn, "Do you feel like they [her parents] have been accepting of the idea of grandparenting the dogs?" She answered, "I think my parents have always taken on that role. . . . If we had to travel or something, we would drive through Fort Worth and drop off the dogs. Because I didn't trust anybody else to take care of them. . . . From my parents, it never would have been an issue to say, 'Hey! Will you take care of the babies?'"

When I asked Wrenn if her husband's parents had supported both her and her husband's parent identities, she noted that they had not but that eventually they had also "come around." She said, "The weird thing is that for years his parents . . . we never did that Grandma, Grandpa thing. But in the last five years they have. . . . It's like they know they are Grandma and Grandpa to the dogs. They do, and they seem to be okay with that."

Reminiscent of Julie, Wrenn's report signifies the presence of a working agreement in which her own parents acknowledge and verify that "parent" is an acceptable identity for Wrenn and her husband to perform across various social contexts.[36] In turn, Wrenn's parents had adopted the grandparent identity, an identity that never would have been present for them were it not for Wrenn's parent-child identity pairing with the dogs.

Hannah's parent identity was emotionally supported by her parents as well, via "parent-grandparent" pairings. Hannah had earlier pointed to the stigma associated with the way her relationship with Sam might be perceived, saying that she had to "be really self-aware": "I mean, social media is like satires constantly, . . . from like [the movie] Dog Show. So I am not going to be that type of owner." Even still, her reported behavior disclosed an intense parent-child identity pairing for which her parents had provided support. Hannah cautiously discussed this:

> We use the terms "Granddog," "Grandma," and "Mom." . . . I moved in with them two years ago, and my mom would take pictures and send them to me during the day and might even share one with our social circle. . . . They [Hannah's parents] will refer to me as "Mom" when talking to her [Sam]. . . . I mean we recognize the relationship, that it's more than just like, "Look there's a squirrel outside . . ." [silence]. I mean, part of it is it's just human nature; part of it is just naming things and making it more of an emotional connection than just Jane, Paul, and Hannah. . . . Sam, I call her my baby all the time. Not in a "I'm going to pick you up and wrap you up in a blanket" kind of way but "my baby" [laughs] . . . and also affectionately. But I think we must recognize that with caveats and limitations, there is very much like a—that she is the creature that I care for, as I would a child, and in relation to them, . . . I think the more that you care for something, it's just exponentially grows. And so we have that with Sam.

When I asked, "How does that make you feel that she has that connection with her?" she answered, "It makes me happy. . . . I really like it. I mean, she sends me pictures, and she loves to say the story when Sam chases squirrels. . . . That makes me happy because to me, it means not only does she recognize that I love Sam, but because now that she lives with Sam, she recognizes these behaviors. . . . She gets that there is a connection between me and Sam. . . . She sees that relationship and then has a connection to that relationship as well."

On the other end of these relationships, four empty nesters who were interviewed for this research also had childfree, adult children with their own dogs or cats. As a result, all four provided the foundation to ask directly if they perceived themselves as "grandparent" or behaved in any way that might exhibit the presence of such a common extended family member identity. Indeed, just because adult children feel supported by their own parents in these identities does not mean that the parents themselves have necessarily internalized the grandparent identity. My empty-nest participants could help me begin to understand if familial identities arising from the multispecies family really did impact the formation of extended familial identity or if this was simply the perception of my childfree and childless animal parents.

Grace was instantaneous in her reply about her son and daughter-in-law's new German short-haired pointer puppy: "She's my grandchild. And I'm her granny." Noting her expedient answer, I said, "You say that very quickly. Why is that?" "Well, I talk to Spring about being her granny and how much her granny loves her. And [her son and daughter-in-law] can have her, and I can be talking to them on the phone, and she might be out in the yard chewing on a bone or playing, and one of them will say, 'Come talk to Granny,' and she'll come run to the phone. And they say that as I talk to her, she gets all excited."

But the emotional support that Grace provided to her son's multispecies family did not stop at simply labeling herself as Granny. Rather, she supported the family domestically as well, providing free, full-time, daily "child care" for Spring as both Grace's son and daughter-in-law worked full-time. Indeed, research on grandparent caregiving, in both the permanent (e.g., abandonment) and temporary (e.g., during the workday) absence of the parent has become an increasing area of interest for scholars.[37]

When I asked Grace why she provided the daily care for Spring, she was resolute:

> I just couldn't stand the thought of her being kenneled all day. She's a puppy, and she's a high-energy puppy. Most puppies are, but because she was going to be a bigger dog, she definitely had energy. And to me, it was a no-brainer. You can't grow like you should, get the exercise that you need, get the love that you need. You know, for a while, she was eating three times a day. There's nobody that can run home in the middle of the day and feed her. The best thing was just for her to come to me and let me spend the day with her, where she could run and play. And she could learn. She could be loved. She could be fed. She could have all the things that she needed as a growing puppy and that I could love on her—you know, things like this, things that it's hard to do when you work all day.

While Grace's narrative reveals a dedicated grandparent, I was curious if she also saw her behavior as beneficial to her adult child and his

Figure 3.2. Grace picking up Spring from home so that she can
take care of her while her parents are at work

new wife. As a result, I asked her if she thought that her support had
taught them anything about being parents. She answered,

> I think that they learned that I will always be there for them, whether it's
> for a puppy or a human child. I'll always be willing to help. I think they
> realized that it was in Spring's best interest. I think that they realized that
> it was nice to have someone else share in the responsibility or offer to
> share in the responsibility. . . . I think they realized that it was a genuine
> offer to help with their child, Spring, to support them and to support
> her—and what was in the best interest for all of them.

Grace's response made two things clear about her grandparent status. First, her relationship with Spring was truly intergenerational in nature. Her narrative reveals a desire to do what is best for both her adult child and his wife as a new "parents." Second, it highlights her need to help Spring develop in all of the ways that Grace feels she should be able to, regardless of the work arrangements of Grace's son and daughter-in-law. Indeed, it is apparent that Grace views her new role as parental in nature—emotional and domestic support of her adult son in a way that allows him and his wife to achieve better work-family balance. Likewise, Grace's interactions with Spring in which she provides socialization, love, safety, and developmental opportunities during the day reveal the presence of a deeply internalized, highly prioritized grandparent identity.

Alternatively, at least one empty nester in my research felt that the grandparent line was not one that she wanted to cross. Gennifer shared that her adult daughter, Holly, had with a previous college boyfriend brought two cats into their residence. Holly had developed a parent identity related to her feline kids, and Gennifer confirmed this, saying, "She would call them her kids. She's a cat mom." "She calls them her kids?" I asked. Nodding her head, she repeated, "She's a cat mom." When I asked, "Does she engage in 'cat-momness' or just kind of call them her kids?" she answered, "Oh no. They all sleep together. She takes photos of them. She always talks about them. Like some people talk about their kids, she talks about her cats." Then I asked her, "Has she ever tried to label a relationship between you or Dan [Gennifer's husband], or does she just leave it at that?" I was interested in her answer, because unlike other empty nesters who had reported varying forms of their own grandparental behavior, Gennifer had made it clear to Holly that her cats were not welcome in Gennifer and Dan's home (part of the reasoning for this stance was concern that her own dogs would kill Holly's cats and part of it was concern about the likelihood that the cats would urinate in her house, leaving an impenetrable and permanent odor). Gennifer answered, "No, she hasn't." Her response made me think that perhaps getting "grandparent" support may not have been so important for Holly's own parent identity. However, Gennifer recalled later in our interview that Holly had been incessant in her requests to bring the cats over for a visit. Steadfast, Gennifer had always said, "No. No, you cannot."

When I asked Gennifer why she thought it was so important to Holly to be able to bring the cats home for a visit, she softened up, sharing, "I think it's something akin to—you know how people are genuinely confused when you don't love their kids as much as they do? . . . It's that. It really is that. She just wants me to think that they're just as great as she thinks that they are. I do think they're great, . . . but I can't really let myself get that invested or the next thing you know these damn cats will be living here when she's in between apartments. And I'm not having that." Gennifer's testimony reinforces two things here. First of all, Holly needs her mother to love her cat children in the same way that she does. She tries to bring her cats over for family visits, which would increase her perception of emotional support from her own mother for her multispecies family. And Gennifer offered that she and Dan do provide domestic support by babysitting the cats—as long as it is in Holly's apartment and not their home. But Holly still makes concerted efforts to engage her mother in deeper-level familial involvement with them because they are like her children. Second, Gennifer appears to be aware of the impact that allowing Holly's cat children to visit would have on her own emotional investments in Holly's multispecies family. Indeed, Gennifer is cogently aware that allowing Holly's cats into her home would cross a line, with regard to her own emotional investment, from which she could not easily turn back.

Empty Nesters, Grandparenting, and Veterinary Expenses

Financial support of adult children and their children is often characteristic of the "grandparent" identity. While participants did not specifically discuss financial support from their parents for the companion animal, empty nesters were much more candid about their own status as "grandparent."[38] For the four participants who had childfree adult children who treated their dogs or cats as children, financial support at the veterinarian was a major theme. In much the same way that a grandparent may provide economic support for a grandchild, these participants all noted either direct experiences in which they had provided financial assistance for their adult children's animals or, in the event that an urgent need arose, would have been willing to do so. Indeed, the willingness to provide financial support in the future even appeared to extend to two

Figure 3.3. Sarah; her dog, Maya (*far left*); and granddogs, Vail (*center*) and Kuper (*far right*), posing for a portrait at Sarah's home

more participants whose adult children did not currently have companion animals.

Sarah provided a cogent testimony to the importance of her "granddogs" to both of her adult daughters. Each child had developed a tightly entangled, intimate bond with each of their respective dogs during their time at college. Sarah's oldest daughter, Cadence, was inseparable from her dachshund, and her friends at the university knew all too well the traumatizing, emotional turmoil in which Cadence was instantly embroiled when she found out that Genesis had developed a debilitating spinal-cord issue. The diagnosis meant Genesis would need to be euthanized almost immediately unless Cadence could pay for a surgical procedure that, when all was said and done, would have cost her over $5,000. Of course, as a poor college student, coming up with so much money was implausible.

Cadence turned to Sarah, distraught, unable to focus on her studies, and as Sarah learned later from Cadence's college pals, "crying all the time because her dog was at death's door." Sarah recalled considering what she should do to support her daughter and Genesis simultaneously. She and her husband debated options as Cadence and Genesis suffered, with Sarah's husband finally acquiescing to her judgment on the matter: "$5,000 for surgery and Cadence to drive her dog down to Texas A&M because of finals. We knew she was going to totally destroy her GPA if we didn't do something. This is my daughter, and I am worried about her well-being." Sarah remembered thinking about the high cost but told herself, "You are going to have to do this for your daughter. She was a mess." Sarah and her husband told Cadence that they would cover the cost of the surgery, and Cadence immediately began the two-hour journey to Texas A&M College of Veterinary Medicine and Biomedical Sciences for Genesis's treatment. The surgical intervention meant that Cadence would have her "child" healing and her multispecies family intact and, thus, be able to focus on completing her schoolwork for the semester.

Grace, "Granny" to Spring, the German short-haired puppy discussed earlier, had not yet seen a dire situation that would require expenditure of large amounts of money for her son's new multispecies family. Furthermore, while Sarah's economic status was closer to upper-lower class, Grace's was far more typical of the average middle-class family in the United States. Sarah made it clear when discussing empty-nest expenditures for her own granddog that she could only do so because of her and her husband's "financial blessings." As a result, I was curious about Grace's position on such support, especially as it might pertain to the presence of a grandparent identity and the appearance of the multispecies family across extended familial networks. After all, as I noted earlier, Grace was a devoted grandmother to Spring, immediately volunteering to "babysit" the puppy over the first summer while both of Spring's parents worked full-time jobs. Would, or even could, Grace consider financial support like this for her son's multispecies family? So I jumped in head first, bluntly asking, "If something happened with Spring, and she developed a chronic illness or was injured in a possibly fatal way, would you offer to financially expend to help them [her son and daughter-in-law] intervene with her health?"

"So, if you are talking about maybe keeping her alive or helping to try to find a cure or pay for medication or find a specialist, I'd definitely be on board. How much? I can't say. But I would do everything within my power to physically, financially, emotionally, and mentally do what I could for my four-legged grandbaby."

When I asked, "Why would that be so important to you?" she answered,

> Because that baby didn't ask for whatever it is that's causing problems. . . . The hurt to watch something that is living, is breathing, is fighting to have to suffer or endure, it's not fair, and if I could make a stand and help make a difference in that, . . . I would. To watch my son and daughter-in-law experience the sadness and grief that they would be going through, of the financial challenge of having to take off work, to be there to give medication throughout the day, or so on, . . . I would have to make it work in my life. I would do whatever I could.

Indeed, it appeared to me that not only would Grace provide financial support to help her son's multispecies family, but she would do whatever else she possibly could to assist as well. And while she qualified her statement about spending by saying she could not say how much money she could offer, she was ready and willing to commit whatever she could to helping. Comparing Grace's and Sarah's stances on financial support makes it apparent that providing monetary assistance for their children's multispecies families was not simply about having the disposable income with which to do so. It was about a deeper connection to both their human children and their four-legged grandchildren.

Partners Verifying Parents

Participant parents were not the only significant family members cited as eliciting positive affect that increased commitment to the animal parent identity. Almost half of participant narratives indicated that partners or spouses also worked to verify the identity. For example, Wrenn discussed the turmoil that nonverification from other actors had brought her with regard to her parent identity, saying, "I have always felt like people don't think that we are family. I think that we are not looked at as a family unit even though we fully see ourselves as a family unit."

Her narrative reveals the key role of her husband's support and the positive affect that this brings to her:

> And because of that [Bob, her husband] said, "We're going to go have our pictures made with a professional dog photographer. . . ." I am almost embarrassed to tell you what we spent. When it was all said and done, we probably spent close to $4,000 on these pictures. But we have these beautiful family pictures. And that's what they are for us, . . . family portraits. We have a big one in our bedroom, [and] we have a big beautiful [canvas] one in the living room—it's just the dogs. I said to [Bob] after we got those, . . . "I have so much joy when I look at those, and I have so much joy when I show them off to other people." And even now the picture is three years old, . . . I just have so much joy.

For Wrenn, her husband's determination to create both a family portrait and a portrait of "just the babies" played a pivotal part in allowing her to feel verified both as a multispecies family and as a mother. His support was integral to her enactment of the parent identity in his presence and paramount to her increasing commitment to the identity across other social situations. Wrenn explained emotionally, saying,

> It was almost like it gave us a validation that I had never felt before. But then I get mad at myself because I don't need that. I've gotten much better at that. But it kind of showed the world. . . . And now when people see that picture in my office, I don't get a lot of those questions. They say, "Are these your dogs?" It makes it much easier for those interactions. All of my patients know I don't have [human] kids, and they will come in and ask, "How are the babies?" They know that they are my babies, and that is how they refer to them.

Wrenn acknowledges the idiosyncratic nature of her relationship with her animal "children." Her narrative makes it obvious that she feels intense pressure to be a family by societal expectations. Negatively perceived reflected appraisals from those outside her family (including her partner, parents, in-laws, and sister) led Wrenn to bring the cultural expectation of the parent identity into alignment with her own

Figure 3.4. Wrenn's husband, Bob, enjoying bonding time with Zen

idiosyncratic perception of "parent."[39] While she reported initially struggling to do this, Bob's effort to verify Wrenn's identity via family portraiture enabled her to enact the identity in her workplace—signaling an increase in commitment to the identity across other networks. In turn, this led to new external support from her clients.

One-third of participant narratives also suggested that they and their partners engaged in reciprocal verification of the animal "parent" identity for each other. Shay reported that her animal "child," Mia, had served to bring her and her husband together as parents:

She links us in a parental kind of way that we didn't have before. So he is her daddy, and I am her mommy, . . . like, "Hey, Matt, you need to go let out Mia. You need to take care of Mia"—what he's never had to do before—and so it kinda is teaching him like, "Oh, I got a responsibility for someone other." You know, someone who can't take care of themselves. Me and him, we are fine or whatever. I can go to this place, he can go that place, and we will be fine. But she needs help. She depends on us. I guess

that's the only thing. Because we were already friends, best friends, partners or whatever, but then we didn't have that parental.

In Shay's case, her partner not only supported her enactment of this
identity, but Shay reported that her enactment, and the labeling of Mia as
"baby," actually catalyzed her partner's enactment of the identity as well,
creating a new identity pair between the two of them, father-mother.
These identities enabled them to experience parenting together, thus
producing, reproducing, and reinforcing each other's performances.

While Shay reported how Mia introduced a new component to her
relationship with her husband, Kathy, who at the time was childless,
explained how Rom's death ultimately prevented a possible custody
struggle within her "mother-father" pairing during a time when she and
her husband were having marital troubles: "It was really sad when Rom
died. My husband and I were young and struggling at that time, and we
weren't sure that we were willing to do the work that we needed to stay
married at the time. And it was like, at the time when Rom died, we
weren't even sure we were going to make it. And in fact, it would be one
of those things where we wouldn't have to worry about who got Rom:
'Who gets the dog?' or something horrible like that." The threat of a custody suit in this case again demonstrates a clear "mother-father" pairing
in which both actors internalized gender-specific parent identities during their marriage and in relation to Rom. The presence of this pairing
not only verified the parent identity for each during happier times but
remained even as they spoke of divorcing, just as it would for a human
child.

Julie discussed how she and her partner worked together "much like
couples who just had a baby" to help their puppy child learn night sleeping by "alternating nights to get Chance to fall asleep." She also noted
that a puppy allowed her and her partner to "have more of an egalitarian
relationship and responsibility": "the potential for being equal in terms
of taking care of Chance is closer to reality, I think, than having a human
baby." She reported that the way in which she and her partner have equal
responsibility for the care of Chance makes her happy about having
Chance as "her baby." Indeed, her satisfaction with her partner about
egalitarian caretaking is reminiscent of the positive effect that egalitarian child care has on marital satisfaction for new parents.[40] That, in turn,

signals that Julie feels verified as a parent because of her partner's equal levels of caregiving for Chance as an animal child.

In a reversal of these patterns, Michelle, a high-powered professional in her thirties, was quite clear that she did not think of or treat Champ as a child. Indeed, in direct contrast to other participants discussed here, she noted that when her father or mother-in-law inquired about Champ's well-being or when her mother-in-law referred to Champ as a "granddog," she felt pitied, surmising, "They don't want me to feel down because I don't have a kid [*laughs*]." Furthermore, Michelle was frank in her disdain for the kinds of high-pressure, symbolic advertising that the pet industry uses to encourage the performance of parent-child relationships among consumers. However, while her interactions with Champ were not suggestive of the presence of a parent identity, discussion of her husband's relationship with Champ revealed that she was a supportive partner in much the same way that the participants discussed previously felt supported by their partners. Michelle shared, "I refer to him as my furry son sometimes just because Nick [her husband] does. I just know how much he cares for him."

Already interested in the fact that Michelle was only one of two participants consistently and adamantly opposed to adopting a parental stance toward their dog or cat, I asked her to tell me more about what she meant. Her response confirmed the kinds of things that had begun to emerge in these interviews about the importance of partner support for the performance of these identities in the multispecies family:

> Well, I think when you are married, you adapt. It's one of those things that makes our relationship successful—that you can become similar in some ways, right? I think if I did not get married to Nick, I don't think I would have a dog because they are messy. Especially bulldogs drool, and they are messy eaters. It's just a mess. Our floors are never clean. I lived on campus for ten years, and I was fine not having an animal. But it was so important for him to do it. So I was like, okay. He just really, really loves that dog.

I asked her, "So when you say, 'That's my furry son' every once in a while, do you think you do that because you want to support Nick or let him think it's okay to call him that?"

"Yeah, I think so. I think it shows Nick that I care for Ace too. It's just speaking the same language."

"Why is that important?"

"Because if I did not want the dog, the dog would be gone [*laughs*]. I think he still thinks of him as a dog, but it's the way he affirms it [the relationship with Champ] and talks about it."

Adult Siblings Verifying Parents

Finally, two participants discussed support from their adult siblings for the parent identity. Wrenn noted that she and her sister, who is childfree, engage with each other and the animal "children" as if they are aunts. When I asked her, "What do you mean?" she said, "Even my sister . . . her dogs call me Aunt Wrenn. . . . That's just how we always refer to each other. In fact, she has a little pug. . . . We don't know why, but this little pug would always get her cell phone and dial my number. And she would always say, 'Kayla [the dog] was wanting to call Aunt Wrenn.' And then she would put her on speaker and say, 'Can you talk to her?' I'd say, 'Kayla?' and talk with her on the phone." This support of Wrenn's parent identity was key to both her enactment of the identity and her commitment across other social situations. Wrenn explained,

> I think that the fact that they [her family of origin] see us as a whole family unit and the fact that we don't have to be embarrassed about that. Or feel like we shouldn't feel like that. Like I said too, I feel like age has really . . . I'm forty-four. . . . We have dealt with it for so long too, we have gotten a lot better at handling it. Even though sometimes we come home and say, you know, it really hurt me that somebody said "They are just dogs" or whatever. . . . In the safety of your own home, you still talk about these things. But it does—it has always made us feel normal that they look at it as normal the dogs are just kids. . . . We recognize that is not the norm, but it is our norm. So I think for them to be as supportive as they have always been, . . . it has made us not feel any "less than" and made us feel like we did not have to justify why we love them so much or explain why we love him so much. Because they just, they got it too.

Wrenn confirms that the support provided by significant others has been instrumental in allowing her and her husband to enact the parent identity, even in the absence of human children. Indeed, the working agreement between her, her husband, her sister, her parents, and her in-laws is one that has shown resiliency over the years. That support is clearly implicated in her own verification of self. This allows her to create an idiosyncratic agreement on social identities that includes animal "children" as children, grandchildren, nieces, and nephews. Further, these familial extensions have created a protective barrier against the stigma with which childless multispecies families like Wrenn's are burdened.

The Power of Support

While I and others have argued elsewhere that it is possible to perceive interspecies intersubjectivity—"doing mind" and developing an identity counter to the nonhuman animal—I have noted that it may be difficult to enact that identity in the presence of other human actors without significant support from them. Indeed, enacting any identity in a situation requires the acknowledgment and agreement of other actors.[41] External support for the performance of an identity is a prominent factor in both prominence and salience hierarchies, the qualitative component for Stryker's commitment, and the positive affect required for the process of identity verification.[42] Although identity theorists have certainly researched the influence of external support in the past, they have not considered whether or how these processes would occur if the identity were counter to a nonhuman entity.

I have examined here what external support for the parent-child identity pairing counter to the companion animal looks like. Participant narratives make clear that other human social actors outside the bonds that they have forged with their animal companions do indeed provide external support for both the parent-child identity pairing and the construction of a multispecies family. Furthermore, this support is far deeper than simple labeling of the animal as "grandchild" or "child." Instead, the behavior of these actors depicts both immediate and extended familial support for the human-animal bond, generating positive reflected appraisals in situations external to their private interactions with their companion animals. Ultimately, this creates a protective social barrier around childfree and childless parents—one that defends the actor against stigma and allows the legitimate performance of parent regardless of judgment.

Also, these narratives demonstrate that acknowledgment of this identity is important enough to the actor to bolster their performance as a parent, while also increasing commitment to the identity across social situations outside of parent-animal child interaction. External support is crucial to the ability of an identity to rise in the prominence hierarchy—a more permanent conceptualization that contains the actor's ideals and desires.[43] Evidence of the importance of that support is clear in Wrenn's narrative concerning the necessity of her extended family's support not only for her comfort in adopting the parent identity toward her dogs but also for increasing commitment in other contexts, such as her workplace. This support also seems integral to performing, especially, the parent identity across contexts, suggesting that "parent" has risen in her salience hierarchy enough to increase the likelihood of its invocation in more than one situation—the comfort of her own home.[44] In fact, she verifies this when she comments on how hard it is when outsiders say "they are just dogs." Wrenn knows her identity is not normative but highlights both family portraits as well as support as foundational to her engagement as a parent in her multispecies family.

Furthermore, positive affect is associated with the performance of a particular identity within any group, serving to increase commitment to an identity.[45] Julie expresses the importance of positive affect emanating from her father's practice of giving her animal "child" a nickname, a cultural tradition typically reserved for human actors. She notes that "it means a lot" and that "it's a big deal" for her father to engage in this activity, revealing a working agreement between the three of them that creates positive affect related to the identity. This allows her to enact and reenact her idiosyncratic parent identity, thus increasing commitment to the identity in social situations involving her father.

Finally, the process of identity verification leans heavily on external praise and rewards as a means of strengthening positive feelings that help to verify one's perception of self.[46] Rewards from significant others, then, help to increase positive affect associated with a particular identity, increasing commitment to that identity. When Lynn contacts her mother because of a medical emergency with her animal child, Lynn's mother's enthusiastic response to the request must be considered as positive feedback to Lynn's enactment of the parent identity. The behavior of Lynn's mother also allows Lynn to increase commitment to her identity, apparent in her willingness to take Roger to restaurants. The lie that Lynn's mother tells restaurant management regarding Roger's service-animal status can only be interpreted as positive feedback, yielding positive affect for Lynn's enactment in that situation. Indeed, Lynn glowed as she recounted these stories to me and shared that her mother would "do anything" for her and her animal child.

Developing our understanding of how external support of a role identity counter to a companion animal, especially for parent-animal child, is important to understand how such relationships are negotiated solely because of the presence of the companion animal. These narratives also highlight the kind of social scaffolding necessary for developing identity meanings that include the companion animal as a family member and ultimately lead to new ways of "doing family." It is quite clear that substantively defining the pet as "child" does not solely reside within the perceptions of one actor. Rather, a performance team of significant others is involved in sustaining both the human role identity that has been formed and the status of family member that has been conferred on the pet.

* * *

Almost two-thirds of the narratives presented here exemplify external support and its influence on participants' selves as partially comprising "parent." More importantly for identity theory, counterstatuses played an important part here as well. That is, external support from significant others highlighted how the people with whom I spoke and those who are important to them reinforce for one another that they are "occupants of counterstatus[es]" such as mother-father and parent-grandparent.[47] This indicates that these human-animal relationships propelled not only the formation of the parent identity but also the formation of other identity pairs commonly developed in American culture. These identities would not have been present were it not for the existence of the parent-child pair developed as a component of participants' selves. Furthermore, it emphasizes that these human-animal relationships have the power to influence identity formation in other significant actors' self-perceptions, creating webs of new familial relationships.

But the power of this external support reaches beyond the multispecies family and its emergent, extended familial identities. And, as with other types of nontraditional families that derive reinforcement for their familial roles from significant others in the face of broader social sanctioning, it reaches beyond defense mechanisms against the negative feelings that arise from stigma. These relationships are produced and reproduced in other interactions relevant to those family members but also outside of the family context. As a result, these new familial relationships become patterned across broader social contexts like Wrenn's workplace, in which she prominently displays family pictures of her "babies" and their "mom and dad" for her clients to see. They become more widespread as grandmothers share pictures of their granddogs in their social circles, as was the case with Jody. They become more ingrained in the cultural fabric when the animal child is defended in public by a grandmother, as Lynn's mother did at the restaurant. And slowly but surely, in the context of increasing diversification of the American family, these multispecies families carve their way into the cultural fabric as family structures that are, albeit unique and still stigmatized, increasingly accepted within broader society.

4

"They Call Me His Mommy"

Families with Human Children

During my earliest visits to the veterinarian clinic in which I conducted my participant observations, I chose to sit out in the waiting room to observe clients and their humans interact with one another as well as with other clients. The clinic manager had given me free rein of the facility, including surgeries, client appointments (with owners' informed consent), the lab, and boarding rooms for both healthy and infirmed clients. The one very understandable caveat was that I remain outside of any appointments that were related to euthanasia. My original intent had been to immediately begin observing appointments in action where the veterinarian staff engaged with small animals and their owners. However, once I was "on the ground," it had just seemed rational to hang out in the front lobby for a while first.

The veterinarian clinic itself is known in the community as having a compassionate approach to veterinary care, both emotionally and financially, for its clients. The management and owner work hard to keep down prices for services. This results in a modestly furnished waiting area. While the clinic is cleaned regularly and thoroughly, its age, the nonstop traffic flow of clients, and the consistent fluffs of stress-laden fur floating around can make it seem dirty. Half of the clinic walls are lined with a plethora of different animals, including a vocal cockatiel, parakeets, ferrets, and fish. In my experience there, it quickly became apparent that this area is an allure for most human children entering the clinic. Indeed, most, upon sitting down with their parents and pets to wait, are almost instantly back up to explore the menagerie of animals.

A resident cat or two periodically roams the lobby area; however, the brave souls who make those rounds usually stay safely above the fray on and behind reception-area counters. Two large, overstuffed photo albums sit next to a hundred-gallon fish tank filled with brightly colored tropical fish. Each photo album is brimming with thank-you cards to the clinic and various staff members for the care that families have received.

Management has arranged foot traffic into and out of the clinic so that clients can only enter through one door to check in at the front end of the semicircular reception counter. When the time arrives, vet techs call owners by the animal's name so that the patient can be weighed on a large floor-level scale—a feat with which many clients have no intention of assisting. Clients exiting exam rooms on the opposite end of the waiting area check out with their owners on the other end of the reception counter's large semicircular counter. This seems to keep both human and animal traffic constantly flowing in one direction—a necessity in a small animal clinic that is consistently jammed with pets and their owners.

While the waiting area here is sizeable, a typical day during the clinic's six-day, sometimes 7:30 a.m. to 7:30 p.m. work week finds a diverse and seemingly unmanageable number of awaiting clients. Because the clinic is widely known in the middle-class community for its affordability and compassion, appointment times are typically booked well in advance, and wait times for walk-ins can be as long as two hours. Staff are constantly running between clients, with vet techs periodically in the waiting area to administer simple services such as annual shots, as a means of decreasing both the number of clients waiting and the wait times themselves. Everyone works fast and hard in this clinic, and most owners, while irritated at the wait that they have endured, leave trusting veterinary staff and satisfied with the visit.

What all of this meant to me early on was that there was goldmine of potential data in the lobby—a fantastic foundation for what I might find in those exam rooms once I began observing actual appointments. I was fortunate enough to observe conversations and interactions between an array of human and nonhuman actors: adults, children, owners, staff, dogs, cats, and occasionally rabbits, rats, and birds. Many mothers also brought along very young and elementary-aged children (occasionally even their teens) with their pets to the clinic. Sometimes fathers were accompanied by a child or two during visits. Periodically, a young couple entered with their dog and/or cat. Elderly owners, sometimes as couples and sometimes by themselves, also frequented the clinic.

One day, I observed what appeared to be an *entire* family. The entourage included a mother, a father, a tween-aged daughter, a younger, elementary-aged son, a preschool-aged daughter, one grown cairn terrier named Willie, and the newest member of their family, a bearded collie puppy aptly named Harry. Initially, the size of this family alone took up almost two vinyl-clad benches, completely eclipsing the front of the fish tank (though this eclipse was a short-lived phenomenon as all three of the children were instantly drawn to both the wall of clinic animals and other clients in the waiting area). The father worked to untangle both dogs' leads, with Harry and Willie working to tangle themselves back up again. The tween-aged daughter asked her little sister, "Did you say hello to the bird [referring to the clinic cockatiel]? I think I heard him say, 'I love you.' Did you say hello?" The little girl's eyes popped wide open, and she ran to the cockatiel cage, where her brother was already standing. He was "rapid firing" questions at her, adding to the acoustic cacophony already present in the lobby: "How are you doing? How are you doing? Hello? Hello?" But the bird had no interest in responding. Both children momentarily lost interest and moved to check out the ferrets.

In the meantime, the older sister took control of Harry's lead and affectionately pet his head, saying, "Awww, you're so cute," but also parentally chided him when he whined nervously at the approach of a small, leashed Chihuahua, nervous and bulgy-eyed, from another family. "Harry, don't be such a baby," she cautioned.

The younger sister returned to her family temporarily to plop down on the dirty, furry floor as the mother sweetly reminded her, "Honey, get off of the floor, please." There was no response from the girl. One more time, the mother said, "Honey, please get off of the floor." The girl got up, twirling her halter dress, a bouncing, blond ponytail wandering back over to the cockatiel to try her luck. "Hello?" she said quizzically.

The boy, who had been kneeling on the bench staring in at the fish, noticed and instantaneously returned to his inquisition of the bird. "Hello?" he questioned. The bird calmly preened her feathers—ignoring the human inconvenience staring in at her.

"Hello? Hello!" the younger sister said.

The cockatiel turned to look at the two children and finally broke her silence with loud laughter. As if they were code breakers having finally deciphered an enigmatic message from some foreign source, both children enthusiastically cheered in unison, "Hello, hello, hello!"

And the bird, finally ready to discuss, said, "Hello back!"

The children giggled uncontrollably. While all of this was amusing to observe, I (as a mother myself to two small children and two German short-haired pointers) wondered why on earth these parents would bring the entire family to a veterinarian clinic. I remember, at the time, with my "mommy cap" on, cringing at the thought of embarking on such an adventure with everyone in tow like this. And then the mother, as if she could read my thoughts, looked over to me (I had been clutching to the very end of the first bench on which they sat—determined to hear and see everything this family did) and said, "It's the first time they've ever been able to get her to speak."

I smiled and said, "They definitely seem excited about it." Silently, I thought to myself, "You've all done this together *before*?"

Harry grabbed his own leash from the oldest daughter, who quickly grabbed it back and commanded, "Down, Harry! Down." Harry ignored her request and turned in a circle, twisting the lead around his chest and hindquarters simultaneously.

"We always bring them to the vet with us. They think it's fun, and they learn so much when we come," the mother explained. And then I realized it: with all of the social chaos going on around us, I had wondered why this mother and father would ever embark on such a stressful outing with their multispecies family. After all, why not a park? How about hiking? Maybe a trip to the grocery store? Anything but this. *This* was parental torture, right? However, ease was not the main parental goal here. Nope. This was about teaching their children—helping them to learn not just about their own dogs but about lots of different animals. *This* was an educational outing.

* * *

One of the purposes of this book is to uncover the varying ways in which the multispecies family has emerged as a new form of family structure that manifests itself across a variety of different family identities. This objective makes it important to move beyond the parent-child and grandparent-grandchild relationships discussed in earlier chapters to address multispecies families in which human children are present. Like childfree and childless families, these families display unique relationships, often only present by virtue of human-animal interaction, that impact the fabric of family life across multiple dimensions. The nature of the identities that emerge in these families also set them apart as family structures from both single-species families with children and child-free and childless multispecies contexts. Children and their four-legged family members take center stage in accounting for identity formation (especially as siblings and best friends). And when the kids leave the nest, empty nesters internalize a new caretaking identity toward their dogs and cats that is not otherwise present in single-species empty-nest families. These multispecies families are far less stigmatized than are their counterparts who do not have children but who do develop parent-child relationships with their animals. However, similar to their counterparts, the functions of family, such as economic expenditure and support, socialization, child care, emotional support, and work-family balance, are distinctively altered because of the identities with which the family dog and cat are labeled.

According to the American Veterinary Medical Association's (AVMA) quinquennial survey for 2018, it is households larger than two members (that is, three or more family members) that appear to own the most pets. Families who have children (or other family members) present constitute the largest percentage of pet owners in the United States, with 43 percent of pet-owning households comprising three or more people.[1] To add to this, the 2018 Current Population Survey (CPS) estimated that almost 42 percent of all households have children of their own under the age of eighteen.[2] The AVMA estimates that 67 percent of family households own some type of pet.[3] The 2013 American Housing Survey (AHS) estimates that 70–75 percent of households with kids between the ages of five and seventeen own dogs or cats.[4]

It has been suggested that growing up with a pet in the household is now more likely than growing up with a sibling in the United States.[5] And while the data do not appear to exist yet to make definitive conclusions, indirect evidence from demographic surveys like the 2018 CPS and the 2017 AHS is compelling. Of all families with children under the age of eighteen in the United States, 42 percent contain only one child—meaning that no siblings are present in the home. If almost three-quarters of all American families with kids between the ages of five and seventeen have at least one pet, and over half of households contain two or more children under the age of eighteen, then scholars can at least *surmise* that more households with children under the age of eighteen have pets than have multiple children (and, thus, siblings) present.[6]

The ability to actually claim statistical certainty with this data will require more data collection and analysis in the future. However, one thing is certain. The percentage of women who have reached the end of their child-bearing years having only given birth to one child doubled between 1976 and 2015—from 11 percent to 22 percent.[7] This percentage currently continues to tick upward in the United States (with no deceleration in sight). If American kids are not already more likely to grow up with a pet than a sibling, then this may well become the case in the coming decades as one-child families become more and more the norm.

A similar contention argues that American children are more likely to grow up in a home with a pet than in a two-parent household due to the increase of single-parent households that arose during the second demographic transition.[8] Problems similar to the sibling assertion discussed earlier also plague this argument. Existing data from demographic sample surveys offer a different picture on two-parent households. For example, the 2018 CPS calculates the percentage of children under the age of eighteen who are living in two-parent families as 69.1 percent of all families with children under the age of eighteen.[9] Children living in single-parent (either father or mother) or "neither" parent households constitute 30.9 percent of all families with children under the age of eighteen.

Furthermore, data from the 2017–18 AVMA survey calculate the percentage of single-mother and single-father families that own at least one pet as 8 percent and 6 percent, respectively, of all households with pets.[10] This lower percentage of ownership makes sense given that single-parent households (especially single-mother households) are far more likely to experience financial hardships than are two-parent households. Indeed, the Bureau of Labor Statistics (BLS) notes that single-parent families with children under eighteen that *do* own a pet spend the least amount of money annually on their animals ($267 versus $412 for two-parent families with kids under the age of six and $536 for two-parent families with kids ages six to seventeen).[11] These data make it difficult to reconcile the contention that growing up with pets in the household is *more likely* than growing up in a two-parent family. As a result, prior scholarship can only descriptively note that there is a higher percentage of households with children under eighteen that also own pets (70–75 percent) than there is of households with two parents and children under the age of eighteen overall (69.1 percent).[12]

Regardless, ensuring that children have a pet in the household is obviously a cultural norm for middle-class parents in American society. Both parents with children under the age of eighteen and empty nesters in my interviews repeatedly confirmed this by positing that children should have at least *one* pet growing up. Both my participant parents and a vast majority of other American parents see pets as a means to achieving multiple goals related to the development of their children. As a result, parents often report that the main reason they have brought a companion animal into the home is for their children.[13] Indeed, over three-quarters of participants with children currently at home and half of the empty nesters whom I interviewed noted that providing a pet for their children was a primary reason for developing or maintaining a multispecies family in the first place.

Dogs and cats especially are perceived by parents as contributing to a sense of empathy, compassion, and responsibility in their children.[14] One of my participants, Britany, who had one son, a dog, and a cat, made this clear, describing for me how she motivated her son—who had had multiple behavioral problems at home and school—to improve his behavior with the prospect of bringing a dog into the family. While he had taken good care of a goldfish for over three years, they worried that the irresponsible behavior that he had been exhibiting recently precluded them from introducing the complexity of a dog into their family sphere. But then Britany said she realized one day that doing so may actually help her son regulate himself better overall. She shared about her son,

> He was having a few issues with his behavior that hindered us from wanting to bring a dog into the family. You know, "We need to be able to trust you. You have to be able to tell the truth. You can't be getting into trouble and having us spend all of this energy just trying to get you to listen. If you want us to bring a dog into the family, you have to have correct behavior, first, so that you can help us be responsible for the dog." It was more our idea, but he got excited about it when we talked about it.

Britany confirmed that her instincts had been correct. The prospect of broadening their multispecies family had contributed to motivating her son to improve his behavior and led to more responsible behavior as he helped to take care of his new pit bull puppy, Fred. Concluding her thoughts about her son's relationship with Fred, Britany said, "I think it has been good for him [her son] to have company—dog company, companionship—to see what it takes to take care of another being."

Multispecies homes bring other benefits beyond responsibility into the family fold for these types of families. For example, the death of a beloved pet can help a child learn to navigate such permanent circumstances long before experiencing this kind of tragedy with one's human family members.[15] Indeed, Zee, a fifty-eight-year-old empty nester, confirmed that when Theo, her twenty-two-year-old daughter's first childhood dog, eventually passes away, it will be Lainey's first real introduction to the grieving process. When I asked Zee what she thought her daughter would learn from Theo's death, she shared,

> She'll have to grieve. . . . She's never gone through it. . . . I lost my dad when I was thirty, and I lost my mom when I was forty [*long pause*]. I don't know. I don't want to sound cruel and cold, but I hope she can go through the process of grieving. . . . I hope this will prepare her in the future because we all have the circle of life. . . . And it drives her crazy when I say, "I'm not going to live forever." She doesn't want to talk about it. . . . Hopefully, [Theo's death] would prepare her for something that will eventually happen.

For the multitude of American families that consider their pets family members, companion animals can also provide unshakeable love and companionship for children. A dog or cat can provide a child on the autism spectrum with measurable benefits with regard to navigating a social world that may be unreachable otherwise.[16] A mother with whom I spoke informally during my fieldwork at the veterinary clinic shared that their family Labradoodle had become her tween-aged daughter's greatest confidant and her youngest son's most avid audience as he practiced reading out loud. Of course, these parental perceptions of the necessity of a companion animal may well be related to participants' experiences with their own childhood pets. Indeed, growing up with pets as a child tends to predict adulthood ownership of pets.[17] This was certainly the case with almost three-quarters of the interview partici-pants in my study (regardless of whether the participant was childfree, childless, currently had children at home, or was an empty nester). This information was sometimes offered in passing as a part of some broader narrative about experiences with pets in general. However, it was most often shared as one reason for deciding to get a dog or cat in the first place. For participants who currently had children living with them or who were empty nesters, there appeared to be an intimate connection between having grown up with a dog or cat and ensuring that their own children would do the same. For example, Victoria, a parent in her for-ties who still had children at home, noted, "I grew up with pets. I've al-ways had animals in the family. So there was no question that we would have them too."

This connection between owning a pet in childhood and introducing a pet into the lives of one's own children was sometimes even present for participants who had not yet had children at all but planned on doing so in the future. Shay, a childfree participant in her twenties who intended to have children eventually, also had plans to include dogs in her future children's lives. When I asked her why she had brought her husky puppy, Mia, into her family, Shay replied, "Because I've always had dogs, and I believe every child, every human, should have a dog. [*Pauses for a moment*] I'm crazy, . . . I know. I think the benefits of having a dog far outweigh the benefits of not having a dog." Later in the interview, she explained her determination to make sure that this happened for the sake of both Mia and Shay's future children.

> I do not want to be one of those people that has kids and totally forgets about their dogs. I just read this really sad blog about a young couple who had a dog, and then as soon as the kids came, they just totally ignored the dog. And that breaks my heart. And she titled the blog "Why Not to Have a Dog with a Family," and I'm like, "No. No, I will make sure that I fight this to the very end." Every child deserves to have a dog. . . . Every kid should have a dog.

Of course, it appears that this parental instinct regarding the import of pet presence for children (even for people who do not have children yet) is not unfounded. Indeed, the scholarly literature greatly reflects the accuracy of this instinct. One of the most common findings that researchers have reported is that pets can provide an avenue of learning how to care for and nurture another living creature. That is, quite in line with parental expectations, pets can teach children the importance of both responsibility for and accountability to another living creature. Children can learn a great deal about what caretaking actually means via hands-on experience with their four-legged family members. As the introduction to this chapter notes, parents see their children as learning these skill sets at the veterinarian's office too.

This kind of learning for today's American youth is certainly not frivolous. Indeed, the American psychologist Gail Melson has pointed out that, in a relatively new child-centered culture, middle-class American parents have taken on the sole responsibility for child care and childcare arrangements within the family unit.[18] This trend overshadows long-standing historical precedent in which siblings were expected to contribute to looking after siblings while parents attended to agricultural duties. Simply put, taking care of one's siblings (especially for girls) was part and parcel of growing up in the eighteenth- and nineteenth-century American family. But twentieth-century children in the United States have increasingly missed out on such opportunities. The disappearance of sibling caretaking opportunities is also probably driven by a decrease in the average size of the American family—which has dropped from an average of seven or eight children in 1800 to just under two today.[19] Indeed, with over 42 percent of families with children under the age of eighteen being one-child families, a dearth of this kind of learning is clearly present in the United States.

The importance of introducing dogs to the one-child family was part of the narrative that Zee shared as she discussed the reason she introduced Theo, a shih tzu puppy, to her family: "My mom was very upset that I couldn't have any more kids. And she didn't want Lainey [Zee's daughter] being an only child. So she said, 'Get her an animal so she has somebody to play with other than a human. And [she can] take care of that animal. . . .' And I promised my mother that I would get her a dog so she could have something or someone to play with. . . . He was the other sibling for her. That's how I looked at it, for her. That's why I got the dog." Providing a companion that Lainey could play with, dress up, and take care of was of central importance to both Zee and her mother. Bringing Theo into Lainey's childhood like this enabled Zee to provide an intimate playmate for her daughter that would not have otherwise been present in their family home. But Theo did not just contribute to Lainey's social world. His introduction also eased the anxiety that both Zee and her mother were experiencing regarding the inability to provide Lainey with a sibling. Zee was clear that, as a child, Lainey never realized that this was why she was given Theo. However, Zee and her husband knew it, and that knowledge eased their concern about their daughter having a constant playmate whom she could "take care of and understand that not only does she take care of herself, but she must take care of other things that are alive."

Beyond the decreasing family size and fertility rates, the cultural value of child centeredness in the United States (that is, the perception that children should be the central concern within the family unit) has also contributed to a decrease in caretaking opportunities for children. Parents are expected to understand how to take care of kids on the basis of only what they experienced themselves as children. And society pressures middle-class parents today to ensure a concerted cultivation of children—one that "develops" academic, athletic, and artistic skills above all else.[20] This has consequences for American youth. Indeed, Melson notes that children in countries in which they are socialized to take care of their siblings as part of their contribution to the family also develop greater skills in the caretaking of others than do children in the United States.[21] However, the multispecies family appears to provide correction for both of these deficiencies. That is, many children identify taking care of their animals as a central part of the relationship that they have developed with their pets.[22]

Furthermore, in contrast to taking care of siblings (which girls are disproportionately called on to do, regardless of society), activities such as feeding the dog and cat, checking on them when they seem ill, providing daily walks, and letting them out to "potty" when needed (or "asked for" in our household) are all gender neutral. Boys can easily engage in this kind of behavior without fear of appearing too feminine and, as Britany's narrative earlier indicates, are eager to do so.[23] More importantly, this kind of training is essential for boys in American society as the traditionally masculine role of father as disciplinarian and breadwinner increasingly gives way to a more modern sensibility that both demands of and respects men as capable nurturers for their own children.

A host of research also points to the socioemotional benefits of pets for the development of empathy and compassion in children. Some research has found that children who have pets in the home show higher levels of empathy, while other work disputes this.[24] For example, research on Canadian elementary students showed that there is a positive relationship between attachment to a child's dog and empathy.[25] The same research has also found that there is no difference in empathy between people who own pets and those who do not and that cat-owning children exhibit lower levels of empathy than do dog owners. This leads one to believe that increased levels of human-dog sociability could contribute to this species-specific finding. Subsequent research has refined these findings, noting that children who own both dogs and cats are more empathetic than those who own one of each or neither.[26] Other scholars have argued, however, that it may well be that positive *attitudes* toward pets in general (even if child respondents do not own a pet) stem from a child who is more empathetic at heart rather than from actual pet ownership.[27]

While findings on levels of empathy for children who own dogs or cats may be ambiguous, other work has shown that owning pets as a child creates longitudinal connections for empathetic behavior into adulthood. For example, anthrozoologists have used the Empathy Quotient to examine "empathic-type" responses in both adults who had pets as children and adults who currently own pets.[28] Empathy scores in this research were far higher for people who had either owned dogs or dogs and cats as children compared to those who had owned neither. But like the research that examines children and their pets, findings that attempt to identify a link between childhood ownership and adulthood empathy are also ambiguous. In an effort to better understand the variables that surround human-human empathy, other research has shown that college undergraduates who had lived with a companion animal as a child (compared to not having had a pet) develop no significant differences in empathy or attitudes toward animals in general.[29]

Over half of the parents and empty nesters in my research pointed to the importance of family pets for teaching their children how to care about the feelings of others. These lessons could be everyday facts of the family's social interaction. For example, my husband and I frequently turn to our dogs (and, in the past, our chickens) as a mode of teaching our boys not just the skill of taking care of others but the importance of being accountable to another living creature who is dependent on them. We do this via all of the different activities discussed earlier but also by giving our dogs, Sam and Sadie, a voice in even the most minor of family discussions. And this has clearly developed both boys' sense of empathy (at least for our dog family). For example, I might ask the boys what they would like to eat that night, and my oldest, Aidan, will "speak for" Sam (an avid lover of carrots): "I want carrots . . . and anything else you make for us to eat" (because Sam is also an avid eater of pretty much anything that he can get his paws on).

Turning an empathetic ear toward Sam's and Sadie's thoughts has become so much the norm in our household that they are often included in our weekly (sometimes monthly, when we get busy and forget) family tradition called "Appreciations." During dinner, each of us (at least those of us who are verbal) lists something unique that we appreciate about other family members at the table. My nine-year-old always includes what he appreciates about Sam and Sadie and often offers, in each dog's voice, what they appreciate about each of us (needless to say, Sam's answer is typically "carrots," and Sadie's answer involves some form of fetch).

But childhood lessons on compassion and empathy in the multispecies family can also be far more serious, peppered throughout childhood and appearing at especially tumultuous moments within the family's life course. Catherine, a fifty-four-year-old empty nester whose father had been a professional retriever trainer, felt that an indispensable part of childhood learning in the multispecies family is learning about compassion in times of pain and suffering. As she spoke about how her children interacted with their dogs when they were younger, she reeled off a multitude of different caretaking activities in which each child had partaken: "I just wanted my kids to see what it was like. I always included them in the care, the feeding, the vet, all that. Even when we put the dogs to sleep, my kids would come with us to that."

Surprised by this last detail, I pressed her: "Why?" She said,

> Because I thought it was important for them to know that it was okay to put a dog out of its misery if it were dying. . . . So, when the vet would

say they had labored breathing or I had them at home until they were incontinent or they couldn't stand, . . . I would say, "It's time . . . ," and I would take the kids, and we would go to the vet. And it was traumatic, and they would stay in the room, and the vet would tell them what they were doing, and they'd start the IV. . . . In a matter of minutes, the pet would expire, and we would have a moment and cry.

I asked her, "Why did you think it was important for them to see that, be a part of it?" She said, "Because, as humans, we have the ability to euthanize. I thought that it was important for them to see that you could take the pain away and not allow them to suffer and that we always had that option. . . . I wanted them to see how peaceful it really is. And that's why I brought them along." Indeed, for Catherine, exposing her children to the death of their childhood pets not only taught them about the grieving process but also instilled in them a sense of compassion about love, pain, and selflessness—both for the animals and for the children themselves.

Children also routinely turn to their pets as confidants, sharing a host of positive and negative emotions with ears that never stop listening and a mind that never passes judgment. Indeed, researchers have found that children frequently label their pets as "confidants" or describe some interactions with pets as confiding in nature.[30] Recent research suggests that some of this disclosure to pets may be gendered in nature, with adolescent girls reporting greater levels of sharing with their pets than adolescent boys do.[31] However, the same research points out that boys and girls are just as likely to share their feelings with their pets as they are with their siblings. Furthermore, both genders report that they feel greater satisfaction and less conflict with their pets than they do with their siblings. Of course, this may well be because pets do not pose the same level of competition for parental attention that human siblings do. It may also be because the family dog or cat (or any other pet, for that matter) is a consistent source of social support, never offering an argument contrary to the child's view and always at the ready with a listening ear. Melson notes that cultural expectations may be responsible for this connection between children and their pets; that is, the expectation that children in the United States become increasingly independent and separate from their parents as they mature may well lead to the choice to confide in pets, because "they can provide uncomplicated and unthreatening intimacy" while still appearing mature and independent to their parents.[32] For example, some scholars have pointed out that when children are looking for someone in whom to confide a secret, they are more likely to turn to either their mothers or their dogs than to their fathers.[33] Furthermore, the tumultuous period of adolescence also proves to be a prime life stage for confiding in one's pets. At a time when teens' "angst" leads to feelings that no one understands them, turning to the family pet to share anxieties and sadness may well have a positive impact on teenagers' well-being.[34]

Other research bolsters the idea that pets can decrease negative socioemotional indicators such as anxiety and loneliness in adolescence.[35] Pet ownership in childhood may actually increase social competence in preschoolers as they interact with peers, though other research suggests that having a pet present may actually encourage children to spend less time with people and more time with their pet.[36] Research has also shown that simply developing positive attitudes toward pets (whether or not a child owns a dog or cat) is significantly associated with lower delinquency rates.[37]

Pets also play an important role for children under eighteen in both dual-earner families (both parents work) and single-parent families. Indeed, with 61 percent of two-parent families classified as dual earner and 82 percent of single-father families and 73 percent of single-mother families classified as employed, pets can be central to a child's "after-school" world.[38] Froma Walsh, a pioneer in the field of family therapy, has noted regarding her own experience as an only child in a dual-earner family, "[My dog Rusty] welcomed me home from school, shared my milk and cookies, and curled up close to help me with my homework."[39] And in my own family, both of our very loud, seventy-five-pound German shorthaired pointers provide both children (and me, for that matter) with a sense of security if I cannot make it home from the university in time to meet their bus after school. For adolescents who are homeless, having a dog not only helps them feel less lonely but also makes them feel safer.[40]

Parent Identity Formation with Pets

With so many agreed-on benefits of raising a multispecies family with children present, one might think that parents internalize some sort of identity related to their dogs and cats. And, in the same way that child-free and childless participants identified their dogs and cats as valued family members, parents with both young and adult human children reported assigning the generalized role identity of "family member" to their pets. Indeed, the one unanimous theme that I found across all of my interviews (and the vast majority of veterinarian visits that I observed in which children were present) was a desire to welcome the companion animal into the family fold. For example, all participants, regardless of family structure, were concerned about leaving their dogs and cats outside in the Texas heat. Gennifer, a fifty-two-year-old empty nester who invited me to her home on a blistering, one-hundred-degree July day, let her two dogs, Simon and Sola, out at least three times during our two-hour interview. Both dogs would trot outside happily, only to return to the door within a few minutes, sending Gennifer up out of her seat to let them right back inside. At one point, she chided Simon, saying, "It's hot outside. You need to stay in for a minute!"

While 27 percent of pet-owning households did not visit the veterinarian in 2016, general veterinary care was also a prominent behavior practiced by all categories of interviewees in my research.[41] Everyone reported keeping vaccinations up-to-date. And while no one reported having veterinary insurance for their animals, all noted that they would take the family animal into the veterinarian if he or she appeared to have a health issue.[42]

Sleeping arrangements, especially for dogs (it turns out that cats sleep wherever they please), were diverse and mixed across all groups. Given the clear-cut parent-child identity pairing that emerged for childfree and childless participants, I originally expected that this group would be far more likely to co-sleep with their animals than would families with children present. However, there did not seem to be a pattern here either. Multiple modes of sleeping arrangements, ranging from crating to co-sleeping to dog and cat beds spread throughout the home, appeared in both types of multispecies homes. The only discernable difference between these categories of participants was that multispecies families with children sometimes reported that their children co-slept with the family pet (though this varied, as well).

However, this general identity formation ("he or she is our family" or "we are all family") seemed to be the deepest identity pairing that parents had developed with the family animal related to themselves (though, as I discuss later, the story was different when parents were asked about their children). While most participants with human children in the home referred to their dogs or cats with names like "baby" when speaking to them (or to others when speaking about them), only one of these participant narratives reflected behavior that indicated an internalized parent-child identity pairing with her dogs. Furthermore, as I have discussed throughout this chapter, the vast majority of behavior by these parents indicated that their four-legged family members were very loved but also very utilitarian in nature. Participants described their pets as babysitters, companions, entertainers, comforters, even as instillers of responsibility and compassion, but not as children.

Some parents with children in the home were stark in explaining the absence of a parent-child identity pairing related to their animals. When I asked Amanda, a thirty-something mother of three children, if she thought of her three dogs as children, she said,

> I don't see them as my children. But I do see them as part of the family. I do have friends who got their dogs or pets as their children. [*Pauses*] . . . If my children want to get ill, and there were ways to help them that were obviously very expensive, I would not bat an eyelash. I would absolutely be doing that. But if my dogs got ill, and it was thousands of dollars, I don't think I would be doing that. Because I have friends who don't have kids that had to do that kind of thing. . . . So I don't have that kind of connection, I suppose. . . . I would die for my children, but not for my animals, I guess.

Sarah, the forty-something mother of three whom I interviewed once as a parent with children still home and then again later as an empty nester, was concise and emphatic in her comparison in that first chat: "I don't visualize them as another child of mine. . . . If I had to choose who to save on your life boat, it's still going to be my kid. . . . It's still a dog, even if I love her very much and I'd be sad if she passed."

These professed boundaries between internalizing the parent identity for human children and for the companion animal are not surprising. Indeed, considering the stigma that childfree people seem to be acutely aware of regarding the parent-child relationships that they develop with their animals, it is no wonder that someone who has a human child makes clear distinctions between their human children and their non-human family members. However, there is more to the story of parental identity than fear of stigma. The American sociologist Barrie Thorne's concept of borderwork makes for an interesting application here. Thorne notes in her book *Gender Play: Girls and Boys in School* that boys and girls either do or do not reinforce and maintain gender boundaries on the basis of the social context in which they interact.[43] She reports that children enact strict, traditional gender roles (and, thus, role identities) when they are at school, in class, or on the playground. However, when girls and boys interact in their neighborhoods outside the context of school, these gendered boundaries become blurred (as do other boundaries, such as age or grade), and many children are far more likely to play with both boys and girls, moving beyond the traditional gender roles that are structurally imposed by school administrations. The reason why children can blur these boundaries has much to do with a lack of adult supervision and the incumbent enforcement of traditional gender roles.

When children are not present, as in the case of the childfree and childless participants in this study, pet owners can blur the boundary between companion animal and child far more effectively than when children are introduced into the family sphere. In much the same way that children of both sexes can engage in play with one another outside the adult gaze of school administrations who reinforce gender roles, people without children in their family context can also engage in far more fluid conceptualizations of what it means to be a parent exactly because they do not have children. Structurally, people without children are not gauged, or even monitored at all, by how well they perform the parent identity because, to broader society, the parent-child relationship does not appear to exist for them. Indeed, this may well be why child-free animal "parents" feel judged in the first place—because they are performing the parent identity *at all*. Further, as pointed out in chapter 3, significant others in their social circles provide support for the internalization of this identity—even without the presence of children—in a way that creates a protective shield against broader social judgment from others about treating their animals like children.

However, the introduction of children into the family sphere changes the context of the family household and brings new social expectations about being a parent into the family fold. The social reality of who counts culturally as "child" in the parent-child identity pairing is greatly restricted, not only by broader social structures but also by the same people who may have supported such a pairing with dogs or cats before human children entered the picture. As a result, parents of human children engage in clear boundary maintenance between their children and their companion animals.

In the Israeli anthropologist Dafna Shir-Vertesh's six-year longitudinal study of childfree couples in Israel, research participants welcomed companion animals into their home as family members and treated them much like small children.[44] Childfree participants in this research not only paralleled their animals with children but also discussed their needs to protect and love their pets as children. Shir-Vertesh's participants referred to themselves as parents, actively enlarging their childfree families while also internalizing an important status within Israeli society. However, once human children are introduced, Shir-Vertesh argues that a "flexible personhood" becomes apparent in the household. Dogs and cats who had previously enjoyed the application of personhood and a parent-child relationship with their owners, now become reduced, demoted in the family structure, and sometimes moved out of the home entirely.

Like the parents in Shir-Vertesh's study, the vast majority of parents in my study who still had human children living in their homes engaged in borderwork as a means of drawing distinct identity boundaries between that of parenting the human child and that of including the companion animal as a family member. A mother of three young children with whom I spoke during my fieldwork highlighted these boundaries nicely. She had brought her three children to the veterinarian that day—a four-year-old daughter and three-year-old twin sons. In the midst of our conversation, and as we waited for the veterinarian to come, her daughter diligently worked to open the door to the lobby. She desperately wanted to see the other animals there, but her mother's firm grip on the exam-room doorknob denied her the opportunity. One of the boys was investigating the otoscope and ophthalmoscope, while her other son sat quietly playing on her phone. Jack, her twelve-year-old Lhasa apso, lay on the floor at her feet, whining and nibbling on the oozing hot spot for which he'd been brought to the veterinarian in the first place. She said, "Jack was my baby before I had kids. He went with me everywhere, and I showed pictures of him to everyone I met. I spent thousands of dollars on ophthalmologists [for cataracts] and dermatologists [for skin allergies]. But then I had kids. And it was either formula or vet bills." She ended her conversation with me as the veterinarian walked in, saying, "I still feel so guilty about Jack—but having kids was a game changer for me. And at least he still has a good home. But my kids are my kids, you know?"

Indeed, this woman's guilt is reflective of research on pre-child "interspecies parenting" and the changes that human children bring into the multispecies family fold.[45] Mary, a thirty-year-old single mother with a two-year-old daughter, a seven-year old dog, and a five-year-old cat, also reported the immense guilt she found with the borderwork in which she felt internally forced to engage when introducing her new daughter to her pre-child "babies." In particular, she felt frustrated by her own internal demands to draw distinct lines between her beloved "little boy," Devon (a cocker spaniel), and Marcy, her daughter. She shared, "Devon is kind of on the sideline now." I asked her, "And how does that make you feel?" After a brief pause, she continued:

> I feel bad, just bad. I have this thing where dogs are not our entertainment. They are there to be loved, and they love us. So let's treat them like our kids and give them time and energy. If you want them, you have to act like you want them, not just throw them in a cage and leave them all day. . . . That makes me feel bad because some days it is like that. I have become that person to him [Devon]. . . . Marcy reminds me he wants to go for a walk, and I'm like, "All right, you are right. He needs this." . . . But then most times I just ignore him.

Mary began to cry softly.

> I guess I am so much less organized now. Like, having a kid, there are too many things to worry about now. . . . My house is a mess, I have dishes all the time, keeping Marcy from spilling milk on the rug and that he [Devon] doesn't eat her grilled cheese sandwich. . . . Devon just went way back on the back burner. And the cat went even farther back. I feel like I am taking care of everything. . . . There is too much going on in the house. It's too much.

Empty Nesters and Caretaker-Companion Pairings

Empty nesters in my research seemed to be a bit more on the fence about their own identities related to their dogs or cats. Indeed, the borderwork used here to maintain boundaries between a "caretaker" identity and a "parent" identity was not as clear as it was with parents who still had children present in the home. When asked specifically if they thought of themselves as "parent" of their animal family members or their family animals as "children," all empty nesters used familial terms to discuss their relationships with their animals. Sometimes they referred to themselves as "mom" in a list of multiple identities paired with their companion animals. For example, Sylvia, a sixty-four-year-old empty nester, had just finished sharing the insurmountable toileting issues that she was having with her French bulldog, Emily. Sylvia had rescued Emily from a puppy mill in which she had been caged and traumatized for years—treated as if she were a piece of reproductive machinery. Sylvia's husband had become agitated with the consistent—and constant—defecation in their home and had said, "Let's just get rid of them [both of their dogs]." When asked why she did not see this as a solution, Sylvia was emphatic: "Because I made a promise to them when I picked them up that I was going to take care of them, and Emily has already suffered so much. I would not put that dog to the curb for anything. . . . I see myself as her protector. I'm her mom. I'm her caretaker, and I'm going to take care of her. . . . It's my job. It's my duty. It's my obligation. It's what makes me who I am to be that to her."

Other times, parent-child identities were tied to participants' spouses. For example, while Zee did not think of her dogs as "children" (or herself as "mother"), she had a different perspective when asked about what her husband thought of Billy, one of their three shih tzus. Zee instantaneously replied, "Oh, he loves him like his son. He just loves Billy. 'Where's Billy? . . . Come, Billy!' [*quoting her husband*]. When Mitch walks in the mudroom, Billy's the first dog to be there. And Mitch is all over him. . . . They sit together every night, and [Billy] just licks his face. And Mitch loves it."

Gennifer offered a similar perspective regarding her husband, Dan, and his parent-child relationship with Simon: "I think he's like the son that Dan never had, because my husband's really handy. He's got all sorts of tools, and he's always doing something because there's always something to do in the house, right? Simon does not care. It doesn't matter how loud, how scary, how big or noisy. He sits right there next to Dan and watches, which Dan loves."

However, all empty nesters but one maintained firm boundaries between themselves as "caretakers" for their companion animals and "mothers" to their children. These participants were able to easily identify specific behaviors that made them "motherly" toward their pets while also making it clear that they saw themselves as "caretaker" rather than "parent" in these relationships. Reported behaviors related to the companion animal typically included taking them outside to play and potty, feeding and watering, and regular medical care. More intensive answers from empty nesters, such as in-depth research on medical care and comforting the animal during thunderstorms (day and night, in some cases), initially led me to wonder if empty nesters would ultimately report similar behavior to the childfree families that I discuss in chapter 2. However, when I asked empty nesters if the dogs in their multispecies families were similar to their children for them, the answers were typically quick and decisive.

Sylvia explained the differences for her, noting, "I'm the caregiver to them, *as if* I am their mother. I feed them every morning, I take them out, I give them fresh water daily, and I take them to the vet. I do everything that a mother would do." Curious if this meant that she thought of her dogs, Emily and Taylor, as children, I asked, "Is this different from being a mother to your [daughters]?" She answered, "Oh, very much. I do care what the dogs think or if they're sad or whatever. But with children, their emotional states and their illnesses impact everything a parent—a good parent—does. I would study with my kids; I would shuttle them back and forth. Their happiness . . . and well-being . . . was paramount."

Focusing on emotional and social development, Zee also unequivocally confirmed this distinction when I asked her a similar question: "No, it's different. I mean, I don't have to advise them. I just see myself as a caretaker to them and as a friend. . . . With Lainey, I had to teach her morals and values and still [be] there for her [now] to support her in some of the decisions that come her way. . . . I think I see it totally black and white."

Catherine homed in on differences in interaction to explain why Matilda, their golden retriever, did not fulfill the role of child for her (even after having shared that Matilda is "a child" to her and her husband, "because she has to be fed and let out, exercised, taken to the vet"). She also simultaneously illuminated the importance that the family dog provided to her and her husband's newly emptied nest and carefully laid out boundary maintenance between the status of child and that of companion: "She's a distraction to how I'm feeling. . . . Because suddenly I have a friend and a buddy to go do things with, and I come home, and she greets me, and I have that sort of presence that she replaces . . . seeing a child." I wanted to know more about what she meant regarding how she was feeling. After all, my husband and I will eventually be empty nesters too. But, for pragmatic reasons, I had not thought about what role our dogs, Sam and Sadie, may play in that next stage of our family life course. And Catherine's descriptor "distraction" in one way or another echoed every empty nester with whom I spoke but one (Zee). So I pressed her, asking, "What would those feelings look like without her, without that distraction?" Pausing for a moment, she answered introspectively, "Quiet contemplation—not depressive symptoms but more lonely quietness—slowly in this quietness in this house, . . . losing the hustle and bustle of the in and out having a child there, the voices, the laundry going at weird hours, the slamming of doors. That all goes away, so it becomes very quiet. . . . She brings an energy and helps take all that lonely quietness away."

"Does she fulfill the role of child for you at all, do you think?"

"No."

"Why not?"

"Because there is a difference between, I think, a human interaction and a canine because I get responses from my children. I get responses more physical from her, but I don't know what she's thinking. Whereas my children are more apt, of course, to have verbal conversations and sometimes know what they're thinking but always be able to talk things out. Can't do that with the dog. She never asks my advice or anything. So no, she doesn't take the place of a child."

Household Composition, Veterinary Bills, and
Financial Boundaries

In 2015, the BLS estimated that the average spending on dogs at the veterinarian was $235 for routine care.[46] For cats, that number was $196. However, if we consider average surgical veterinarian visits for dogs, Americans spent $551 on their dogs and $398 on their cats. Only spending on food and boarding facilities (which are often at the veterinarian anyway) was higher for dogs. For cats, on the other hand, the only thing that exceeded veterinary spending was food cost. Needless to say, veterinarian visits can require large outlays of cash and credit for all multispecies families.

There are, however, differences in family composition that impact levels of spending at the veterinarian. Comments by participants like those earlier by Amanda, Sarah, and Jake's owner at the veterinarian clinic make it clear that this is one area of behavior in which boundary work for child and pet identities is robust. Intensive veterinary expenses, such as the $3,000 back surgery (and subsequent CareCredit loan) that Becky had done for her suffering dachshund or the $200-a-month seizure medication that Kathy, who thought she and her spouse would never be able to have children, purchased for Rom never made an appearance in conversations that I had with people who had children present in the home. While participants with young kids wanted their animals to be healthy and would do the best that they could with medical emergencies that arose, most could not justify expensive treatments or foods for their companion animals.[47]

Examples of this resistance to expensive treatments for pets among participants with children were present in my fieldwork as well. For example, one male owner shared with me that he and his wife had a ten-year-old and an eight-year old child as well as two rescue dogs at home. I observed as he was advised by the veterinarian that Ally, one of his rescues, had fairly severe hip dysplasia, a debilitating, genetic malady in which the hip socket forms atypically, causing chronic arthritis and lameness. The owner, deeply concerned about the pain that his dog was suffering, asked how much it would cost to fix the issue. The veterinarian said "$4,000 to $5,000 for a hip replacement." The man's face dropped in astonishment. Unphased, the veterinarian continued on: "*But* there are other, more cost-effective options that will minimize pain and improve her quality of life." And, just like that, veterinarian and owner seamlessly moved to discussion of and choices between alternative (and far more affordable) treatments such as Rimadyl, an anti-inflammatory drug, hip and joint supplements, and muscle-building exercises.

Obviously, spending on pets in general appears to be a mode of boundary work that parents maintain between their understanding of what a "child" is and what a four-legged family member is.[48] The BLS notes that average spending on pets within households that contain children ages six to seventeen is $536 per year.[49] For households with children under six, the amount drops to $412. And for single-parent households, expenditure on the family pet plummets to the lowest of all household compositions: $267.

Half of my empty-nester participants, however, seemed more willing to cross the financial boundaries that most other parents either could not or would not cross at the veterinarian.[50] In fact, according to the BLS, empty nesters (or at least those couples with children over the age of eighteen) spend the second highest amount on their animals, laying down an average of $644 per year.[51] In keeping with my research, the only category of household composition that exceeds this amount is family units that contain only spouses who are childfree or childless.[52] Indeed, empty nesters in my research were willing to outlay larger amounts of money than were their counterparts with children still in the home. Catherine noted that Matilda was currently on a medication that cost $3 a pill, per day (with a monthly expenditure of over $90 on medication alone), for an allergy that causes skin inflammation, itching, and fur loss. When I asked her why she was willing to spend so much on medication, she quickly responded, "Because of what she provides us, all the things I've told you about: the companionship, the ability for her to bring happiness, to take the loneliness away when the children leave. In that regard, I would not want to have to lose her to sickness. . . . I would rather treat it so she can always be around us." Indeed, Catherine relates the importance of her status as an empty nester to Matilda and expenditures to keep Matilda healthy.

Because of the longitudinal nature of my interviews with Sarah, she also provided interesting insight about veterinary expenditure. During her first interview, while her children were still home, she did not report having spent large amounts of money at the veterinarian for her dog (though she did discuss the expense of boarding). However, when I returned to speak with her four years later, after all of her children had moved out, she discussed having spent upward of $5,000 ($3,000 on multiple surgeries and then another $2,000 on emergency-room visits, medications, follow-ups, dehydration therapy, etc.) on her shih tzu, Maya, when she upended the garbage can and "swallowed tampons." Sarah was out of town with her husband when this happened—a three-hour car ride away, in another state—for Easter weekend. Her husband immediately drove her back home to attend to Maya. Maya was sick for two weeks after that but recovered—only because of Sarah's fast return and involvement with the veterinarian.

When I asked Sarah if she had ever spent such a large amount on a pet when her kids lived at home, she said, "No. Because we couldn't afford it. We haven't been financially blessed until the last ten years. There's no way we could have afforded that. Being able to afford things—it dictates what you can and cannot do. If I could only afford kids or taking care of the dog, I would choose my children over any pet—my kids, hands down, versus pets." And with that, Sarah made it clear that the boundary work that is involved in delineating between "child" and "pet" is also financial in nature. The increased disposable income that comes when children finally do move out of the home makes it possible for empty nesters to blur financial boundaries in ways that are reflective of a parental identity, even as they engage in careful borderwork that separates "parent" of child from "caretaker" of a generalized family member.

Child-Pet Identity Formation

The clear borderwork separating pet from child that was present for parents with young children appeared to be quite different when they were asked about their children's identities related to companion-animal family members. Of course, this would not be surprising. Children can establish close emotional bonds with their companion animals that result in the internalization of various identities for themselves and the assignment of relevant counteridentities to their pets. Empirical evidence indicates that children rank their dogs and cats in the top ten *social* relationships constituting their social networks (alongside parents, siblings, and best friends). Dogs and cats are identified as companions, playmates, comforters, and protectors (functions also included with the status of sibling) and consistently rank above other nonimmediate family members (for example, aunts and uncles or grandparents) in importance.[53] The perceived forging of both friendship and kinship with pets is a common narrative for kids, while adults under the age of forty have retrospectively reported the same about their childhood animals.[54] Other research has pointed out that some children label their pets as "siblings."[55]

Considering "sibling" as a potential identity for the family pet is in alignment with scholarly literature that highlights the functions of a sibling in Western (and American) society. As researchers have pointed out, siblings and pets are logistically similar in that both are accorded "family member" status, reside in the home, and depend on parental support. Furthermore, the culturally expected role set for the sibling identity within the United States includes characteristics such as cultural and social educators, nonparental social support, companionship, playmate, and where required contextually, caretaker.[56] These characteristics also appear for the companion animal in the multispecies family framework within my own work here and in that of others.[57] It would make sense pragmatically that parents recognize these intimate relationships and try to make meaningful sense of them.

As a result, the parental narrative in my research was much different when participants spoke about identities that their children appeared to have internalized in relationship to their animals. Indeed, participants' recounting of the different identities with which they saw their children interacting with the family pet divulged multiple possibilities, including companion, friend, and even mother, in one case.[58] The presence of the pet as quasi-sibling was a common identity that parents related to their children having with the family pet, with seven out of eighteen participants (both with children present and empty nesters) commenting on this status in some way. For example, while Riley, a participant in her forties with two daughters, made it abundantly clear that she did not think of their King Charles spaniel as a child, she also commented that her two daughters, Danica and Iliana, felt otherwise.

I asked her, "Would you give Snickers any kind of label in relationship to you or your girls?"

Figure 4.1. Danica, Riley's daughter, cuddling next to her brother, Snickers, as she scratches his tummy

"To the girls, yes."

"How so?"

Thinking for a second, she responded, "The girls always explain that [Snickers] is their brother. Then they say, 'You're the mommy, right?' So I'm the mommy." Her daughters' perceptions of Snickers's familial status extended to Riley because her children also said that she (Riley) would be the dog's "mommy." However, it was clear that the sibling identity and the connections to other human family resided solely with Riley's children, as Riley repeatedly explained that she was disappointed in Snickers as a pet. This was especially the case regarding the way that he acted toward Danica and Iliana. Riley explained, "He's very grouchy to people. He's not social. When the girls approach his cage, he growls really bad. It's awful, . . . but they [still] want to be with him, . . . love him, . . . ask for toys for him." Snickers's failure as the kind of dog that Riley had hoped her daughters would have led to Riley's resentment of Snickers, even as she still classified him as a member of the family.

Building on Melson's ideas of the importance of family companion animals in providing caretaking opportunities, Amanda argued that her own children thought of the dogs in her household as "siblings."[59] When I asked her why she thought this, her response focused on the responsibilities her children had related to the dogs: "They think of them as siblings. . . . But there is still kind of a separation. There is an understanding that . . . [at least] I believe that there is an understanding that they are not the equivalent but as close to that as you can get." She contemplated for a moment after saying this and then added, "Because they have to take a lot of responsibility for the dogs. My son picks up their poop and helps me feed them, my daughter helps me bathe them, things like that."

Sometimes, the identity pairing of sibling-sibling was placed on the dog by parents themselves as a means of providing guidance to their children about how they should interact with their companion animals. This was a common mode of meaning making for some parents as they sought to educate their children about the nature of pets. For example, when Victoria discussed whether her relationship with her cats changed when she had her first child, she was confident that it had not. Straightening herself in her seat, she said, "I have always had animals around.

So integrating them in, I don't overemphasize their importance, nor do I push them aside and treat them like they have a lesser role. The cats were just their usual place, and the children were allowed to play with them gently. They learned from the beginning that you have to be gentle and touch them with respect like a sibling. We treat our pets like siblings."[60] In this case, parents used the status of sibling as a means of providing guidance on appropriate interaction with four-legged family members.

It is important to note that three empty nesters, when asked to remember how their children would have labeled their family pets, were emphatic that their children had *not* thought of their dogs or cats as siblings. Indeed, Paula, a fifty-five-year-old African American mother with one college-age daughter and two toy poodles, offered an example. Amanda, her daughter, had just begged her parents the day before our interview to let her bring her "best friend" Splenda (one of their family dogs) back to university with her for company. However, Paula also shared that one of the main impetuses for getting the now sixteen-year-old dog, Splenda, had been the euthanasia of an earlier family dog and the subsequent despair from a then three-year-old Amanda:

> We were eating at the table when, out of nowhere, Amanda started crying. And we were like, "Oh my God! What is wrong?" And she says, "I don't have a brother, and I don't have a little sister. And now I don't even have a dog. . . ." That broke my heart because we weren't going to give her a brother or sister. And I thought, "She's right." Because she did everything with [the dog]. And my husband said, "Well, you're not going to get a brother and you're not going to get a sister, so what kind of dog do you want?" And so that's how we wound up getting Splenda."

Although Paula and her husband did not provide Amanda with Splenda to take the place of a sibling, they were very much reacting to Amanda's desire to have that level of constant social interaction present in her home life. And Splenda has remained an integral part of Amanda's life ever since.

Figure 4.2. Paula's daughter, Amanda, holding her dog, Splenda, at age five; in a family portrait at age ten; and home from college at age twenty

"As Close as You're Going to Get"

Two parents thought of the family pet as the closest that they would ever get to providing a sibling to their own children. Both instances were connected to the unique roles that companion animals can play in the one-child multispecies family, especially when infertility or some other inability to have more children is present. Zee, who could not have any more children after Lainey, provided a good example when she commented, "Theo was the other sibling for Lainey." Kathy, a forty-something mother, was starker about this comparison in her experience. She and her husband had been told for years, by multiple doctors, that they would never have children. When Kathy unexpectedly became pregnant with their only child, the pregnancy was difficult, and her son was born with multiple, chronic health problems.

Kathy described the importance of their family dog and cats to distract from the required intense focus on her son's health, sharing, "He [her son] comes first. He comes first. He comes first. But animals were a way of finding a little bit of balance around that because, no matter what medical needs your child has, if you don't have a sibling—and this [the family dog] was as close as we were going to get to a sibling—that balance is hard to achieve. In fact, I think that any level of intensity towards the animals would balance my son's perspective of being part of a family team. That's what I hoped for." Indeed, for Kathy, their family animals were very much substitutes for siblings. That is, their presence distracted from the constant focus (and pressure) that would have otherwise been present for her son (because of his medical issues) had there been no one else, like a sibling, to demand and absorb some of that intensity. Similar to Paula's daughter, who actively sought the social interaction that a sibling would have provided, Kathy, as a parent, pursued the same for their entire family unit. Indeed, having an animal "sibling" present was imperative for both the mental and emotional well-being for Kathy, her husband, and their son as they navigated his health issues.

Kathy's focus on the family as a "team" uses a common cultural moniker for the middle-class family. However, her perception is important in another, unique way that sets Kathy's multispecies family apart from those families that are not dealing with chronic pediatric illness. Research on pediatric illnesses has shown that focus on a child who is ill can bring the family closer together.[61] Whereas for human siblings who are not ill, such a focus can cause emotional strain and trauma later in life, an animal sibling may well circumvent these issues while still working as a member of the family team to bring balance to the family's life together.

* * *

While it is clear that the multispecies family with human children (either present in the home or having flown the nest) engages with its dogs and cats as family members, the specificity with which distinct familial identities are internalized or assigned varies by context. While parents who currently have children in their homes discuss their animals in human terms such as "family member," "companion," "protector," and "educator," they are typically careful not to assign childlike statuses (e.g., baby, son, daughter, child) to their animals that represent anything more than a superficial label. This may well be because, while multispecies families are increasingly permeating the cultural fabric of what counts as family in the United States, there are also very clear identity standards associated with statuses like "parent" and "child." Violating those standards by behaving as if your dog or cat holds the same status as your human child would presumably generate far more stigma for parents—both from their significant others (e.g., partners, parents, and adult siblings) and from society in general—than would be the case for childfree and childless persons who choose to blur the boundaries between animal and child.

Indeed, as I discussed in chapter 3, it appears that both the childfree and childless may feel supported by significant others to blur these boundaries, even as their counterparts with human children engage in careful borderwork to maintain separation between the two. In fact, Michelle, a participant in her thirties who owned an English bulldog, provided support for this contention. Michelle was one of two childfree participants (both married women with high-powered careers) who did *not* exhibit a parental identity counter to her companion animal. Her narrative revealed that her dog, Champ, was a beloved family member but one that maintained the clear status of "family dog." Alluding to the idea that childfree people who treat their animals as children may receive support (rather than stigma) for their behavior, Michelle noted,

> I never try to treat him like a baby or anything like that. I care for him, I worry about him, but he is a dog. He is not a human. He will never be able to take care of himself. . . . He is not like a baby because he is never going to grow out of it. We don't dress him up. He is just a dog. We can love him and care for him, but he is not our son. When I talk to people like that, sometimes I think they think I am cold or not caring."

Interested in what appeared to be a contradiction to the perceived judgment that other childfree participants had reported for behaving as if their animals *were* children, I asked her, "Why do you think people think that?" She answered, "Because the industry and society treats animals like they are little babies, little kids. But he is not. We think he loves us, but he would never show love like a human does. . . . I don't think a dog takes the place of a kid. . . . It's completely different. There are similarities because you have to take care of it like a child. But sometimes I just think the whole industry of animals is wacky and out of control." And although Michelle does not specifically reference the industry and others as focusing on families without children, her childfree experience leads me to believe that she feels pressure for not having a child.

Michelle continued, "Society tells us as a woman you should have it all . . . [*crying and laughing simultaneously*]. There is social pressure to get married, you are supposed to have a child, you're supposed to have a career. . . . And I don't think I need a kid to feel complete. . . . I don't think I need to check that box." But she also feels pressured by industry and society to treat her dog like a child—something she does not feel comfortable doing. This suggests that the expected parental borderwork that separates human child from family animal is not expected in the same way from those who are either voluntarily or involuntarily childless. Perhaps due to the pronatalist culture endemic in the United States, people without children look for a way to perform family through their animals.[62] For Michelle, not engaging in this blurring of identity boundaries between human child and animals while also *not* having children means that others think of her as "cold and not caring."

However, for those who *do* have children, there is strong social pressure in the United States for "child-centeredness" and attachment parenting that is self-sacrificial.[63] As a result, clear-cut borderwork that acknowledges the "child" identity (in human form) as an appropriate counterpairing to "parent" is required. This cultural imperative simultaneously supports the multispecies family with children present, with the caveat that the companion animal maintain a generalized "family member" related to the parent. This makes sense given the empty-nester narratives in my research. With children gone from the home, grown and on their own, the cultural imperative to engage in this borderwork appears to ease for empty nesters, who are then able to blur these boundaries somewhat more freely (but not so freely that they once again appear to be childfree in their parental performances).

With regard to multispecies siblings, these frameworks appear acceptable and even encouraged within the family structure. And the presence of dog and cat siblings in these families, compared to families with children who are not multispecies, makes these family structures unique for research on the sociology of family. Indeed, family networks and identities adjust in relationship to the dogs and cats with which children have identified as siblings. These relationships, which cannot exist in single-species families (especially one-child families), can provide protective and loyal support for children as they progress through the trials and tribulations of childhood and adolescence.

5

"This Is My Son Rosenberg"

Advertising in the Age of Pet Parents

"Budweiser has an awesome PSA about drinking and driving!" one of my students offered enthusiastically. I had tasked students in my Animals and Society class with finding and analyzing different advertising representations of companion animals. Our analysis was centered on the anthropomorphism of pets by advertisers as well as if pets were depicted in familial roles with statuses such as "child," "sibling," or "friend" or more traditional "pet" roles in which the pet is present in the household but without the intimate, familial human-animal bond that has been the topic of this book. The organic flow of our large group discussion had drifted toward a televised Budweiser public service announcement.

"So . . . forgive my ignorance, but what Budweiser PSA?" I asked.

One of my students piped up immediately: "It will make you bawl uncontrollably over and over again," she said, quite sincerely. Some other students in the room murmured in agreement.

Titled "Friends Are Waiting" and produced by Momentum Worldwide Advertising for Anheuser-Busch, the spot was released digitally online on September 19, 2014, immediately went viral, and—on the heels of that success—was subsequently televised during the Major League Baseball playoffs and World Series that same year. By the end of 2014, Momentum Worldwide reports that the ad had received over twenty million views online and been named the "Ad of the Day" by *Adweek* and "Ad of the Week" by *Advertising Age*.[1]

The ad initially introduces viewers to the heartwarming story of a twenty-something man and his new golden Labrador retriever puppy, Buddy. Viewers are then taken through a series of life-sharing experiences between the two as the pup grows up. Buddy and his man are shown hugging, playing on the floor together, romping in the park, indulging in beer (for the man) and spoonfuls of peanut butter (for Buddy), and co-sleeping. The ad is set to the following song lyrics:

> You and me we were made for love,
> A lifetime is not long enough to show you
> what you mean to me.
> Ohhhh, I'll be waiting here for you
> When you come home to me.

At the twenty-second mark of the sixty-second spot, the mood changes substantially, as the now adult dog follows behind his man, who is leaving home with friends for the evening, holding a six-pack of Budweiser, and saying, "I'll see you later, Buddy." Buddy spends the next fifteen seconds of the ad expectantly staring out the living room window, lonely, then noticeably despondent, as he cuddles with what appears to be a piece of clothing. At the thirty-five-second mark, copy appears on a black backdrop reading, "For some, the waiting never ended." The dog whimpers in the background despairingly, suggesting that the dog's man never came home again—a victim of drunk driving.

Cue the tears. I was literally forced to turn my back to the class so that I could hide my crying at that point. The ad is poignant and touching and misery-inducing—in much the same way it would be were the advertisers to have shown any family member (human or not) making the same realization. The good news for Buddy is that, with fifteen-seconds left to the spot, his man returns home the next morning, with Buddy beside himself with joy and the man explaining his absence: "Hey! I'm sorry! I decided I shouldn't drive home last night. I stayed at Dave's." Copy on a black backdrop appears again, reading, "Make a plan to make it home. Your friends are counting on you." Buddy licks his man's face, warmly welcoming him home in an emotional return, and the ad ends with his man saying, "I'm back. . . . I'm back. . . . Yeah, I'm back."

There appeared to be more than one tear-stained face in the room when the clip ended, and I (having hastily wiped a sleeve across my face) turned back around to face the class. "So, what do you guys think? Are they using Buddy the dog as a metaphor for a person in this ad? Is he anthropomorphized?"

Doug raised his hand and said, "I think so. They show the dog as an emotional creature, sad, happy, playful, attached to his owner."

"Plus," Mandy added, "this seems like exactly what a person would go through if they thought they'd lost a loved one. And the man is talking to Buddy as if he speaks English." Good. They understood anthropomorphism and could apply it here.

But it was what Steph said next that really stuck out for me: "It's obvious Buddy is anthropomorphized. But I really think that misses the bigger point. Advertisers are reaching out to Millennials and trying to speak to who we think of as family. When I think about my cat at home, it hurts to even imagine how she'd feel if I made this kind of stupid mistake." A muffled "yep" sounded off in agreement with her. And with that, students began packing up their things, signaling that our fifty minutes together were up for the day.

* * *

One of the main goals of this book is to highlight how society-wide, demographic changes have impacted identity formation within the multispecies family (and the accompanying behavior associated with it), leading to a new form of family structure. However, another equally important goal is to connect micro-level behavior to macro-level, cultural expectations regarding family. As I mentioned in chapter 2, cultural expectations of particular statuses like "parent" develop over a long-term course of repeated, widespread, and patterned behavior within groups and between social actors.[2] These expectations do not evolve overnight but, rather, *gradually* adapt to micro-level changes that are spread broadly across a variety of groups in a patterned way that eventually begins to alter the understanding of affected identities (as well as, in this case, who may be included as "family") within society as a whole.[3] Indeed, the struggle for single-mother families, single-father families, and LGBTQ families to be recognized as legitimate, successful forms of family in the United States is demonstrative of the gradual and often tumultuous nature of culture-wide changes regarding "family."[4]

This connection between micro-level behavior and macro-level institutions is a key hallmark for structural symbolic interaction and, thus, identity theory. Indeed, it is requisite within the perspective to show how the internalization of identity by individuals both influences and is influenced by broader cultural demands about how the status should be performed. However, a depiction of the link between micro and macro is also imperative to show how micro-level interactions are intertwined with culture-wide expectations, causing adaptations, new meanings, and unique structures to emerge within cultural constructs related to family.

Human-animal interaction scholars have investigated relationships between humans and companion animals at the macro-level from several angles. Research has examined natural-disaster response related to nonhuman animals in the home, on factory farms, and within research facilities.[5] Other work has explored the legal evolution of companion animals from "property" to "quasi-citizens," with armies of animal rights advocates working to see them assigned legal personhood and membership status within society.[6] Other scholars have explored the use of animals in scientific research, depictions of such within scientific and political realms, and perceptions of human lab workers.[7] Still other studies have analyzed American consumerism as reflective of family status for cats and dogs.[8] In a similar vein, this chapter aims to uncover how the meaning of the multispecies family today, complete with assignment of typically human identities to the dog and cat, is produced and reproduced via print ads designed between 2000 and 2019.[9] This reproduction in advertising highlights how the institution of mass media has embraced the multispecies family as a unique structure, with needs distinct from single-species families and in need of targeted marketing attention. As a result, I move from the micro-level analysis of the multispecies family itself, presented in earlier chapters, to demonstrating how these same relationships are depicted at the macro-level. For identity theory, this is an important piece of the bigger social picture that enables us to see how patterns in human-animal relationships have traversed across groups to further diversify the kinds of family structures that have become increasingly accepted in society.

Anthropomorphism, Advertising, and Animals

Animals are used prolifically and universally within the advertising industry.[10] With respect to companion animals, the diversification of the American family over the past forty years to include the multispecies family has certainly been noticed by marketing executives. Indeed,

Figure 5.1. Luke readying in his uniform with Maeve to watch his dad referee a football game

the American pet product and service industry alone has grown from a $21 billion industry in 1996 to one that topped $95.7 billion in 2019.[11] In 2018, Americans spent $46 billion on pet food and supplies and an additional $18 billion on veterinary care alone.[12] Spending growth on pets in the United States is robust and fast-paced. And while most Americans were cutting back on spending during the Great Recession, spending on companion animals between 2007 and 2012 grew an astounding 28 percent, making the pet industry apparently recession-proof.[13]

Of course, spending on pets in the American household is nothing new. The development of pet products and services between the mid-nineteenth and twentieth centuries highlighted a growing market for mass-produced dog foods, over-the-counter remedies, cages, beds, and accessories such as collars, harnesses, and leashes.[14] But companion-animal spending has not only increased at an incredible pace in the past twenty-five years but has also changed dramatically in nature. Purchases exceed what has come to be the expected minimum in many families: trips to the veterinarian, beds, and food. Designer clothing, health-care insurance, pet party organizing, and organic and gourmet food options

Figure 5.2. Sarah's granddog, Kuper, at his second birthday party held in a Dallas dog park that rents space and supplies for multispecies family birthday parties

are but a few of the kinds of items and services for which consumers, both human and animal companion, have become keen.

It comes as no surprise, then, that dogs and cats have become prolific parts of the advertising regimen in society. At a minimum, the use of animals in our language (e.g., "scaredy cat" or "stubborn as a mule") to symbolize mood, emotion, and social relationships and structure has always been a widespread practice. Indeed, animals are constantly used as metaphors to reinforce the existing social structure.[15] For example, they are an omnipresent force in children's literature for teaching life lessons that might otherwise not be fully understood developmentally.[16] Parents use visits to the zoo and symbolic imagery related to the animals to instill a better understanding of gender roles in their children.[17] Companion-animal narratives in particular are a cultural staple within American society—used for the transmission of values regarding gender, family, and parenting.[18]

The widespread process of attributing what would normally be considered human traits to nonhuman animals in such ways is called "anthropomorphism." When we anthropomorphize, or apply human traits to nonhuman animals, a clearer understanding of what it means to be a human, to be a part of society, and to draw anthropocentric lines between human and nonhuman animals arises.[19] There is a strong tradition in both American films and advertising of using the animal metaphor for humans, human relations, and the solving of human problems. For example, extant literature has successfully shown how animals are used by filmmakers as parallels to human society and behavior.[20] Animal metaphors are also used by advertisers to instruct consumers about gender and racial boundaries within society, building social relationships, and the importance of family formation and reproduction.[21]

However, there is a difference between simply assigning human characteristics to animals (e.g., a televised Subaru ad in which a golden retriever family dubbed "The Barkleys" drives a Subaru vehicle around town) as a means of representing something about human nature and placing an animal as an actual family member. Consider the following two examples. The classic Camel cigarette ad often depicted a camel dressed in a black leather bomber jacket or a suave black tie and tuxedo with a Camel cigarette hanging coolly from his lips. This imagery was used to symbolize aloof masculinity that could transfer seamlessly to all

Figure 5.3. "I and Love and You" ad copy in which a kitten and puppy label their human owners as "moms"

male smokers who purchased the product. Another, much more recent ad for "I and Love and You" natural pet food shows a puppy and a kitten on a white background exclaiming, "Voted Best Looking!" and "By Our Moms" (see figure 5.3). The second ad also anthropomorphizes the kitten and puppy by attributing speech and affectivity (both anthropocentrically believed to be human traits) to each animal.

While both ads have anthropomorphized the featured animals, anthropomorphism in the "I and Love and You" ad displays dogs and cats as having literal familial relationships with their human moms. The copy provides the counterstatus of "mom" and immediately imbues the identity of "child" in each animal because cultural code embeds these two identities as complementary of each other. This process "levels up" from metaphorical anthropomorphism by actually placing the cat or dog in the legitimately held position of child. Furthermore, this second ad demonstrates the increasing marketing tactic of targeting the cat or dog as an actual consumer in much the same way that other human "statuses" are (e.g., parent, child, or grandparent).[22] This is done by ac-cessing the cultural "status quo" for who counts as family in the United States today—in this case, the multispecies family.[23]

In the ads that I examine here, dogs and cats are different in nature than in previous metaphorical usages. That is, they are no longer al-ways metaphorical representations of how humans interact and what so-cial relations should be performed in interaction with other humans.[24] While animals continue to be used in a metaphorical fashion through-out film, advertising, and literature, they no longer appear to always *stand* for humans in these narratives. Instead, dogs and cats in particular are increasingly depicted as legitimate family members in and of them-selves, in human positions, with human roles and rights being conveyed via their human family members. This is apparent in advertisements in which the companion animal is represented as the consumer in much the same way that the human child is—as one that asks their parents for products that are intended for them.

Copy in the ad that is anthropomorphic in nature is not needed to accomplish this assignment of status either. For example, one particu-lar ad for Zurich pet insurance depicts a presumably single woman of child-bearing age holding an umbrella over her small dog to protect him from the rain (see figure 5.4). The ad copy reads, "Zurich insurance. For those who truly love." The metaphor here is not found in the animal but rather in the rain—paralleling the challenges that the woman must overcome in protecting her "family" (the dog) with the umbrella (which represents the veterinary insurance being marketed by the company). The dog is a literal family member here, benefiting from the protection in the same way that a human child would from traditional health in-surance. Of even greater significance is the way in which the woman sacrifices her own needs for that of her animal child—an expectation of "intensive mothering" long in place for the ideal contemporary Ameri-can mother.[25] And while some people may argue that the dog's mere presence in a human capacity is anthropomorphism, I argue that this is beside the point. The more important issue is that the dog *is* family (indeed, with the status of child), not *representative* of family.

The idea of "animal capital" explains how these anthropomorphized depictions are perceived by many Americans as more than the use of animals to imitate people.[26] Instead, because many Americans have a

Figure 5.4. Similar to intensive mothering, a Zurich pet insurance ad depicting a woman sacrificing her own comfort for that of her dog

deeper, more intimate connection with their dogs and cats, they see these images as reflective of the particular human statuses that they have assigned to their pets. Pet owners who do not think of their animals as affective, communicative, and intelligent family members probably will not see these kinds of ads as "speaking to them" about their animal children, grandchildren, or siblings. However, consumers *without* animal capital are *not* whom advertisers are targeting with these messages.

Instead, the kind of ad in which the companion animal *is* family rather than *representative* of family speaks to the cultural status quo that now defines "family" in the United States as inclusive of the multispecies family. This, of course, would include all of its human and animal members and all of the requisite statuses that have historically been identified as familial in nature—in the past restricted to humans but now available to pets as well.

Familial Identities

Leaning on research about familial identities in the United States, I analyzed eighty-eight ads for the presence of at least one of these statuses. Fifty-one of the eighty-eight ads (approximately 58 percent) contained some sort of direct or indirect identity or identity pairing within the image, copy, or both. I identified four discernable familial identities used by advertisers to connect with the "multispecies family" segment of the market: (1) child (n = 42, or 48 percent of total sample); (2) mother (n = 28, or 32 percent of total sample); (3) father (n = 11, or 13 percent of total sample); and (4) sibling (n = 3, or 3 percent of total sample). However, the sibling identity, while represented in the sampled ads, was not significant enough across the sample to warrant a thematic discussion here. Each of these themes is firmly entrenched in images and copy that are clearly geared toward the multispecies family. Paralleling these ads with the cultural expectations for each identity helps us to see both how the multispecies family is acceptably performed within the family and also how it is reproduced within mass media as a distinctive form of doing family.

Mother Identity

Middle-class American motherhood in the late twentieth century and early twenty-first century has been defined as one in which a woman puts her child's needs over her own. "Intensive mothering" is "child-centered, expert guided, emotionally absorbing, labor-intensive, and financially expensive" and has become the stalwart for what being a "good" mother entails in the United States.[27] More specifically, intensive mothering is visually apparent via activity such as organic feeding, co-sleeping, and baby wearing. Mothers are further expected to protect, socialize, and nurture their children, regardless of one's socioeconomic status or culture.[28]

These cultural ideals regarding how to be a "good mother" began to find their way into American advertising in the 1970s and 1980s, when good mothers were generally depicted as child-centered nurturers (versus domestic caretakers) for the first time ever within advertising. By the 1990s, "intensive mothering" had made its way into print images and copy. Ads of this decade showed mothers not only as "child-centered" but as mothers who "play with them and become involved in their daily lives, their ups and downs, their comings and goings, . . . informed by the experts who endorse the advertised products, . . . plac[ing] the 1990's mom firmly on an ideological path of intensive, expert-guided mothering."[29] Furthermore, mothers in advertisements (versus women portrayed as not having children) are overwhelmingly shown engaged in "caring consumption," in which their consumption goals are all about taking care of others via "intensive mothering" with "assistance" from the relevant product.[30]

Ads in my sample in which women are "mothering" their companion animal (n = 28, with a total of thirty-three female representations included) seem to exhibit much in common with the "intensive mothering" ideal culturally expected of women in the United States.[31] The behavior represented in this theme visually depicts women in multiple ways, including directly, by themselves with their animal (n = 18); directly, alongside a male partner and the animal (n = 4); or indirectly, with only the animal present (n = 4). Women are shown engaged in a variety of activities with their dog or cat (only one representation shows a woman with more than one pet), including cuddling, lovingly touching, or holding their animal (n = 13); kissing their animal (n = 4); cleaning up after their animal (n = 2); or playing with their animal (n = 1). A total of eighteen ads (64 percent) in this theme use copy to refer to the woman in some sort of maternal capacity. Eleven of the eighteen ads (61 percent) refer to the woman as a "pet parent," while seven ads (38 percent) refer to the woman as "mom" or "mother."

One 2006 ad from PetSmart, a pet-supply retailer, exemplifies the mother identity within the multispecies family via both copy and imagery (see figure 5.5). The image shows a woman playing ball with her

Figure 5.5. PetSmart ad depicting a dog playing with his mom

aging dog in what appears to be a park. The woman wears the casual clothing characteristic of "mother" imagery used in advertising that encourages intensive mothering. Both dog and mom appear to be intensely focused on engaging in play with each other—neither looks at the camera, nor do they stare at anything else in the image. They are running side by side, in very close physical proximity, reminiscent of the general "family" themes found in advertising with companion animals starting in the 1980s.[32]

The copy reads, "He's 70, and he still lives with his mom." Later copy reinforces the idea that she "parents" the dog by leaning on the expert advice that is available via PetSmart. In this ad, PetSmart provides expertise to "pet parents." That this is something that should be desired by pet owners is an obvious acknowledgment of the multispecies family type and the growing concern among such families that their animals are not only healthy but happy, nurtured, and expertly raised. However, further examination reinforces the idea that a specific "mother" identity is reproduced here. A parallel to the cultural ideal of American "intensive mothering" is clear here, suggesting that behavior toward the dog is similar to that of a mother to a human child. Indeed, expert guided assistance for mom as she raises her child is a hallmark of intensive mothering. Rigorous communication to women of this "necessity" began appearing in ads in the 1990s regarding human children.[33] Now, with cultural entrenchment of the multispecies family, in need of unique socialization solutions, PetSmart fully levels the same services at these moms as well. Targeting moms like Kathy, who, in chapter 2, noted spending copious amounts of money on trainers to help her and her husband raise Rom, PetSmart promises to do its best to mitigate parenting problems in the twenty-first-century multispecies family.

Another recent ad, from 2019, for Paws4You.org, a "dog adoption" house, depicts an image of a woman in a short, white dress cradling what appears to be a white dog at her abdomen (see figure 5.6). The woman appears on a traditionally gendered pink background, and although she has no apparent facial features, the positioning of her head and face suggests that she is looking down lovingly at the dog. The only copy here (beyond the organization's information in the bottom-right-hand corner) reads, "Expecting unconditional love."

As with the PetSmart example, both image and copy are notable here. The ad promotes "adoption," a term that has historically referenced human children. However, past research has already noted that shelter and rescue organizations have used terms such as "adoption" in a way that not only anthropomorphizes the animal but also suggests that pets should be a part of the family (thus encouraging people to take in otherwise-unwanted pets). However, this ad takes that several steps further. The woman stands in profile—a pose stereotypical of pregnant women so that they can show off their "baby bump." The dog is the same color as the woman's dress, in a spherical position inside the woman's arms and resting at her abdomen. At first glance, the woman appears to be pregnant, holding her hand protectively over her abdomen—a position that is also typical of pregnant women. The word "expecting" in the copy reinforces this interpretation of the image. The woman literally,

Expecting unconditional love.

✿PAWS4YOU.org
Dog adoption house

Figure 5.6. An adoption ad in which a woman initially appears pregnant but, upon closer inspection, is actually holding a puppy

visually, becomes the dog's mother here. In keeping with intensive mothering, she is protective and nurturing. However, because the background is blank (with the exception of the pink coloring), the suggestion is also made that the dog is the woman's only concern at the moment. Furthermore, the phrase "Expecting unconditional love" reminds consumers that, as with human children, ideal American mothers should love their animal children unconditionally, making the intensive mothering ideal requisite in the multispecies family. Adoption is key here, suggesting that there are babies (of the canine persuasion) who need homes (and are not being sold by breeders) in the same way that there are foster children in need of families. Such ads touch moms like Lynn, one of my childfree interviewees, who adopted Roger rather than having children of her own (or, presumably, buying from a breeder) because "there are enough children in the world and way too many animals." Offering depth to her explanation, she added, "I would rather take in a fur baby than create a new life. . . . The world is overpopulated with both animals and people. I am trying to do my part and not add to this."

A 2019 BarkBox ad also clearly depicts the identity of the "intensive" mother to the animal child via both imagery and copy (see figure 5.7). BarkBox is a subscription service that sends a monthly selection of toys and treats for the resident dog(s). The imagery in this ad shows a younger woman both holding and kissing her dog, her eyes focused on his face. The dog stares at the camera, while the woman holds a sign with copy that reads, "#1 DOG MOM." The product advertised is a limited-edition "Mother's Day" BarkBox, promised for delivery by Mother's Day.

The mother identity is apparent in this ad if only because of the constant reference to the woman as "mom," "mama," or "mother" and the limited-edition product available for Mother's Day. However, a deeper, culturally entrenched message related to "intensive mothering" is also present. Initially, the contents of the advertised gift is puzzling given that this is purported to be a gift for the "#1 DOG MOM." The copy reads, "Mother's Toys and Treats," with an arrow directing consumers' attention to the basket beneath it. The BarkBox pictured shows two bags of treats and two, presumably squeaky, dog toys (one in the shape of a basket of flowers and one in the shape of a pair of shorts). What appears to be fresh (or perhaps fake) flowers are also included in the basket, though it is unclear if these are actually part of the advertised product

Figure 5.7. BarkBox ad promoting the celebration of Mother's Day as a dog mom

that the consumer receives. The gift is clearly meant for consumption by the dog. However, the intensive American mother—the ideal mother, even in the multispecies family—is one that is self-sacrificial and child-centered, even on Mother's Day.

These exemplary ads as well as others in the theme all have some component of the "intensive mother" present, via image, copy, or both. The ads show behavior characteristic of the intensive mother—related to her animal child rather than a human child. Imagery and copy go well beyond anthropomorphizing the dog or cat. This reveals that internalizing an identity such as "mother" related to the companion animal and performed in the context of a multispecies family is not only acceptable now but reproduced at the macro-level via advertising as a means of drawing in potential customers who identify in such a way.

Father Identity

Advertisements in which men are depicted as "fathers" adhere to what multiple scholars on fatherhood, fathering, and men and masculinities have referred to as the "new father role" that has emerged in the United States.[34] In contrast to the traditional "fatherhood" identity characteristic of the mid-twentieth century and earlier, in which masculine gender norms define the father as the breadwinner, disciplinarian, and socializer of boys to masculinity, the "new father" role defines expected behavior as well beyond the traditional father described here. Instead, dads are now also expected to provide day-to-day care for their children that involves interactive and physical caregiving, emotional support, and nurturing, making them involved and competent parents.[35] While scholars disagree about how well this expectation has been integrated into masculinity within the family in the United States, the "new father" role has indeed been incorporated into postmodern ideals about being a father and coparent in the United States.[36]

The advertisements that I coded as "fathering" (n = 11, with a total of fifteen male representations included) use images and/or copy showing men performing some version of this postmodern conceptualization of fathering—only in the context of the multispecies family. As with mothers, the behavior represented in this theme visually depicts men in multiple ways, including directly, by themselves with their animal (n = 7);

directly, alongside a female partner and the animal (n = 4); or indirectly, with only the animal present (n = 2).[37] Images show men engaged in a variety of activities, including being concerned about nurturing their animals with good diets (n = 4), lovingly holding their pets physically close to their bodies (e.g., holding them in their arms, on their shoulders, snuggled close; n = 9), or playing interactively and physically close to their animals (n = 1). Eleven of the total representations in this category contain some sort of paternal reference to a man. Four of these eleven representations (36 percent) use copy to refer to the man in the image as "dad." Three (27 percent) use copy that refers to the man in the image as "pet parent." One adoption ad with just the dog present (9 percent) refers to "dad."

Figure 5.8 shows an ad for Glycoflex Plus by VetriScience, a supplement for feline joint support. A man is in the bathroom brushing his teeth. A cat is draped over his shoulders, clearly comfortable in the position, with one leg gently hanging down over the man's neck. The man is smiling and appears to be glancing upward in the mirror—potentially more interested in looking at his cat than at his teeth. The copy reads, "Take good care of your little shadow."

In this ad, image and copy perform the identity pairing of "father-child" directly, and both symbolically communicate what, in American culture, men often do with their children—carry them on their shoulders. The cat's obvious calm with her position shows that she trusts him enough to stay there. His apparent affective state communicates a warmth toward the cat that expresses endearment and enjoyment in their relationship. The copy really drives home the message that this is a direct father-child identity pairing. Indeed, just as a human child is often referred to as a parent's "little shadow," the cat in this picture is too. As a result, the cat is not a metaphor for a human child but rather actually holds the counteridentity of "child" in the ad. Her positioning on her "dad's" shoulders, his adoring facial expression and visual gaze toward her, the phrase "little shadow," and the private nature of the setting (a bathroom) all confirm this. Furthermore, the fact that the product is geared toward maintaining the cat's health with an expensive, high-end joint supplement highlights the importance of taking care of her health, a key expectation of the postmodern father identity.

Figure 5.8. Ad copy that uses a common euphemism for human children, "little shadow," to refer to the man's cat

Another sample from this theme is an advertisement for Dick van Patton's Natural Balance Limited Ingredient Diets dog food (see figure 5.9). A lab scientist for Natural Balance sits on the ground with his dog in what appears to be a park. His body is physically intertwined with the dog's body, with one arm wrapped under the dog's hind leg and his hand rubbing the dog's belly. The man's other arm is laid gently on the dog's neck, possibly patting him there as well. The dog's jaw is loosely holding onto a band on the man's arm. Because of the positioning of the dog's hind legs and jaw, he may be gently wrestling with the man. Finally, and similar to the "little shadow" ad in figure 5.8, the man gazes down adoringly at the dog, suggesting a tight social bond between the two.

The imagery in the ad indicates a father-child identity pairing—confirmed by the physical closeness, playing, and a visual emotional bond between the two. The copy in this ad is particularly telling, referring to the man as a "pet parent" twice, with one of these references being an actual quote from the man himself: "As a pet parent, I believe it's important to have food I can trust without a doubt"—confirming that the man has internalized a "father" identity. The focus on trusting a company to help him provide the best nutrition possible is a common concern for postmodern dads, who are expected to engage in day-to-day physical caregiving and nurturing of their children.[38] Furthermore, discussion of total trust in the company to help the pet dad achieve this goal makes it clear that he has prioritized his animal child's nutrition. Pride in this status (and presumably in his multispecies family) is made apparent in the copy, in which two salient identities for the man are noted: "Natural lab scientist and proud pet parent of yellow lab Riley."

This ad takes on special significance in relationship to the idea that internalizing a parental identity toward your dog or cat might be stigmatized by society. As I noted in chapter 3, multiple childfree participants in their interviews mentioned concern about being perceived as "crazy" for interacting with their dogs or cats as a parent might with a human child. This was also a sentiment sometimes echoed by empty-nester participants in my research who had heavily invested in their pets—both financially and emotionally. Yet this Natural Balance ad makes it acceptable to be proud of investing in the animal child, to embrace it. More important, the expression of pride in this father-child pairing as a strong theme in the ad indicates the reproduction of the status quo within the

Figure 5.9. Ad copy that uses a testimonial in which the commenter refers to himself as "pet parent"

cultural definition of family. Indeed, advertisers are in the business of connecting already culturally accepted ideals to their products to produce interest and positive attention in the consumer.[39] While some of my participants worried about the stigma attached to internalizing a parental identity related to their animals, macro-level data such as this advertising suggests that their concern may be a product of past stigma rather than current stigma. This in no way delegitimizes participant perceptions but rather highlights the rapidly growing cultural acceptance of the multispecies family alongside increasingly public performances of mother and father counter to the animal child identity.

Child Identity

As a counteridentity to the "mother" or "father" identities discussed earlier, far more ads depict animals as legitimate family members who are specifically acknowledged as "children" within the family (n = 42). As with the "mother" and "father" code, the behavior represented in the "child" theme visually depicts dogs and cats in multiple ways, including directly, with their "dads" (n = 7); directly, with their "moms" (n = 20); directly, with only the animal present (n = 17); or indirectly, with no animal or human present (n = 2). Only five of the forty-two ads (approximately 12 percent) in this theme used copy including some variation of "child" in reference to the animal.

Ads in which the mother-child or father-child identity pairing is present use both imagery and copy to communicate familial identities. The presence and positioning of the dog or cat, copy that includes some version of "mother" or "father," and messages that communicate information about the "new father" role or "intensive mothering" in relationship to the companion animal all serve to highlight the presence of these identity pairings within the cultural ideals guiding marketeers who craft these ads. As a result, twenty-seven of the ads coded under "child" were also coded under the appropriate parental identity.[40]

However, as mentioned earlier, a subsample of ads coded under "child" (n = 17, 40 percent) showed only the animal. An ad for obedience training from Petco, another pet-supply retailer, is especially demonstrative of the child identity (see figure 5.10)—without ever actually using the label "child" or "kid" (though the copy does refer to the dog as

Figure 5.10. Dog depicted in a traditionally human child role, going to his first day of school

a "furry family member"). A picture frame displays a golden Labrador retriever puppy wearing a blue bandana with "future leader dog" emblazoned on it. The background of the photo shows an institutional setting of some sort (perhaps a school?). Copy in the ad exclaims, "Comet's first day of school!" and exalts the fact that the puppy has learned to sit so that you—presumably a parent, based on counteridentities—can take a photograph in order to memorialize this particular "milestone" in Comet's life.

From the idealized middle-class standard of child rearing in which parents strive to put their kids on the fast-track to future success to the idea that Comet's developmental milestones (in this case, sitting still) are of utmost importance, the ad copy repeatedly reproduces the American child identity for the dog within the multispecies family.[41] The photograph itself is a nod to the cultural tradition that the first day of school for children is one to be remembered. Furthermore, both copy and image contribute to the middle-class ideal that American parents should be child-centered, concerned with following these milestones closely, socializing to good behavior, providing a good education while being excited to do so, and able to provide "all of the products that [their] growing furry family member will ever need."[42] While the copy does not expressly label Comet a child, all of these factors directly identify him as such while simultaneously (but indirectly) labeling his owner "parent." Indeed, for the targeted consumer parent here, "the best decision was bringing [Comet] home."

Of course, most interview participants in my research, whether they were childfree or childless, had human children at home, or were empty nesters, made it clear that they did not think that their pet was an *actual* human child in the way that this ad portrays. For example, when I asked Gennifer, a 52-year-old empty nester, what the difference was between raising her dogs and raising her daughter, she noted, "I don't worry about their futures. . . . There are no decisions or relationships that they need guidance to navigate, and I am not trying to groom a human being for adulthood," all items that primary and secondary schools in the United States help to address. Hannah, a childfree participant, also reminded me that she is "not responsible for [Sam, her dog] to go out and be a productive member of society." But Hannah also continued with, "Okay, I took her to obedience school," signaling that the marketeers in this ad

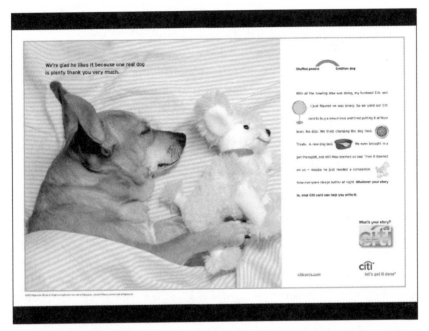

Figure 5.11. An ad depicting a dog in a childlike environment (in bed snuggling with a stuffed dog), with copy that describes disruption in human sleep for the dog's comfort

are targeting their audience correctly while also capitalizing on the idea that people with animal capital may well perceive their pets as similar to human children in needing socialization via obedience school.

Another ad, for Citi credit cards, owned by Citigroup, Inc., advertises the benefits of its service with only a dog present in the image. The copy is narrated by a married partner who refers to a "husband" named Eric (see figure 5.11). The dog, Max, is sleeping peacefully in a pink-striped bed, covered by a matching sheet, with his forelegs wrapped around a stuffed animal.

Citigroup heralds the benefits of consumer credit by showing consumers how their lives, and their family's lives, are made easier by having an extension of the company's credit. As with the Petco ad, the copy does not use the word "child" in any variation (and "dog" is prominent throughout). But, as is also the case with the Petco ad, all of the behavior shared by the narrator indicates that the couple is "child-centered" in their attentiveness to the dog's needs—interactions typically seen in relation to the American child. As is culturally expected of American parents, the narrator and partner, Eric, work tirelessly to solve an initially unidentified problem with which Max seems afflicted. The narrator expresses the depth of their commitment to solving Max's issue via their multiple purchases, sharing, "We even brought in a pet therapist, but still Max seemed so sad." The problem is clearly night oriented, judging from the imagery used of Max in bed with the stuffed poodle and the purchase of a new dog bed. The copy confirms this: "Now everyone sleeps better at night," indicating that the issue of sleeplessness for all has been resolved.

Furthermore, as I noted in chapter 2, a willingness to disrupt parental sleep for children when they are potty training, ill, or otherwise afflicted is a common cultural expectation of the American parent. As a result, the couple's actions toward Max in this ad indicate that they think of him in childlike terms and that he holds an important place in their family. Just as Julie and her fiancé were willing to adjust their sleeping patterns to accommodate young Chance's sleep training in chapter 2, the same is reflected and reproduced in the Citigroup ad. Indeed, the vast majority of childfree, childless, and empty-nest participants in my research noted willingness to engage in night care when presented with chronic or acute illness, sleep or potty-training issues, or anxiety in their pets. For example, Wrenn, a childless participant, recalled chronic illness in her own dog, saying, "She had stopped sleeping, . . . and of course, we were up all night with her. She was not sleeping. We were not sleeping. We were all falling apart. She was suffering." As with the Natural Balance ad discussed earlier, in which the "father" identity is invoked, the Citi card ad not only reproduces the multispecies family form in the United States but also reinforces the idea that engaging with a pet in the way that one might with a human child (and thus assigning the "child" identity to the pet) is increasingly normative.

For two adoption ads from SPCA San Francisco, symbolic imagery is clearly used to parallel kittens with human infants in the multispecies family—but with no actual animal present in the image. Both reproduce symbolism stereotypically representative of the human infant: pastel colors, a pacifier, and a mobile. Figure 5.12 shows a pacifier on a pink background—only a mouse is in the place of the rubber nipple that the human infant would commonly use to orally soothe. Figure 5.13 shows

Figure 5.12. A San Francisco SPCA ad for kitten adoption depicting an infant's pacifier on which the nipple has been replaced by a stuffed mouse

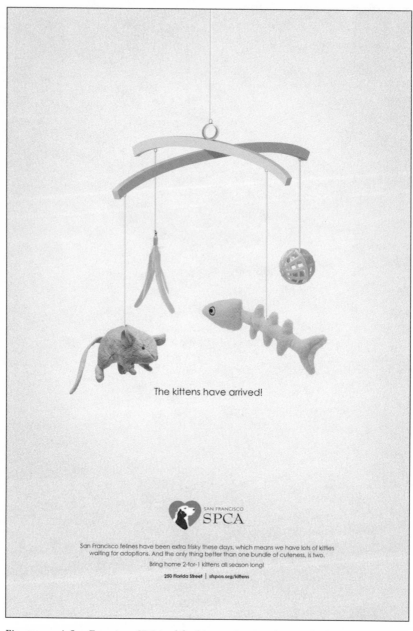

Figure 5.13. A San Francisco SPCA ad for kitten adoption depicting what would normally be an infant's mobile but with various kitten toys attached instead

a traditional mobile used to entertain the infant but similarly replaces infant toys with kitten toys: a stuffed mouse, a fish skeleton, a catnip ball, and feathers.

The imagery here is clever in how it symbolically evokes the "child" identity for kittens within the multispecies family without ever depicting the actual animal. Cultural symbolism in advertising is a means of connecting the consumer to the product (or here service) by evoking particular feelings or ideas about the product.[43] Both of these ads use visual symbols to evoke the cultural definition of the "infant" status in order to connect the ideal warmth, love, and joy culturally associated with having a baby to the adoption of a kitten (or two, as the small-print copy notes, "2-for-1 kittens all season long!"). As with other examples from this theme, the marketeer accesses the cultural foundation for both family type and actual familial identity to successfully pitch the multispecies family, complete with a kitten "infant." In doing so, the imagery and copy again reproduce the acceptability of defining the kitten as a "child" within the family domain. Indeed, Leandra, a sixty-four-year-old empty nester, compellingly confirmed this interpretation when asked why she called her dogs and cats her babies. She shared, "I treat them as babies, as I would my children. . . . You don't really own them. You adopt them into your family, and they become part and parcel of your daily life. . . . They're the babies."

Gender, Race, and Species

As advertising scholars have noted, depicting the American family pet as an actual family *member* has become a fairly common practice in marketing, depending on the product. Historical examinations of companion animals in print advertising have found that, especially by the 1980s, advertising imagery had moved to depicting pets in this role.[44] Elements of this industry movement are apparent in my own data. For example, animals in my sample rarely wear leashes, are always in close proximity to their owners (assuming their owner is present in the ad in some way), and maintain residence within the home if the ad is in this type of setting (sometimes even in the human's bed).[45] Indeed, ads in which either the dog or cat could be coded as a family member in some way constituted seventy-one of the eighty-eight sampled ads (approximately 81 percent).[46] Advertisers are driven to reproduce the cultural status quo for consumers in order to evoke a positive affective state toward the product—these representations would not exist if consumers were confused, irritated, or alienated by animals portrayed in such a way.

Furthermore, with 58 percent of the total ad sample portraying some specific form of familial identity, these ads are not just simple anthropomorphic depictions of animals. They also go well beyond including the pet as a generalized "family member." Advertising messages in this sample convey clearly acknowledged identities that have been stereotypically reserved for humans in the past. This is indicative of the growing tendency to assign human identity to pets within the family (e.g., "child" instead of "family pet"), while also depicting humans as internalizing the related and appropriate counteridentity (e.g., "mother" or "father" instead of pet owner).

However, as a sociologist, I see other important variables to attend to in these data, such as representations of gender, race, and species type. Including these variables in my analysis allows us to consider if the multispecies family, and the familial identities that arise within it, is more prominent for certain groups of people. Indeed, because advertisers are in the business of reflecting and reproducing cultural drifts (in the hopes of drawing consumer interest), advertisements offer a good opportunity to examine what demographic categories are perceived as prominent for this kind of family. These variables also allow us to conceptualize whether there are gender, racial, or species gaps present in currently accepted forms of the multispecies families as well as why these gaps might be present.

Gender

Images from my data of "mother" and "father" paired with the animal "child" provide important information about whether women or men (or both) are seen by marketeers as more likely to internalize such identities. Ad representations coded under the "mother" identity outpaced representations coded under the "father" identity by 220 percent (n = 33 and n = 15, respectively). Initially, this appears to suggest that men may not be as likely to adopt a "father" identity in relationship to their pets as women are to adopt a "mother" identity. And this is not terribly surprising when we consider nationally representative surveys that ask about human-animal relationships within the American family. For example, a 2006 Pew poll found that there was a 9–10 percent difference between the number of men and of women who reported thinking of their dogs (men = 80 percent; women = 89 percent) and cats (men = 72 percent; women = 82 percent) as family.[47]

A Harris Poll completed in 2015 supports this contention as well. When asked about things that pet owners do for their pets, fewer men than women reported purchasing a holiday gift for their pet (58 percent versus 70 percent), allowing their pet to sleep with them in their bed (69 percent versus 73 percent), and cooking especially for their pet (29 percent versus 33 percent).[48] Furthermore, scholarly literature appears to reinforce this analysis, finding that men feel less intense attachment with and psychological kinship to pets compared to women.[49] Self-reports like this suggest that, at least to some degree, men may be less likely to internalize a parent identity toward their animals. Additionally, the 142 percent disparity between men and women on mean annual spending for pets, combined with the greater likelihood of women thinking of their companion animals as family members, is a likely motivator for advertisers to depict women as "mothers" to their pets at a higher percentage than they depict men as "fathers."[50] That is, advertisers may simply be reflecting these gendered preferences by focusing on women as "mother" more often than men as "father" in the multispecies family.

However, some data suggest that men are more likely than women to engage in certain types of kinship behavior with their companion animals. The same 2015 Harris Poll found that a higher percentage of men than women reported taking their pet to work with them (16 percent versus 9 percent) and purchasing a health/medical insurance policy for their pet (15 percent versus 9 percent).[51] A 2018 nationally representative poll cosponsored by the Harris Poll and Volvo Car USA reported that more Millennial men than women engage in the following behaviors: "spoiling their pets by buying organic food (39%); throwing them birthday parties (30%); and taking them to daycare (22%)."[52] Indeed, some research has noted that men underreport their emotional attachment to their pets as a means of maintaining traditionally masculine gender roles that deter the appearance of emotional sensitivity at all.[53] Similarly,

I had a paucity of male participants who were willing to be interviewed for this research, although men in my fieldwork at the veterinary clinic were just as likely as women to allow me to observe their visits. Perhaps this explains why men have been depicted by advertisers as "father" in some capacity, albeit muted in relation to the "mother" identity.

Another idea may help explain the quantitative difference in ads with either identity present. Existing literature that examines media representations of men as fathers to human children suggests that, culturally, the "new father" identity is still somewhat nascent in its evolution within the media.[54] This leaves the "intensive mother"–child pairing far more represented than the "new father"–child pairing within advertisements aimed at families.[55] It would only make sense that the same would be the case for the "father" identity within the multispecies family.

Race

Another interesting pattern, regarding racial depictions, emerges within this sample. When coding for *perceived* race or ethnicity of owners in ads that convey the "mother" or "father" identity, multiple categories arose. For a sample of fifty-one ads with sixty potential racial representations, coding included forty White representations (four from the same ad), seven Black representations (three from the same ad), and two Asian representations (both from the same ad).[56] Another category, labeled "indiscernible" (n = 11), was created because the person's body was turned away or otherwise obstructed or was artistically rendered without racial markers. White representations were present 571 percent more times than Black representations, the next highest category.

As with gender, the racial distribution present in ads coded with familial identities is not surprising given the tendency of marketeers to reproduce current cultural trends. While there is a paucity of work regarding the effects of race and ethnicity on people's relationships with companion animals, the work that is present suggests that there are qualitative differences between Whites and Blacks in the United States with regard to companion animals. For example, research on White and African American veterinary students notes that, while all White respondents had pets at home, only 86 percent of African American students reported having pets. White students (70 percent) were also far more likely to co-sleep with their pets than were African American students (53 percent). An administered pet attachment questionnaire also revealed that there were significant differences in agreement between the two groups on scale items such as "no family is complete without a pet, having feelings affected by how people react to your pet, taking pets to visit friends and relatives, and keeping a picture of your pet in your wallet or on display in your home or office."[57]

African Americans are also the least likely among Whites, Latinos, Asians, and African Americans (in that order) to own a dog or cat, with only 29 percent of African American families reporting that they have any type of pet at all.[58] Dog ownership among African Americans is even lower (22.8 percent), while it is the highest among Whites (53.7 percent), with Latinos following Whites (44.1 percent).[59] These differences may well be because "many forms of racialization have . . . long relied upon a discourse about human-animal boundaries, namely the dichotomous division of sentient beings into categories of 'human' and 'animal.'"[60] Indeed, critical race scholars have noted that historically, dogs have been used by police in the United States to violently repress Blacks (and other persons of color) across eras such as slavery, the civil rights movement, and desegregation.[61] These cultural memories for persons of color serve to socially construct dogs in a much different light than the way in which Whites, specifically, now define their canines.[62]

Indeed, these memories may well show up in human-animal relationships within multiracial neighborhoods, especially those that are gentrifying. Critical race scholars have argued that dogs in particular are socially constructed by Whites in gentrified urban areas to claim "quasi-exclusionary spaces" (e.g., dog parks, dog bakeries) that serve to separate new upper-class groups from poorer residents of color.[63] Dogs are often seen as a major source of conflict between original Black residents and Whites who are presently moving into the neighborhood.[64] And Whites in multiracial neighborhoods may use their dogs to maintain racial boundaries between themselves and Black and Latino persons.[65] Other scholars have argued that African American men continue to be framed as "less-than-human," even as dogs are elevated by an ideological shift in "White" thinking that advocates for the civil liberties of dogs while ignoring the plight of Black men, who are disproportionately incarcerated and unemployed in the United States.[66]

Findings such as these suggest that African Americans may not be as likely to perceive their pets as general family members, let alone to internalize human identities related to their dogs and cats. That is, Whites may well be far more likely than persons of color (and Blacks, in particular) both to grow these kinds of multispecies families and to internalize familial identities related to their pets. This could be because of the qualitatively different sociohistorical and current experiences between racial groups in relationship to animals (and specifically to dogs). As with gender, advertisers who are necessarily fine-tuned into cultural definitions and symbolism are not likely to stray from those meanings for each demographic. Ads in my sample indicate that, at the macro-level, advertisers are reproducing racial features in their product communications about the American multispecies family.

Species

Finally, one other observation bears discussion regarding how advertisers comprise animal members in the multispecies family, especially with regard to species. I coded ads in this sample on the basis of whether they used a dog, cat, or both. Ad representations across all seventy-one ads (in which dogs and cats were coded for specific identity pairings or coded as a general family member) that were coded under "dog" outpaced representations coded under "cat" by a ratio of over six to one (n = 76 and n = 12, respectively). The discrepancy within species representation is probably explained by a couple of things. First of all, a smaller percentage of Americans own cats compared to dogs. A 2015 Harris Poll found that 71 percent of pet owners own a dog, while only 49 percent own a cat.[67] This is in line with other polling that indicates that 38 percent of households own a dog, while only 25 percent own a cat.[68] So the greater number of ads depicting dogs in the multispecies family may simply reflect a stronger market for canine-based products, leading to the larger percentage of ads in this sample targeting that niche. Second, this discrepancy in species representation may reflect a slightly smaller percentage of families who report thinking of their cats as family members versus their dogs.[69]

On the other hand, Shelly Volsche, an anthropologist interested in pet parenting in childfree homes, has noted that the "archetypal pet for a parenting analogy is the domestic dog." Other scholars have noted that dog owners have a qualitatively different relationship with their dogs compared to those who own cats or other pets.[70] Dog owners spend far more time with their dogs engaged in behavior such as talking to them, exercising with them, going on rides outside the household (75 percent of dog owners versus 8 percent of cat owners), and taking them to boutique dog bakeries.[71] Some dog owners are increasingly looking for work benefits such as "pawternity" leave when they adopt a new puppy.[72] Dogs depend on humans for physical requirements such as food and shelter and emotional needs for security, companionship, and play (in contrast to the independent and perceived aloof nature of cats). Indeed, these needs may well contribute to the idea that dogs are in greater need of "parenting" than are cats.

Some research indicates that there is no difference between cat and dog owners in the level of intimacy achieved with their pets and that cats may be a better source of social support in times of chronic illness.[73] However, other scholarship disputes this finding. For example, cat owners appear to be less attached to their cats than dog owners are to their dogs, and dog owners report stronger relationships with their dogs than do owners of other types of pets.[74] Recent work suggests that adult cats, as autonomous individuals, do not develop secure attachments to their owners, while dogs appear to engage in attachment behavior, and perhaps attachment bonding, with their owners.[75] Indeed, Beth, a childfree interviewee in my research, provided a frank assessment of how her feline children's unique behaviors suggested both aloofness and autonomy. Noting that both of her cats' (one of which had recently passed away) had distinctive personalities, she explained, "Angel was 'I will let you worship me. . . .' You couldn't go from petting her [*purring*] to petting her feet because she would turn and be hissing and glaring at you. It wasn't so much affection as she was saying, 'You're under my power, and I am holding you down.' Whereas Owen is very much 'Come pet me. . . . Rub my belly.'"

With regard to assigning family membership, a 2006 Pew poll revealed that 85 percent of dog owners thought of their dogs as family, while a smaller percentage of cat owners, 78 percent, felt the same way.[76] While a 2015 Harris Poll found that the difference between thinking of dogs or cats as family is far smaller (96 percent versus 93 percent), it also found that behavior related to pets that might generally be perceived as parental in nature is more prominent for dogs than for cats. With the exception of co-sleeping (73 percent of dog owners versus 81 percent of cat owners), behaviors such as purchasing holiday presents (70 percent versus 61 percent) or birthday presents (52 percent versus 40 percent) are more prominent in dog owners. The poll found the same species differences in cooking especially for one's pet (38 percent versus 26 percent), dressing one's pet in some type of clothing (28 percent versus 19 percent), and taking a pet to work (16 percent versus 11 percent).[77]

All of these differences in human behavior toward dogs and cats may well suggest what this sample of ads exemplifies: a greater focus on assigning actual familial identities to dogs than to cats in the multispecies family. Considering that identity formation in humans takes place in social communication with other actors, this makes sense. After all, research has found that dogs appear to understand human language via tone and word sorting and are perceived to accurately respond to human facial expressions—both symbolic interactionist prerequisites for the formation of identity.[78] Like gender and racial variables, species may well be another variable used by advertisers to reproduce the status quo in multispecies families.

* * *

While I have focused exclusively in this chapter on print advertising, dogs and cats across multiple modes of advertising are increasingly depicted not just as family members in the multispecies family but as family members with specific human identities. Research has shown that companion animals have moved into the family sphere within television commercials as "loved ones." But now, dogs and cats appear in television commercials with human family members who have internalized familial identities counter to their pets. For example, a 2015 PetSmart television commercial shows a young man and woman (with no human children) shopping for toys at PetSmart when an employee asks them, "What's it like to be new parents?" The "dad" answers, "We know nothing," while the "mom" answers, "We know absolutely nothing." The spot finishes out with a female voice-over: "PetSmart has all you need to take care of your kids." Another ad, for Sprint, shows a man named Topher Brophy sitting with a dog on his lap. An off-screen voice asks him, "Who's that?" The man answers, "That's my son. This is Rosenberg." The next scene shows Brophy from behind, walking down a city street, carrying a fully clothed Rosenberg in his arms. Rosenberg stares over his shoulder in much the same way that a small human child might.

Structural symbolic interactionists have long argued that we must connect micro-level behaviors to macro-level output in an effort to show how they impact one another. Data from advertising provides an important indication of what current cultural trends are. Advertisers are taught early on in their profession to reproduce the status quo as a means of both ensuring positive affect toward their products and reassuring consumers that prior purchases of the product were excellent choices. As a result, advertising media, such as the print ad, provide an interesting, macro-level means of measuring cultural standards of who is counted as family in the United States. Findings such as these make it increasingly apparent that sociology of family scholars, who have been reluctant to include companion animals in the way families build and maintain ties, need to consider not only group behavior within the American multispecies family but also macro-level entities that help to produce and reproduce such definitions.

Conclusion

Recently, a colleague of mine mentioned that a couple with which he is friends had completed an international adoption. This had occurred in the aftermath of Hurricane Maria, and the pair had flown to Puerto Rico to adopt one of the many dogs who had been left homeless and without their human families. My colleague reported that the couple did not have children, but they did have a burgeoning multispecies family of the sort that I discuss in this book (two humans, two dogs—including the new adoptee—and a cat). They had been compelled by the sheer devastation of the catastrophic storm, the endless disruption to family life on the island, and the countless—now homeless—dogs who would need a new family with which to heal.

The story, of course, is not unusual anymore. International adoption of dogs especially (and cats, to a lesser degree) has grown exponentially in the past decade, with plenty of agencies to choose from that specialize in the process. For example, International Pet Rescue, housed under Animal League America, works to bring together abused, abandoned, and ailing animals from around to world to multispecies families within the United States that are eager to adopt from other countries. The organization's website promises to provide "better lives for as many homeless animals as we can, regardless of the lengths we have to go to do so."[1] The International Street Dog Foundation heralds a mission to assist dogs in extreme need from around the world by bringing them to families in the United States.[2] The Sato Project takes aim at rescuing abused and abandoned dogs in Puerto Rico to place them in "loving homes" in the United States.[3] The organization's website notes that it was instrumental in placing over two thousand dogs with new, mainland American families after Hurricane Maria. Airlines and pilots have also jumped in on this international philanthropic effort. Southwest Airlines is known to donate airplane space and transportation to rescue endeavors like the Sato Project. Pilots N Paws connects rescue personnel with pilots who are willing to transport pets to their new foster or adoptive families—with especially poignant stories to tell of air lifts from disaster zones in order to save dogs and cats.

Although the scope of this book does not include the examination of animal rescue and the attendant organizations involved in the United States, the stories are certainly interesting with regard to who counts as family. If nothing else, it reminds me of the comments made by another colleague, who respectfully questioned the utility of sociological research regarding the American multispecies family. The lengths that many Americans are willing to go to for their companion animals make it robustly apparent that dogs and cats hold a special place in the family sphere. How and why that came about can be tied to sociohistorical mechanisms found in the emergence of a postmodern society fueled by the burgeoning surpluses made possible by the Industrial Revolution. The resultant recognition of companion-animal sentience and agency and the diversification of family structure within the United States, propelled by the second demographic transition (SDT), have undergirded the emergence of the multispecies family.

Asking what the point is of such research is like asking why family sociologists should care about other nontraditional family structures that have become increasingly more common in the United States since the 1970s. Indeed, each family structure contains unique familial relationships, interactions, and challenges. The relational composition of actors within the unit is important to understanding everything from emotional support to financial expenditures to after-school care and activities to physical care and so on. Laying an additional level of actor complexity to that unit (in the form of the dog or cat in the United States) does not somehow negate its importance because it is nonhuman. Rather, examination of this unique form of diversification within the American family is required in order to understand how the multispecies family has emerged hand in hand with the SDT in similar ways to that of other nontraditional structures like childfree families, single-parent families, grandparent families, and LGBTQ families.

Importance to Family Scholarship

While multispecies families are of increasing interest across an array of fields, including human-animal interaction, anthropology, social work, and psychology, sociology as a discipline (and family sociology as a subdiscipline) has a paucity of research in the area (unless the family researcher happens to be a human-animal interaction scholar). Indeed, mainstream family sociology is typically concerned with the traditional family type, exploring marital relationships, the impact of socioeconomic status and racial and ethnic variation in family formation, family-work balance, child and youth sociology, and parenting. To a lesser degree, research on nontraditional family structures and processes have increasingly included areas such as cohabitation, divorce, single parenting, LGBTQ families, unmarried parents, and teenage parents. Intergenerational families, childlessness, stepfamilies, and adoption as nontraditional family structures have received very minimal attention in the sociology of family literature.[4] This is despite the fact that each of these family forms has seen dramatic growth since the 1970s and within the context of the SDT.[5]

I have shown in this book that the emergence of the multispecies family is a result of a combination of many factors, including postmodernity; a recognition of companion animals as beings of agency with emotions, thoughts, intentions, and desires; and the diversification of family in the United States alongside the SDT.[6] These factors have produced the multispecies family with attendant and unique identities that exert influence across both nontraditional and traditional family structures. The multispecies family, with scant representation in the premier academic journals within sociology, needs increased attention alongside all of the other nontraditional family experiences and household arrangements that Betty Farrell and colleagues identify in their research.[7]

Future potential research in this vein should include analysis of the impact of the "parent-child" identity pairing related to the companion animal on fertility intentions within the childfree experience. This has implications for family structure, fertility intentions, increasing age at first childbirth, and opting out of having children entirely—all important, *mainstream* areas of interest for both family sociology and demography. The total fertility rate (TFR, an estimate of lifetime fertility based on what current fertility patterns bear out) in the United States has hit a historical low of 1.73 (anything below 2.1 is below replacement, meaning that it takes 2.1 births per woman to replace the current population in a society).[8] Age at first childbirth for women has also been steadily increasing in the United States, with 26.9 as the mean age in 2018 (compared to 21.0 in 1970 and 24.9 in 2000). Anything that impacts these rates is of importance to the scholarship of family and family demography.

The demographic transition theory tells us that these changes are intimately related to a societal increase in women's status, including access to contraception and power over reproductive capacity, educational attainment, and occupational earnings since the mid-twentieth century.[9] However, as I have argued elsewhere, the role of the companion animal in the childfree multispecies family may well incrementally contribute to delaying, or even eventually opting out of, childbirth. Indeed, prior research has noted that childfree families may satisfy a need to nurture with their animals or may engage in cost-benefit analyses comparing the human child to the companion animal that may support additional delays in (or even eventual opting out of) childbirth as women continue to develop professional careers.[10] This may be even more the case if, as I note in chapter 3, extended support from other family members reinforces a parent-child relationship in this kind of multispecies family.

Future research should also investigate data contained in the most recent General Social Survey regarding pet ownership because this is the first time that nationally representative data surrounding pets in the United States have been made available to researchers.[11] Doing so will provide family and human-animal interaction researchers a means of better understanding how human-animal relationships are experienced across a multitude of variables. Indeed, we already know via descriptive statistics that varying levels of income and family size are correlated with the amount of money that multispecies families spend on their dogs and cats.[12] However, we do not know if that is indicative of a decreased likelihood of considering the pet a member of the family. Furthermore, we can see descriptively that African Americans have a much lower rate of ownership for dogs and cats, but we do not know if race predicts the likelihood of the formation of the multispecies family discussed here.

Likewise, while analysis contained in this book indicates that many childfree individuals and couples have internalized a parent identity related to their cats and dogs, we do not know if there is a statistically significant relationship between family structure and integrating dogs and cats into the family fold. Nor do we have literature based in statistical analysis that explores family structure, time use (both involving and not involving pets), and the identification of pets as family members. Furthermore, questions that address the relationship between the ideal number of children reported by a respondent, pet ownership, and the likelihood to think of the dog and/or cat as a family member could provide insight into the impact of the dog or cat as family on future family structure. Use of the most current General Social Survey would be integral to ferreting out answers to these kinds of questions while also providing a more methodologically rounded understanding of the multispecies family in the United States.[13]

Finally, I have described the emergence of the present-day multispecies family as being partially dependent on attitudinal shifts related to the diversification of family structure that arose with the second demographic transition in the United States. Indeed, Ron Lesthaeghe has argued that characteristics of the SDT are also prominent in other industrialized nations, in northwestern Europe, Canada, Australia, and Japan.[14] If this is accurate, then there is a need for cross-cultural comparisons of the evolution of multispecies families across high-income countries with diversified family structures and below-replacement fertility rates. Furthermore, Adrian Franklin's argument regarding the evolution of the pet to family member extends to Great Britain in his analysis, as well.[15] That analysis rests on the societal shift to postmodernity that is integral to Dirk Jan van da Kaa's analysis of shifts in fertility preferences that are characteristic of the SDT.[16] It would seem that the kinds of familial identities that arise in the context of the multispecies family discussed here may well extend to other societies that have experienced the diversification of family structure brought on by the SDT.

There is evidence for this contention. For example, in Britain, with a total fertility rate of 1.8, 90 percent of Britons identify their dogs and cats as family members.[17] In fact, 15 percent report that they love their pet more than their partner, while 16 percent chose to include their pet as a family member on the official United Kingdom Census in 2011.[18] People in Japan (TFR = 1.44) also increasingly appear to regard their companion animals as family.[19] In the shadow of a declining birth rate, some reports in Japan suggest that pets are becoming increasingly preferable to parenthood among the youngest adults.[20] Two-thirds of households in Australia (TFR = 1.81) contain at least one pet, and over 60 percent of dog and cat owners there (63 percent and 60 percent, respectively) think of their companion animals as family members.[21] And similar to the generational differences inherent in the United States and the United Kingdom, Australian members of Generation Z are far more likely to consider their pets family compared to Baby Boomers.[22]

Future research would do well to consider how the emergence of the multispecies family is connected to broader demographic trends in family formation that are appearing in various countries around the world. I am not arguing that the multispecies family, and its attendant familial identities, is a major contributor to decreasing fertility rates in these countries. However, as in the United States, the trends may well be symptomatic of broader changes in attitudes toward self, society, and family in general. Mediated by these trends, the multispecies family is an important area of study for scholars interested in declining fertility rates and potential contributing variables to this decline.

Importance to Identity Theory

The findings in this book also signal a need for a specialized focus within identity theory on the influence of nonhuman animals on identity formation, a point that is not readily apparent within the current theoretical or empirical literature. As Sheldon Stryker notes, when someone internalizes these cultural expectations as part of their self-concept, an identity forms linking the individual to the larger social structure via the cultural expectations for that identity.[23] While identity theory addresses role identity as sourced from interaction with other human actors, participant narratives in this research suggest there are also other sources.[24] The identities discussed here (e.g., "parent," "grandparent," "sibling") developed only through interaction with a nonhuman counterpart who was perceived as a family member. In keeping with Clinton Sanders's contention that lingual actors engage in "doing mind" with alingual actors, my data show that participants developed a parent identity as they sought to better understand the animal child's emotions, preferences, and intentions with others.[25] However, these childless narratives not only depict instances of "doing mind" for the companion animal but also highlight an identity that would not have been present in the everyday life of these participants otherwise.

Another implication of these findings is consistent with George Mead's not-often-discussed depiction of the relationship between humans and nature as being mutual, rather than dualistic, suggesting the presence of "sociality" between objects, organisms, and systems.[26] While childless participants and their animal children in this research may not share the lingual, symbolic language that is spoken by human actors, *at minimum*, actors "doing mind" for their animal children in this context perceive a mutuality. "Doing mind" is an important mode of translation between companion animal owners, the animal, and other human actors. But, going a step further here, the perception of the companion animal as an agential social actor also directly led to the development of an idiosyncratic parenting identity among the participants in my research.

Perception is a key component of identity theory, as all behavioral input is perceptual in nature.[27] George McCall and Jerry Simmons describe this nicely: "It is in this sense that we can be said to interact, not with individuals and objects, but with *our images of* them. We do not, after all, deal with them directly as physical 'things' but as *objects* that we have clothed with identities and meanings. We act toward them on the basis of their meanings for us, the implications they have for our manifold plans of action."[28] If this is the case, then how a person perceives behavioral input, not just from human sources but from nonhuman sources as well, must be considered when theorizing the formation of identity. The meanings that actors associate with both human and nonhuman animals in their capacity as "objects with identities and meanings" is integral to understanding how the actor derives meaning for self.

For example, Becky, a childless female who spoke of the absent "pitter patter of little feet" in her home and her idea of "human replacement theory," also discussed how the relationships with her two dachshunds had helped. She noted, "They have helped in that regard because you hear their little feet, and they always have the little smiling faces looking up at you." Behaving toward her dogs as young children, she "does mind" in a way that allows her to enact the parent identity in response. This makes the animal-parent identity real in itself and thus real in its consequences.

The same can be said for other family members who ultimately verify the parent identity in their adult children. This leads to the formation of extended familial identities, such as "grandparent-granddog."

Internalizing the "grandparent" identity is a function of the presence of child(ren) in an adult child's life. As the node needed for the "grandparent-grandchild" identity pairing to emerge, the adult child, having internalized the "parent" identity, plays mediator in the formation of this pairing. Grace, the empty nester who was self-professed "granny" to Spring (her son and daughter-in-law's German short-haired pointer puppy), epitomizes how the grandparent identity present in this research is real, in and of itself, with concomitant consequences and regardless of the species. Indeed, in relation to Grace's childfree son and daughter-in-law, she shared, "I wouldn't want them to get a dog so I could be 'granny.' I wouldn't want them to have a child so that I could be 'granny.' I want it to be a part of their life, something they've accepted, something that they're willing to take on. And then, once they've made that decision, I want to be fully on board. I want to step up, whether it's got four legs or two."

Of course, it may be argued that these behaviors (and resulting identities) are simply a reflection of time use and opportunity for those who choose to tap their resources in such a way. I would argue otherwise. The meanings that an actor applies to a particular identity not only have implications for how that person behaves but also provide critical information for understanding the identity in that person.[29] In my research, a strong social connection has clearly been built between a multitude of actors (human and nonhuman) across a variety of family relations and structures. This connection signals important information about self and identity for those who are internalizing identities based on these relationships. Arguing that the human behavior exhibited in the context of family pets is simply a result of the way one chooses to spend one's time does not negate the fact that a role identity has been formed as a result.

I argue here for the need to have an identity theory with theoretical avenues that are unimpeded by "human exceptionalism" and that can extend to the companion animal as a source of identity. However, this need is not merely confined to the human–companion animal relationship found in the multispecies family. Certainly, nonhuman entities in general may well contribute to the formation of identity in humans. Likewise, living nonhuman actors may well engage in their own forms of communication, without the verbal discourse on which human exceptionalism is based. While it is not within the scope of this book to substantively discuss other areas of inquiry germane to a less anthropocentric identity theory, diverse examples of a need for reconceptualization abound. For example, researchers at MIT working on robotic artificial intelligence (AI) as a social intervention for children with autism have developed a "deep learning" process in AI that allows the technology to assess children's responses somewhat better than a human researcher can. Autistic children, for their part, appear to interact better with the AI than they do with human children—and they react to the human-shaped technology "as if it is a real person."[30] How might this research offer information on the formation of a childhood "friend" identity with AI?

Another example can be found in broader examples of human–nonhuman animal interaction and intersubjectivity. Noting that nonhuman animals are political actors tightly entangled with humans in multispecies, democratic communities, recent scholarship has argued that their speech goes unheard even as their actions coconstitute the political realm within human society.[31] Other research has emphasized the impact of invertebrates such as horseshoe crabs on human society via biomedical research, geological understanding, agricultural applications, and, ultimately, career trajectories for those who are entangled with these animals.[32] How might identity theory contribute to understanding how these nonhuman-animal voices situate themselves as active social actors with the propensity to impact the sense of human self—whether that be in the form of role-identity pairings such as "protector-protected," "antagonist-protagonist," or "researcher-researched"? And how might these potential identity pairings connect with a structural symbolic interactionist approach in which these seemingly micro-level conversations between human and nonhuman impact macro-level social institutions like polity, medicine, and economy?

Likewise, virtual social spaces (e.g., Second Life, Active Worlds, and World of Warcraft) and the avatars that inhabit them have received increasing attention from both symbolic interactionists and phenomenologists. At issue in these investigations is how "self" is impacted, developed, and liminally connected to (or not) the users who create them.[33] For example, some research explores how social norms and sanctions work within virtual reality to impact identity formation.[34]

Other work examines how the virtual social world is created by its residents, who develop virtual selves meant to engage in growing, vibrant social communities. Recent research investigates how emotions and virtual life experienced parallel to the avatar experience impact the "self" and interaction in reality.[35] How might we see the formation of identity in these virtual social worlds impact identity hierarchies and commitment in the real world, especially as we see creators combine the two worlds together?

Finally, if we are considering intersubjectivity as part and parcel of traditional symbolic interaction, an example can be found in old-tree communities that contain social networks with extensive, mature root systems. Mature forests appear to have a chemical system of communication in which trees can warn one another of impending danger, share nutrients with those that are ill, and actively protect the youngest saplings from disease in a social unit similar to that of a family.[36] How might this research point to the importance of alingual communication in the social preservation of nonhuman social groups?

All of these examples provide rich areas for exploration via an identity theory approach. But as is obvious in each, the theoretical underpinnings of the perspective would have to be reconceptualized in a way that permits consideration of the nonhuman actor as impactful on human self and identity and communicative in ways that are beyond spoken language. Indeed, the approach would have to move beyond thinking that only human social action can be influential in the formation of identity.

Some Final Words about My Experience

I began this book by recounting my own, childfree (at the time) multispecies family that had comprised me, my husband, and our dog, Chewbacca Bear, with whom I had developed an intense parent-child identity pairing. My narrative explains the impetus for what would ultimately evolve into this book. Scholarship on death and bereavement has long demonstrated that the severity of grief accompanying the loss of a companion animal is, in many ways, similar to the loss of a close human being.[37] Certainly, I remember feeling lost when Chew Bear passed, angry that we had not somehow beaten the lymphoma but ultimately relieved that she took the burden of euthanasia off my shoulders. When we found the "blood" patch on her abdomen the day before she died, the oncologist told me it was time to let her go, that she had not suffered but that she would now if we did not do something. That night I looked into her eyes. Our shared histories together, all of the intimate knowledge that we had of each other, told me she was at peace. I lay with her on her bed—she had not wanted to get on mine that night—probably knowing how horrible it would be the next morning. Both my husband and I knew that euthanasia, while traumatic for us, was the only option we had if we truly loved her.

Strangely enough, I had no idea what her plan would be as I loaded her gently into the back of the Honda Pilot, rolling down all of the windows for a few last sniffs that I knew had always been so fulfilling for her. When we got to the vet, I did not have to make that final decision—even though I already had. She passed before the vet could inject her with a lethal dose of pentobarbital, on the table but loving me enough to do it on her own. I knew then, somehow, that she knew that that was what I would need. And as always, she offered it. Loyal, loving, knowing me better than I did—she died changing who I was yet again, and as I sat clinging to her lifeless body on that exam table, with a clipping of her bright red mane in my hand, delicately trimmed by the tech and gifted to me, I knew she would always be a part of me. She was my first four-legged child, my first time performing "mother." And, while that identity has changed substantially for me in the subsequent years after having my two boys, I will always remember the first inkling of what it was like to love someone as I would my own, *human* children later on.

Today, I have a multispecies family of six: me, my husband, our two boys, and Sam and Sadie (and, for a while, the two roosters who loved to attack our legs). My relationship with Sam and Sadie is dramatically different from what I had with Chew Bear. I love them dearly. We all view them as integral members of our family. We are cognizant and respectful of each of their distinct personalities (and distinct they are!) and love the shared history that our entire multispecies family has built together.

I think that none of us could imagine our family without Sam and Sadie. Occasionally, my tender-hearted, now ten-year-old son will pensively ask when Sam is going to die—choking up as he asks the question. Of course, I do not know the answer to that. But I reassure him anyway, telling him that Sam is only ten years old and that we have a long road ahead of us together as a family. He hugs Sam tightly, momentarily forgetting that dogs do not typically appreciate this kind of affection because they feel trapped. But he remembers quickly and draws his arms away to stroke Sam's liver-colored ears. Sam, for his part, returns the affection by leveraging his seventy-six pounds against Alex, leaning on him as dogs will when they hug.

"I love you, Sam," my son murmurs endearingly, and I realize how much he and his older brother have learned about compassion, responsibility, empathy, and taking the role of other with these two dogs in our family. Sadie, realizing Sam is basking in my son's attention, moves quickly to his other side, pushing her long, pointed nose into his hair to announce her presence.

"You want some love too?" he says, as he scratches her head. We all learned very early on after we adopted her that her ears are off limits for her.

I suggest that he take her outside for a run and fetch, to which he stands up quickly and whines, "Aww, Mom! Do I have to? I was about to go play with my toy soldiers."

"Yes! You have to! How would you like it if I didn't want to play with you?"

And with that, he glumly looks to Sadie and says, "C'mon girl. Let's go." I realize that we (dogs included) still have so much to teach our boys before they grow up and leave the nest. And I wonder what it will be like when they leave home for college and we become empty nesters. Sam looks at me pensively—I swear he is wondering the same thing.

ACKNOWLEDGMENTS

Writing this book has been a five-year journey that has traversed across time in my doctoral program as well as my subsequent experience as a professional sociologist. My plan for *Just Like Family* has always been one that would challenge preexisting sociological thought about the importance of companion animals to the ways in which society operates but, more importantly, to the ways in which we define our families. To this end, I am indebted to a number of humans and nonhumans who have provided unremitting support, encouragement, advice, and generosity along the way. Indeed, this book may never have come to pass were it not for the commitment and collaboration offered by so many others.

I have been immensely fortunate to have the mentoring of Leslie Irvine, who has always generously offered me a seemingly endless array of expertise in human-animal interactionism, symbolic interactionism, and sociology. She has repeatedly provided me with insightful critiques of multiple iterations of the chapters in this book, given me guidance that has continually strengthened its message, encouraged me as I sought the perfect home for its publication, fostered my growth as both a symbolic interactionist and a human-animal interactionist, and patiently reminded me time and again that taking up these kinds of challenges is a worthy cause in our discipline. I hope that one day I can do two things: return the favor in some never-likely-to-be-equal way and pay her scholarly and professional kindness forward to another junior scholar endeavoring to place their proverbial brick in the wall of academia.

I owe a tremendous debt of gratitude to New York University Press for publishing this work. In particular, Ilene Kalish has been an indispensable source of editorial shaping and molding. Her excitement about this project, continued support, and patient guidance have all allowed the narratives in this book to shine as they so deserve to. I also appreciate the help of her editorial assistant, Sonia Tsuruoka. I am grateful to

Colin Jerolmack, the series editor for Animals in Context, for seeing the potential in my proposal and forwarding it on for serious review. I am also quite grateful to four anonymous NYU Press reviewers who took the time to provide in-depth ideas on increasing the impact of my work.

Multiple scholars have provided their time and expertise to the development of this book. Beth Montemurro has repeatedly provided careful reading of my work, providing constructive feedback to me every step of the way. Her endearing friendship, comradery, scholarship, and willingness to carve out time for a junior scholar have been a constant source of encouragement. I also appreciate Celia Lo for her nonstop friendship, support, and pride in my work. Her perspectives on ways in which to constructively critique statistical analyses have contributed greatly to pieces throughout the book. I thank Liz Grauerholz for reviewing my writing on family and theory and for providing insightful suggestions on the same.

This book would not have been possible without the anonymized participants who so graciously allowed me access into their multispecies families and experiences. Whether this was through my fieldwork at the veterinary clinic, chatting over a cup of coffee at the library, or sitting in participants' homes to interact with their cats and dogs, I am in awe at their willingness to break bread with a sociological researcher about whom they may have known very little.

I am indebted to those who have supported, advised, and taught me throughout my graduate education and beyond, especially the chair of my dissertation committee, James Williams. Scott Coltrane and Misako Ishii-Kuntz also provided me with a solid foundation of knowledge regarding family and contemporary theory. Much of what I learned from these scholars is embedded in this book in often hidden, but very influential, ways.

My continued research in this area and the writing of this book have been supported by multiple colleagues in my department at Southern Methodist University. Matt Keller has provided both logistical and scholarly support of this work. Anne Lincoln has offered her own book-writing expertise and friendship, listening to me toil and burble in the next office with good humor. Likewise, Alicia Schortgen, Leslie DeArman, Nancy Campbell, and Karen Delk have given their encouragement and support, especially when I was positive that there simply were no more hours in the day, month, or year to complete all of the tasks that I needed to complete. Parts of this project were also funded by a Sam Taylor Fellowship from the Division of Higher Education, United Methodist General Board of Education.

Of course, there have been so many others who have provided encouragement and emotional support along the way. Liz Cherry, John Pruit, Maggie Bohm-Jordan, Bob Young, and Carol Thompson have checked in on me at conferences, via email, texting, and Zoom to press me on in this endeavor. I also appreciate Colter Ellis, who as chair of the Animals and Society section at my very first ASA meeting in 2014 welcomed me with open arms to human-animal interaction scholarship, assuring me that there was space for all perspectives in the section. Many other individuals have also mentored me in various ways over the past seven years, including offering professional advice, various reviews of other human-animal interaction manuscripts, and countless other things that have made me who I am as a scholar today. I am beyond grateful for their investments in me.

Without the contributions and love of countless dogs and cats—in my participants' families, at the veterinary clinic, across mass media, within my own home, and across so many other contexts—this book would not have been possible. A special thanks goes to Chewbacca Bear, whose undying love and equally stubborn personality was the driving force behind writing this book. And I thank Sam, Sadie, and Tickles, who along with Chew Bear continue to be primary motivators for writing about the unique nature of different kinds of multispecies family structures in the United States.

Finally, I would especially like to thank my husband, Mark, and our two boys, Aidan and Alex, for their endless sacrifices of time with and help from me. Thank you for your continued acceptance of my prolonged absentmindedness as I tried to balance work and family, often in miserable fashion. But more importantly, thank you for your perpetual support, creative ideas, and open-mindedness. Mark, thank you for your good-natured love and humor as I have written this book. You have happily shared in taking care of our multispecies family and home; engaged in never-ending reviews of chapter drafts, paragraphs, and even sentences; and willingly helped me, often very late at night, check and double check references throughout this manuscript. Aidan, thank you for challenging your teachers about anthropocentric thought and for your inquisitive nature about all things nonhuman. Alex, thank you for your keen observations of the ways in which others present and interact with their dogs and cats. Our entire multispecies family has made me who I am today, both as a person and as a scholar. For that, I am eternally grateful.

METHODS APPENDIX

This project was mixed methods in nature, using a variety of qualitative methodologies that culminated in an investigation of the American multispecies family and its attendant identities. In-depth interviews, participant observation, and content analysis were all used to triangulate data regarding the ways in which familial identities emerge within varying family structures. I also draw on my own experiences within both a childfree, multispecies family and a multispecies family with young children present. Four distinct projects constitute the data and analysis used for this book. While I did not initially plan to develop multiple projects in this manner, each project informed the design of subsequent projects, with the last two projects being directly and intentionally informed and influenced by the first two. For example, one of the themes that emerged from Project 2 was "grandparenting." The creation and design of Project 3 was directly informed by this theme, and the interview guide was drafted to include questions reflective of the behavioral output that we might expect to see from grandparents in the United States. In the following sections, I discuss each project separately, providing readers with information on the method, time frame for data collection, participant parameters and recruitment, and data analysis.

Project 1: Veterinary Clinic Observations

The initial plan for my dissertation was inspired by Arnold Arluke and Clinton Sanders's[1] contention that people "speak for" their dogs and cats in the veterinary environment. I found this fascinating from a symbolic interactionist perspective and decided that I would build on their ideas by paralleling this speech with the concept of language brokering—a process used by immigrant children who translate and interpret messages for their nonfluent parents. In the process of doing this, language brokers can both influence decision-making and become the decision-maker in interactions between their parents and other social actors. It seemed to me that "doing mind" for and "speaking" for the companion animal was translational in nature, obviously leading to decision-making within the veterinary environment (albeit with the parent-child roles reversed).

The design of this initial project was qualitative in nature and used participant observation. As Danny Jorgensen has noted, participant observation is useful in "studies aimed at generating theoretical interpretations," one of the goals encapsulated in crossing over from the "language brokering" of immigrant children to "speaking for" nonhuman animals in the veterinary environment.[2] This methodology is particularly useful when what is being examined is hidden from public view, as is the case with exam-room interactions in the veterinary clinic.[3] However, securing a veterinary clinic that was willing to allow me to enter exam rooms and observe veterinarian-client interactions was not easy. Starting close to my residence, I contacted approximately ten veterinary clinics, either by phone or in person, to pitch my project to the clinic manager. Responses were negative across the board. Sometimes I was not allowed to speak with the clinic manager at all and told instead to leave a card for the manager to get back to me (none did). In the rare instances that I was allowed access to the clinic manager, I was told that, unless I was a client of their clinic, they would not consider allowing me to engage in research at their facility. Indeed, such resistance made it clear that learning more about interactions between owners, patients, and veterinary staff in the exam room was indeed held by professionals as restricted from public view in much the same way that medical staff might restrict observations of human patients' exams.

The insistence that I be a client of the clinic eventually led me to approach my personal veterinarian, who wholeheartedly agreed to allow me "behind the scenes" and into his exam rooms (as well as unfettered access to the rest of the clinic, except for euthanasia appointments). It is interesting to note that at some time early in the process, my personal veterinarian asked me how many clinics were allowing me access. He was not surprised when I told him that his clinic was the only one that had consented. Rather, he offered that veterinarians were anxious about such research because of concerns regarding disruption in client flow, the misrepresentation of data and findings to other clients, or even attacks in the press over euthanasia, rising costs of care, or refusal to treat an animal (regardless of the reason).

Data collection commenced in early June 2015 and went through mid-July 2015. I was at the clinic four days a week, four (occasionally five) hours each day, for approximately one hundred hours of observation time. Before I began this process, the clinic manager, owner (who was also my personal veterinarian), and I agreed on a process by which I could observe clients' exam interactions, respect the efficient business flow of the clinic, and maintain institutional review board (IRB) expectations for the project. First, clinic veterinarians and vet techs were all given the opportunity to opt out of observations—meaning that when their turn came up to take a client (or the client was theirs), I would not proceed into the exam room. I met with each veterinarian and veterinary technician to explain the project, to present the informed consent form, and to emphasize anonymity and confidentiality. Of twelve staff members (five veterinarians and seven vet technicians), four veterinarians and seven vet technicians agreed to be observed. Such a high rate of veterinary staff participation made it quite easy to know which appointments I could sit in on, as almost all had consented. Vet technicians were instructed to let me know when a client had entered the exam room, when the attending veterinarian would be the member that had opted out, and when euthanasia was either imminent or a foreseeable potential.

The second step entailed gaining consent from the client for observation. Once I was informed of a potential observation by the assigned veterinarian technician for that client, I would enter the exam room before the veterinarian technician came in for a preliminary visit (or to perform routine procedures like vaccinations) to explain the project and ask for consent from the owner. Potential participants were provided a brief synopsis of the project and, if they expressed interest, were presented with a consent form. I explained each portion of the consent form in detail and answered questions that arose. All forty-five owners consented to be observed.

The exam for one consenting individual involved the quickly degrading health of the dog of his very recently deceased mother. The participant was already visibly and emotionally distraught by his mother's death. The high cost of veterinary intervention required for her beloved dog's survival appeared to push him to a limit that caused extreme, visible distress. I removed myself from that observation because of ethical consideration for the owner's psychological state. This reduced the number of observations to forty-four.

Once consent was obtained, the owner, any other humans who accompanied the owner (e.g., children, roommates), client(s), and I would remain in the exam room, informally chatting. Often, owners, unsolicited by me, would share integral information regarding their history and interactions with the animal. I found these narratives particularly interesting because of their voluntary nature and paid close attention to transcribe them into my notes. Indeed, Howard Becker has emphasized the importance of this kind of voluntary discourse in participants because it provides a far more accurate assessment of participants' experience than when participants have been asked specific questions by the researcher.[4] Confirming Becker's guidance, spontaneously shared stories were often just as poignant and informative (if not more so) than observations that occurred in interaction with veterinary staff. Indeed, Jack's owner, discussed in chapter 4, who felt bad for the subordinate position that he had taken on in the family since the births of her children, or Carmella's owner, discussed in chapter 3, who shared her intense concern about increased viral loads due to clinic exposure, are exemplary of the necessity of unsolicited statements for the discovery of new information.

Owners sometimes asked what had prompted me to conduct the research—to which I promptly provided detail that expanded on the consent synopsis. I was also periodically asked what I had found so far in my research. These questions were somewhat more difficult to answer for a few reasons. Analysis was ongoing, making it difficult to provide any sort of real findings in answer to their questions. Second, and related to the first, sharing findings with participants runs the risk of altering their behavior during observation. Finally, not providing a suitable answer (at least suitable to the participant) risks irritating them or making them suspicious of my motives, endangering their trust in me as a researcher and destroying any precious rapport that we may have already developed. Ultimately, I simply explained that "analysis was ongoing, making it difficult to say much for sure at the moment." I usually followed that up with something disarming, along the lines of "the most obvious thing that I know now is that people love their animals and work hard to take care of them."

Once the vet tech and/or veterinarian entered the room, I fell to the back of the interaction against a wall to observe interactions among all actors. I took this time to make detailed notes about stories of interest that had been shared in our wait for clinic staff and any other observations that I had made during that time. I also simultaneously watched for interactions that transpired as the staff examined the client(s) and discussed plans with owners, taking notes as these occurred.

Occasionally, I was called on for assistance in the exam. This usually occurred when the vet tech had left the room for something. Participation typically entailed helping the veterinarian by restraining a dog in either a sitting or standing position, either on the exam table or not. I felt quite comfortable engaging in basic restraint like this. I had learned how to properly restrain a dog as a teenager in the course of helping my parents, who had professionally bred Chinese shar-pei throughout my adolescence. I was never asked to do this with animals who were behaving aggressively in any way, as the veterinary technician was always present in these circumstances.

I helped more frequently by simply speaking to the dog or cat in a quiet, calming voice as the vet tech restrained the animal and the veterinarian performed the exam. Rarely, when both the vet technician and the veterinarian left the room, an owner asked a medical question of me or asked that I further explain a procedure presented for consideration by the veterinarian. When this happened, I gently reminded them that I was not an expert in veterinary medicine but that we could ask for clarification when veterinary staff returned.

Exam observations ranged anywhere from forty-five minutes to two hours. How long I engaged in these interactions depended on several factors, including the reason for the client's visit, how many animals the owner brought in for exam, if labs or x-rays were required, how busy the clinic was, whether the appointment would be handled by just a vet tech or also by the veterinarian, and wait time for veterinary staff.

As mentioned earlier, I was not always in the exam room. Often, I sat in the lobby to observe families interacting or owners discussing their animals with one another. When I could, I sat on a corner bench in the lobby, inconspicuously taking notes. However, when the lobby became crowded, being discreet became difficult. I often found myself drawn into conversations with curious owners who wondered why I was there (probably because of my note taking) or where my animal was at the moment. When this occurred, I openly offered the purpose for my presence by explaining the project to them. Other times, I followed veterinary staff through the sick bay and kenneling areas, the x-ray room, and lab.

Project 2: In-Depth Interviews, Eighteen- to Forty-Four-Year-Olds

Shortly after I received IRB approval for Project 1, I designed another project with the goal of comparing human–companion animal interaction in families, both with and without human children. Further, the project was meant to probe into the effect that having companion animals may (or may not) have on fertility intentions of the childfree. As I gathered data simultaneously for both projects, I moved toward using this second project as the basis for my dissertation.

As with Project 1, Project 2 incorporated a qualitative research design for data collection but used semi-structured, in-depth interviews rather than participant observation. This type of data works well for informing researchers of participants' "views, feelings, and actions as well as the contexts and structures of their lives."[5] As such, I chose in-depth interviews to gain detailed narratives concerning the sociorelational bonds between owner and animal.

Participants were recruited via a two-pronged approach. First, fliers were placed in North Texas veterinary offices and on the campus announcement boards of a southwestern regional university.[6] Fliers noted that the study examined "the role that pets play for people both with and without human children" and specifically asked for participants "between the ages of 18 and 44, with or without human children, and with either a dog(s) and/or cat(s) . . . who [were] willing to be interviewed about their relationship with their pets." Those who contacted me were screened for sample parameters discussed shortly and were included if they met study requirements. The vast majority of participants were recruited in this fashion. Second, at the end of each interview, I used snowball sampling for further recruitment by asking participants if they would distribute a flier or two to contacts whom they thought might also be interested in taking part in the project. However, only one participant resulted from this type of recruitment.

Participants in this study were required to meet certain parameters. As mentioned earlier, both people with and without human children who also owned at least one dog or cat at home were included. I chose to limit the "companion animal" to either dogs or cats because literature cites these species as having the greatest level of familial bonding with humans.[7] Further, participant animals could not be service animals (animals specially trained to assist humans with disabilities such as blindness, deafness, or autism) because of the specialized work relationships entailed in these kinds of human-animal interactions.

Participants were required to be between the ages of eighteen and forty-four because I assumed that people under the age of eighteen would not be actively, intentionally making fertility choices. The age range was capped at forty-four in order to avoid "empty nesters," as I believed that this population could significantly blur the symbolic boundaries between human and animal child.

Project 2 included seventeen participants who were either childfree or childless. Twelve participants were childfree, while the other five were either involuntarily childless or had been told that they would never have children, only to find out later that this was incorrect. One female participant had adult stepchildren but identified herself as childfree because she had married her husband well after his children had left home. Female participants constituted the majority of the people with whom I spoke, with fifteen women and two men agreeing to be interviewed. Five participants fell into the twenty to twenty-nine age range; four participants fell into the thirty to thirty-nine age range; and eight participants fell into the forty to forty-four age range. Participants were mainly White (n = 13), with two Latinas and two Asian Americans.

I also interviewed eleven participants who, at the time of interviewing, had at least one human child under the age of eighteen at home. Ten of these people were female, and one was male. Participants with children were somewhat more racially and ethnically diverse than the group without children, with seven White, two Asian American, and two Latina participants. Two participants fell into the twenty to twenty-nine age range; four participants fell into the thirty to thirty-nine age range; and five participants fell into the forty to forty-four age range.

Data collection occurred across summer and fall of 2015. Five additional interviews were collected in summer of 2017 as a means of bolstering data in anticipation of writing this book. A semi-structured interview guide was used to ask questions such as "When and why did you first bring your pet into the family?"; "How do other family members (for example, partner, parents, or children) think of your animal?"; and "How would you define or label your relationship with your animal?" Questions that inductively arose during the course of interviewing were also asked, such as "Have you taken your animal into consideration as you have made serious life decisions involving relationships, career, or financial expenditure?" While I use the terms "pet" and "companion animal" interchangeably here, during data collection both terms were adjusted by how the participant referred to the animal (e.g., "baby" or "girl"). These adjustments were made to avoid damaging researcher-participant rapport—the last thing I wanted was to make my participants feel conspicuous about calling their pets "babies."

Participants were each interviewed one time, ranging from forty minutes to two and a half hours and generating large volumes of rich, thick description. Data analysis was ongoing throughout the data-collection phase for both Project 1 and Project 2. Following the methodologists Herbert and Irene Rubin's "responsive interviewing" technique allowed for adjustment of the interview guide in Project 2 in response to unexpected emergent themes produced by participants' narratives.[8] Themes that emerged during my analysis were incorporated into the interview guide as additional probes or sometimes entirely new questions. For example, after analyzing the first few childfree transcripts, I realized that participants' narratives revealed a tendency to make major choices about their relationships, occupations, and/or careers with their dogs and cats playing substantial roles in those decisions. To learn more about this, I added a question to the interview guide that would allow me to better understand the relationship between these decisions and the companion animal. The question was posed to all participants in Project 2, whether or not human children were present in the home. Likewise, questions that consistently appeared to garner very little data were pruned from the guide as a means of maintaining an efficient process as well as re-specting participants' time.

Responsive interviewing was also useful, cross-project, as a means of guiding observations being conducted for Project 1. For example, an early amendment to my methodology for Project 1 came as a direct result of Project 2's focus—relationships between family structure and human–companion animal interactions. As the theme of intensive par-enting came up more and more in interviews with people who did not have human children, I decided to amend the IRB for Project 1 to ask owners at the vet clinic if they did or did not have human children. This resulted in the ability to look for similarities in themes on family struc-ture across both Project 1 and 2 and culminated in using Project 1 data to bolster findings for Project 2.

Project 3: In-Depth Interviews, Empty Nesters

Eventually, I will collect data from across the entirety of the American family life course regarding the multispecies family. To that end, a cur-rently ongoing project that engages empty nesters has also been a source of data for this book. Design for Project 3 began in fall 2018, with data collection commencing in spring 2019.

As of the writing of *Just Like Family*, there are two major goals for Project 3. One is to discern the role that companion animals play in the empty-nester stage of the multispecies family. For example, do empty nesters, now beyond the young-child phase of family life, develop a parent-child relationship with their companion animals in ways that they did not when their human children were at home? Do they inten-sively parent their dogs or cats by engaging them in socialization classes and protecting them emotionally and physically? Do they invest large quantities of time and money into their companion animals' health? Just as importantly, how does the empty-nester multispecies family provide support to parents as they transition from a household with children to one without? What does this support look like? And how integral is it to the human's mental and physical health upon entering this next stage of the family life course?

The second goal of this new project entails triangulation of data with the childfree and childless data discussed in chapters 2 and 3 of this book. A major theme in Project 2 highlighted external support for the parent-child identity pairing in these family types. Because participants' narratives regularly identified their parents as providing social and emotional support for their own multispecies family identities, Project 3 examines whether this is simply the perception of participants or as a result of the internalization of the "grandparent" identity in their parents. Firsthand narratives from empty nesters, many of whom have childfree adult children who also own a companion animal(s) (or deeply desire to do so), address identity formation related to their adult children's dogs and cats (rather than simply depending on the adult child's perception). These narratives also allow me to further probe the multispecies family with human children via retrospective reporting of experiences that occurred in the family before participants became empty nesters. Pursuing both of these goals provides a useful, qualitative data set that bolsters my analysis from Project 2.

Participants have been recruited using the same strategy in Project 2. Again, fliers have been posted in North Texas veterinary offices and on the campus announcement boards of a private southwestern university (but different from the one in Project 2). Fliers note that the study purpose is to "understand the role that pets play for both people with and without human children in order to better understand what roles companion animals play in different types of families." Fliers also specifically ask questions such as "Do you have adult children who have all flown the nest?"; "Have you ever thought about how your adult children without kids of their own treat their companion animals like kids?"; and "Or have you ever thought about how you and your pet interact with each other now that your children have grown up?" For those who volunteer, sample parameters (discussed shortly) are screened and checked for inclusion in the project. However, at present, most participants have been recruited either via word of mouth from others who thought they would be suitable for the project or snowball sampling (so far, only one participant has emerged this way).

Currently, required parameters define two avenues for participation in Project 3. Regardless of the avenue under which one qualifies, all participants are required to be forty-five years of age or older; to have had at least one biological, step-, or adopted child in residence in the past; and to have all children grown and no longer living in the participant's residence. In addition to these umbrella parameters, Option 1 requires that the participant have at least one companion animal in residence (either a dog or cat, for reasons already discussed earlier). Option 2 allows participants to be without a companion animal in residence. However, with Option 2, the participant must have at least one biological, step-, and/or adopted child who is at least twenty-two years old, owns at least one dog or cat, and does not have any biological, step-, or adopted human children.

The age requirements for both participant (forty-five years or older) and at least one child (twenty-two years or older) is derived from the assumption that children younger than twenty-two are likely to still be attached to their family of orientation. This could be because the child is still in the midst of transitioning to adulthood via college/university or other types of young-adult life-course transitions. I also assume that children younger than twenty-two are not as likely to have (or be intentionally trying to have) human children of their own.

Furthermore, a child younger than twenty-two could feasibly alter a potential participant's identity formation with the companion animal, especially if the participant is more heavily engaged in intensive parenting practices, increasingly expected of those with kids present in the home. While there are few data on age at last birth for women in the United States, the overall mean age at first birth of US women (aged forty to forty-four) is 26.3 years. Setting the youngest participant age at forty-five years ensures that the project can capture the younger end of the demographic.

To date, seven participants have provided interviews for Project 3. Five participants fall into the forty-five to fifty-five age range, and two participants fall into the fifty-five to sixty-five age range. All are female. Five participants are White, one is Asian American, and one is African American. One of the seven women is also a part of Project 2, as she had teenaged daughters at home when I first spoke with her. As of 2019, all of her children had permanently moved out of her home.

As mentioned earlier, data collection is currently ongoing for Project 3. And while I have not gathered enough information from this project to write reliably about emergent themes on the impact of companion animals on the transition to the empty nest in the American multispecies family, these interviews have been integral in bolstering data and analysis in Projects 1 and 2. For example, empty-nester participants have provided valuable retrospective narratives regarding their experiences as parents with young children in a multispecies family. These data have worked nicely alongside data gathered in Project 2 from families that have young human children present.

For participants who have adult, childfree children with their own pets, I have been able to glean information about behavior that is consistent with the presence of a grandparent identity in my empty-nester participants. Indeed, this information has provided nice support for the findings from Project 2 in which childfree and childless participants discuss receiving social reinforcement from their parents for their relationships with their animals. And, finally, themes have emerged in these interviews that, while secondhand in account, provide valuable support for the idea that "parent" identities do emerge within familial contexts that are devoid of human children. In all but one empty-nester interview, strong themes of caretaking identities (rather than parent identities) have arisen, allowing me to theorize that the multispecies family and the identities that it evokes in its human participants may well evolve along the family life course in much the same way that family researchers have noted occurs in human-human relationships along the life course.

A semi-structured interview guide, informed by the responsive interviewing technique discussed earlier,[9] asks questions about the empty-nest experience, such as "Have you ever taken your animal into consideration when making major decisions about yourself and/or your family?"; "If so, what were those decisions, and why did you make the decision that you did?"; "How is taking care of your pet similar to and/or different from raising your human children?"; and "How has the presence of your dog or cat impacted your transition to an empty nest at home?" Questions that consider adult children's pets and the relationships that have developed as a result are asked as well. These items include "Can you describe what you think your child's expectations are of you for how you should interact with their pet?"; "How does your child refer to you in relation to their animal?"; and "If you were to put a family label on this pet related to *your* experience with him or her, what would it be and why?" As with Project 2, the terms "pet" and "companion animal" are used interchangeably in these examples. However, during data collection, both terms are appropriately adjusted to correspond to the words the participant uses to refer to the animal (e.g., "baby" or "girl").

To date, interviews have ranged from fifty-five minutes to two and a half hours.

Data Analysis: Projects 1, 2, and 3

Data analysis for Projects 2 and 3 was identical in nature. Once transcribed, interviews were loaded into NVivo, a software program specifically developed for qualitative data analysis. Each participant in Project 2 was assigned demographic traits for ease of categorization based on the following characteristics: race/ethnicity, age (twenty to twenty-nine, thirty to thirty-nine, forty to forty-four), gender, fertility status (childfree, childless/infertile, thought infertile initially), species of participant animal(s), and how the animal had been procured. For Project 3, I coded for the same variables as Project 2 but added marital status and whether or not the participant's adult children had companion animals. Age ranges (forty-five to fifty-five, fifty-six to sixty-five, sixty-six and over) were different from Project 2 because of differing life stages between the two groups (child-bearing age versus empty nesters).

Transcribed interviews began with a brief skim of the transcript, followed by a more thorough read of the transcript, to simply think through the data without coding, helping me develop a general overview for later coding. Once I had done this, data went through a two-step process that involved both initial and focused coding.[10] I used this process as a means of developing themes that would allow me to address the research questions while still allowing for the emergence of unexpected findings. While I used identity theory from the outset, I also engaged in inductive analysis, yielding initial codes that were a hybrid of identity theory and themes generated from participants' responses. I moved line by line through the data looking for ideas that could be used for categorization later. Some of these initial codes failed to produce much information and were eventually abandoned for more substantive codes that had deeper and more contextualized significance for particular family structures.[11]

Once a transcript had gone through the initial coding process, I went back through the data for focused coding that would allow me to bring all of the bits and pieces of earlier coding into major categories.[12] This enabled me to make connections between many of the earlier initial codes, creating more meaningful, substantive categories. This process was ongoing, allowing me to theoretically sample subsequent interviews as a means of refining major categories until reaching saturation.

Data analysis for the participant observation data in Project 1 was nearly identical to that of Projects 2 and 3. NVivo was used again to aid in coding of themes throughout the data. However, there were a few differences. Because the methodological nature of the project called for handwritten notes of my observations, these were scanned into the program as PDFs rather than imported as Word documents. The way in which NVivo works meant that I was forced to code as if each document were a photograph rather than a Word document. That is, rather than coding pieces of text (as with transcribed interviews), I coded by "cropping" pieces of my notes into relevant themes. While the logistics of this was, at times, a slow-going, frustrating process, the means by which I analyzed for both inductive and deductive themes in observational data were not otherwise changed from the way in which I analyzed data from Projects 2 and 3.

Also, because I was engaged in participant observation for Project 1, I was not able to gather all of the same demographic information that I did with Projects 2 and 3. However, I did manage to record gender (although this was based on my perception rather than participants' report), the presence of children in the family or not (I amended my IRB fairly early on in data collection to allow for request of this information in informal conversation before the arrival of veterinary staff), and species of animal(s) (limited to dog or cat, also asked of the participant before veterinary staff arrived in case there were more animals at the participant's home).

Project 4: Content Analysis of Print Ads

Project 4 used qualitative methodology via content analysis using a convenience sample. I designed Project 4 with the data and analysis from Projects 1 and 2 in mind. As I have noted elsewhere in this book, a key component of structural symbolic interactionism is to demonstrate how widespread patterns of behavior across groups are connected to gradual changes in macro-level social structures that can impact the cultural expectations associated with relevant statuses in society. Print advertising offered a good opportunity to connect the rapidly growing $95 billion pet-product industry to the growing acknowledgment of dogs and cats as family members in the United States. After reviewing what little research had been done on animals in advertising, I used Jennifer Lerner and Linda Kalof's research on animal themes in television advertising as an additional justification for narrowing my focus to ads that only portrayed dogs and/or cats as family members.[13] Furthermore, in relation to other animals in the American family home (e.g., guinea pigs, rabbits, birds, snakes), dogs and cats have repeatedly been found to have the highest percentage of people identifying them as family members.[14]

Data Collection

Initially, I planned to use the search engine Google to locate print ads with companion animals featured in some way. My parameters for inclusion in the sample were simple: ads from the United States with dogs and cats depicted as having some sort of familial (or friend) relationship with a human. However, I soon found that to be a difficult endeavor, at best. Regardless of search terms used, a few weeks of searching had secured only a handful of advertisements. Furthermore, I was often unable to ascertain the markets (domestic or international) in which the ads had appeared, nor was I able to determine the year of their release.

Looking for guidance, I consulted with my university's advertising and marketing librarian. She quickly filled me in on why it was so difficult to find ads in this manner. Apparently, advertising agencies do not classify ads by keywords in the way that peer-reviewed literature is cataloged in digital libraries such as JSTOR or multidisciplinary indexes such as the Social Science Citation Index. Instead, searching for particular kinds of ads means searching large volumes of metadata that may or may not use seemingly obvious (to me, anyway) search terms (e.g., dog, cat, pet, companion animal) as a part of their advertisement profile. Furthermore, I learned that the representation of "family" was often contained in the subtext of ads in a way that would not necessarily pop up in a keyword search (such as the woman holding an umbrella over her dog's head in figure 5.4).

After several online advertising databases were suggested to me, I decided to use AdForum and WeLoveAd (both databases used by professionals in the advertising industry) to add to the small collection of ads that I had already gathered for analysis. Searching these databases, as mentioned earlier, was arduous. There was no standard way to locate samples using keywords, even in these professional databases. There were, however, key elements that made data collection easier, including the ability to search by country (United States), medium (print ads), industry (e.g., pet products and services; alcohol and wine; household), and date range of release (2000–2019). Once I narrowed my search with those parameters, I used a variety of terms to create a convenience sample, including "dog," "cat," "pet," "parent," "pet parent," "sibling," "family," and "fur baby."

There were several parameters in place to guide selection of advertisements. First, because the project examines familial identities in the American family, I only included advertisements that were targeted at markets located in the United States. Images whose agencies were located outside the United States were still included as long as the ad was for the US market. Project parameters did not limit the kinds of products being advertised. This resulted in an array of consumer goods and services, including pet products and veterinarian services, footwear, alcohol, cleaning supplies, veterinary services, pet adoption, and credit cards. Advertisements were only selected if at least one dog or cat was included. The pet was required to be (or at least appear to be) in close proximity to a human while also appearing to be "part of the family."

Ads were determined to depict the companion animal as a family member for a variety of reasons. Ads with copy that referred to the animal as "family" or labeled the animal with a family status (e.g., "baby" or "kid") were included in the sample. Likewise, ads that showed the animal in a physical position similar to that which a human child might be (such as the cat sitting on the man's shoulders in figure 5.8) were coded as "family." An ad also qualified for inclusion if a dog or cat was not present but either the image or the copy made it clear that one or both of these species had been included as a family member (such as the pacifier with a "mouse" nipple in figure 5.12).

Finally, as mentioned earlier, I restricted the data range of the sample to reflect advertisements from 2000 to 2019. I based this parameter on prior literature that had already examined the use of companion animals in print ads but had done so using date ranges prior to or including the year 2000.[15] I was able to find only one study that extended the date range of analysis into the new millennium, but only by four years, covering the decade 1994–2004.[16] Further, and in addition to the need for new analysis in the literature, I assumed that the date range used in my design was the most likely to substantively depict dogs and cats as members of the American family. I based this assumption both on my own research and also on prior sociohistorical research. Indeed, extant literature has robustly demonstrated the continued sociohistorical growth (especially throughout the twentieth century) of acknowledgment by American families of the companion animal as a legitimate family member in the United States, both generally and across varying mass-media platforms.[17]

Data Analysis

My final convenience sample had a total of eighty-eight advertisements. I began analysis by examining each advertisement for the presence of the following identities: "parent," "child," or "sibling." An ad was coded "parent" (n = 39) if one or more of the following conditions applied: the copy mentioned parental status (e.g., "mom" or "dad"); the behavior of the human in the ad was aligned with that of a parent; or the subtext of the ad's imagery suggested the presence of a parent-child relationship. An ad was coded "child" (n = 42) if one or more of the following conditions applied: ad copy utilized a child status to refer to the dog or cat (e.g., "baby," "son," "kid"); ad copy used a cultural colloquialism typically reserved for a child (e.g., "little shadow" or "little buddy"); the behavior of the pet was in alignment with that of a child; or the subtext of the ad's imagery suggested the presence of a parent-child relationship. An ad was coded "sibling" (n = 3) if one or more of the following conditions applied: ad copy utilized a sibling status to refer to the pet (e.g., "brother" or "sister"); at least one human was depicted alongside the pet in a way similar to that of human siblings (e.g., arms around each other); or the subtext of the ad's imagery suggested the presence of a sibling relationship.

I further coded each ad for gender (man or woman), race/ethnicity, and species. Absent any other firm data to the contrary (such as more preferable self-reporting of the persons depicted or *at least* the advertising agency's representational intention), I based each category on my own perception of these characteristics. Indeed, Nancy Denton and Glenn Deane note that "definitions of race and ethnicity are far from clear cut" in society and that race is a social construct linked to biological markers.[18] While subjective measurement of gender and race is problematic from a methodological perspective, I had no other way to code for these variables.

Based on "mothering" and "fathering" codes, thirty-nine sampled ads provided forty-eight representations that could potentially be coded for gender. The other forty ads either did not provide imagery that would allow even a subjective analysis of gender or did not include humans at all. Of the forty-eight representations to which a potential gender code could be applied, thirty-three were coded "woman" and fifteen were coded "man."

Fifty-one sampled advertisements provided sixty representations that could potentially be coded for race or ethnicity. The other thirty-seven ads either did not provide imagery that would allow even a subjective analysis of race or did not include humans at all. Of the sixty representations for which a potential race code could be made, forty were coded "White," seven were coded "Black," and two were coded "Asian." Eleven representations, while containing a person who might be coded for race, positioned the person in ways that made race indiscernible (e.g., the person's back is turned to the camera and the focus is of a puppy being held over her should the way a human infant might be).

I coded for species (dog or cat) subjectively but with full trust in my ability to use culturally defined characteristics about what defines a dog versus that of a cat in the United States. Seventy-one ads contained the physical representation of a dog, a cat, or both. This resulted in a total of seventy-six dog representations with which to work. Twelve representations were coded for cat.

My Own Experiences

My own experiences as an adult in two different types of multispecies families over my own family life course has informed my analysis throughout each of these projects. I began my first adult multispecies family with Chew Bear when I was a twenty-year-old, single woman in my third year as an undergraduate student. My future husband and I met shortly thereafter and were married a year later. As I note in the introduction to this book, my relationship with Chew Bear was one that was intense and tightly bonded. And it informed familial decisions in countless ways, including where we would live (as college students and later young professionals, we were highly transient), how we would budget our finances, what types of vacations we would take, our daily exercise schedules, family that we would visit, and how we would spend our time with each other. Chatting with participants and observing clients during my fieldwork, and then later analyzing my data, I was often struck by how much data from childfree families reflected my own experiences.

It took me a long time to grieve Chew Bear, and it would be another six years before we created a new multispecies family, but this time with young children present. Sam entered our world in 2012, but not without some convincing. A good friend had contacted us, sharing that her neighbor was about to take a beautiful, kindhearted German short-haired pointer (GSP) boy to the local animal shelter because he no longer had time to take care of the dog. At first, Mark, my husband, and I said, "Nope. No dogs. Especially no hunting dogs." We had thought that a GSP would be too boisterous, even with the two acres that we lived on, for three- and six-year-old boys and did not want to deal with it. But my friend convinced me to visit the dog to see what we thought. She had been right. Sam was a dream. And we knew it from the moment we locked eyes with his gentle, hazel gaze. The boys were in love too, especially our younger, more extroverted son, who spent many waking hours thereafter lying with and piling on top of Sam to "be part of his pack."

The first night that Sam was in our home permanently, and after the children had finally collapsed in exhausted but joyous heaps in their beds, Mark and I sat side by side on the family-room floor with Sam. In what we now know is typical Sam fashion, he had used his long, pointed, liver-colored head and incredibly flexible girth to pry his way into the small, narrow space where our hips and legs came together. As we stroked his long, brown, velvety ears, he rapidly wagged his white tail, short from docking when he was six days old. After a few minutes, it wagged a bit slower but still rhythmically, then with increasingly longer pauses, until he simply went to sleep between us. He was a wonderful, passionate, pensive boy who would fit perfectly into our family from that point on.

Two years later, Sadie entered our family. At that point, I had been increasingly working outside the home, and Mark traveled frequently during the week for business. With the boys in school all day, Sam was often by himself for eight hours at a time. I felt awful for him, convinced that he needed some sort of companionship while we were gone. This time, it was my husband who took some convincing. But after finding a picture of Sadie on the Texas GSP Rescue website, her big, brown head cocked inquisitively at the camera as she daintily crossed her front legs, the boys and I were able to convince him to drive all five of us down to San Antonio for a meeting in her foster family's home. She and Sam immediately romped around her temporary living room, and she became the second nonhuman member of our multispecies family on the spot.

I have accessed these relationships throughout data collection and analysis, memoing about these memories throughout each project, referring to journal entries that I kept, especially during our time with Chew Bear. I have occasionally shared some of this experience here where it seems appropriate and in ways that answer questions about the project's motivation, my own identity formation, and that of my children.

NOTES

INTRODUCTION

1. Irvine 2004.
2. For a more in-depth treatment of methods deployed for this book, please see the Methods Appendix.
3. Weber 1947:104.
4. Parsons 1937.
5. Durkheim 2005.
6. Goffman 1959.
7. Alger and Alger 2003a; Wilkie and McKinnon 2013.
8. Mead 1967.
9. Mead 1967:182–83.
10. Alger and Alger 2003b.
11. C. Bryant 1979:399.
12. Murphy 1995:691.
13. Sanders 1993, 2003.
14. Irvine 2004.
15. Alger and Alger 2003a.
16. Franklin 1999; Charles 2014, 2016.
17. Grier 2006; Melson 2001.
18. Arluke et al. 1999; Flynn 2000b.
19. Burke 1980; Burke and Stets 2009; McCall and Simmons 1978; Stryker 1980.
20. Lesthaeghe 1995; van de Kaa 1987.
21. Ariès 1980.
22. Blackstone 2019; Shir-Vertesh 2012; Volsche 2018.
23. See, for example, Elder, Wolch, and Emel 2009; Tissot 2011; Wall 2014.
24. Farrell, VandeVusse, and Ocobock 2012:283.
25. Smith 1993; Farrell et al. 2012; Harris 2008.
26. US Census Bureau 2017; APPA 2019.
27. AVMA 2018.
28. Shannon-Missal 2015.
29. Farrell et al.'s (2012:287) research on the presence of nontraditional family types within four prominent, peer-reviewed sociology journals confirms this distinct omission. Attempting to examine how the nontraditional family is represented in these venues, study authors coded for the following: "non-resident parents";

"teenage parents"; "unmarried parents"; "cohabitation"; "gay and lesbian"; "divorce"; "single parents"; "comparative" work (in which two or more family types were compared); and "traditional." "Other" was an additional category with which Farrell et al. attempted to capture nontraditional family types with "very low counts" in the four journals. This included "articles on widows, stepfamilies; intergenerational households; separation; childlessness, adoption and foster care" (288). The multispecies family (or at least something akin to it), apparently making nary an appearance in their analysis, could not even be included as "other" regarding family type due to its absence.

30. APPA 2020.
31. Stryker 1980:57.
32. Burke and Stets 2009.
33. Sanders 1993.
34. Carter and Charles 2018.
35. Orwell 1946.
36. Irvine 2004.
37. Meijer 2019:30.
38. Linzey and Cohn 2011:viii.
39. Hankin 2009.
40. In Defense of Animals USA 2019.
41. Francione 2000.
42. AVMA 2019.
43. Matheson 2011.
44. Irvine 2004.
45. Arluke and Sanders 1996:51.
46. It is quite possible that I also spoke with LGBTQ families. However, I overlooked asking about this this type of family structure during interviews and only asked those whom I observed in my fieldwork if they had any young or adult children in their family. Sexual orientation was not a data point, though it should be an important family type for research on the multispecies family going forward.
47. See Blackstone and Stewart 2012 or Blackstone 2019 for a more nuanced treatment of this.
48. Dye 2010.
49. Mathews and Hamilton 2002; CDC 2020.
50. Thorne 1993.

1. HAS THE AMERICAN FAMILY GONE TO THE ANIMALS?

1. Taylor, Funk, and Craighill 2006.
2. Shannon-Missal 2015.
3. AVMA 2018.
4. Duffin 2019.
5. The American Veterinary Medical Association (2018) notes that cat ownership appears to have actually dropped from a peak of 37,500,000 cat owning households

in 2006 to the current household number of 31,896,077. However, the organization also contends that this drop is probably not due to an actual decrease in the number of cat-owning households but rather statistical error contained within the survey. Indeed, AVMA statisticians note that they oversampled women in their data; women notoriously are far more likely to own cats than are men. This skewed the 2006 and 2011 data such that it appeared that more households owned cats than actually did. As noted in this chapter, cat ownership has increased since 1996.

6. Rogers 2018.

7. Stump 2018.

8. Olick 2018.

9. Indeed, 71 percent of Generation Xers now own at least one pet, while 65 percent of Millennials report the same (Shannon-Missal 2015).

10. Instagram, for example, is particularly popular with Millennials and Generation Zers—those between the ages of eighteen and twenty-four—constituting the second-largest age demographic for the platform in 2019, at 22.9 percent of all users (Statista 2019b). As social media users in general go, 88 percent of the eighteen- to twenty-four-year-old demographic use social media at least once a day, making it the leading social media user age demographic in the United States (Pew Research Center 2019).

11. Mars Petcare 2016.

12. Mediakix 2018.

13. Khalil 2018.

14. APPA 2020.

15. Schaffer 2009.

16. Semple 2018.

17. CareCredit 2019; APPA 2019.

18. Selman, Nussey, and Monaghan 2013.

19. CareCredit 2019. Just as food preferences of owners for their companion animals reflect human nutritional consumption patterns, canine and feline obesity reflects the growing epidemic among human population in the United States. Indeed, the Association for Pet Obesity and Prevention estimates that a full 59 percent of cats and 54 percent of dogs can be categorized as obese in the United States (Ward 2017), surpassing the 39.8 percent of adult men and women in the United States who can be classified similarly (CDC 2019).

20. APPA 2020.

21. Marquand 2016; Springer 2019.

22. Dewey 2018.

23. The Dogtopia franchise is the leader in this industry, with record growth in 2017. With 65 locations already open around the United States, the franchiser has another 110 stores in development now, with a goal of reaching 400 locations by 2021. The franchise attributes its fast-paced growth to the growing demand for professional pet-care services (Franchise Chatter 2018).

24. At the 2018 Atlantic Coast Veterinary Conference, one veterinarian noted, "The human-animal bond is a pretty strong thing. They truly are a part of the family, and people want to have a piece of their pets around forever." The pricing noted here appears to make this pet trend a thing of the most affluent, but veterinarians see the level of human-animal bond as the most influential, saying, "It's those clients who love their pets the most, who are the most compliant with your recommendations for regular office visits, screenings, and year-round parasite prevention," who are most likely to pay (McKinney 2018). While the ability to actually pay for this kind of genetic guarantee without debt clearly remains with the wealthiest clients, it is also apparent that pet-cloning companies like ViaGen see the importance of getting the cost down so that cloning becomes "available to all dog (and cat) owners" (ViaGen 2019).

25. Haraway 2008.

26. For example, a purebred akita can cost anywhere from $1,500 to $5,000, while a purebred rottweiler may set one back between $2,000 and $8,000. The English bulldog, a breed that has been selectively bred for a short snout and legs that are responsible for the breed's chronic respiratory issues and degenerative spine disease, has a price tag that can range from $2,500 to $9,000 (Harleman 2015).

27. Smith et al. 2018.

28. US Census Bureau 2017.

29. Multiple human-animal interaction scholars have examined the family relationship. See, for example, Charles 2014; Franklin 1999; Melson 2001; and Power 2008.

30. Cain 1985; Power 2008.

31. Powell et al. 2010.

32. Gray et al. 2015.

33. Kurdek 2009a.

34. Blouin 2013; Franklin 1999; Gray and Young 2011; Laurent-Simpson 2017a; Turner 2005; Walsh 2009.

35. Volsche and Gray 2016; Peterson and Engwall 2019.

36. Owens and Grauerholz 2019.

37. Walsh 2009.

38. Laurent-Simpson 2017b.

39. Flynn 2000a; Strand and Faver 2006.

40. Cowan and Hodgson 2016; Mahoney 1991.

41. Tipper 2011.

42. Arluke and Sanders 1996; Hirschman 1994; Melson 2001.

43. Cassels et al. 2017.

44. Kurdek 2009b.

45. Turner 2005; Walsh 2009.

46. Melson 2001.

47. Serpell 2005.

48. Serpell 1996.

49. See, for example, Charles 2014; Herzog 2010; and Thomas 1983.

50. AVMA 2018.
51. Franklin 1999; Ritvo 1987; Thomas 1983.
52. Grier 2006:160.
53. Brandes 2010.
54. See Grier 2006 for a full treatment on the historical development of American consumer habits related to companion animals.
55. Olson 2015.
56. Bianchi 2014; Cherlin 2009.
57. Franklin 1999; Anthony Giddens, a British sociologist interested in the evolution of modern society, argues that ontological security engages one's trust in other people to help the individual navigate the risk and uncertainty characteristic of the postmodern era. As a protective barrier for emotional safety, ontological security provides a "protection against future threats and dangers which allow(s) the individual to sustain hope and courage in the face of whatever debilitating circumstances she or he might later confront" (Giddens 1991:38–39).
58. Bianchi 2014; Franklin 1999; Lesthaeghe 2010.
59. Cherlin 2009.
60. Coontz 1997.
61. Franklin 1999.
62. Carson 1962.
63. Ehrlich 1978.
64. Franklin 1999.
65. Franklin 1999.
66. Franklin 1999.
67. Franklin 1999.
68. Irvine 2004.
69. Irvine 2004.
70. It is important to stress here *nonverbal* abilities because of the historical, scholarly emphasis that has been placed on lingual capabilities as being requisite for the development of a core self. Irvine (2004), like other influential human-animal interaction scholars before her (see, for example, Sanders 1993, 2003; Alger and Alger 2003a), argues that, much like human infants who are alingual but still accorded a meaningful "self" by their caretakers, dogs and cats also exhibit nonverbal indicators of selfhood. These arguments are direct challenges to the traditional interactionist position that the presence of language indicates a symbolic system of thought—necessitating the presence of a core self that could have only been developed in *linguistic* interaction with other social selves (Mead 1967; Blumer 1969).
71. Irvine 2004:133.
72. Alger and Alger 2003a.
73. Holbrook and Woodside 2008; APPA 2020.
74. By family "status," I mean the kinds of labels that human family members use to identify and classify their relationships to one another, including "parent," "child," "sibling," or "grandparent." These culturally bounded statuses each come attached

to a set of society-wide expectations for specific behavior related to those statuses. When an actor regularly performs one of these statuses in the presence of other social actors, identity theorists argue that that actor has internalized the status and created a role identity for self that is accessed in relevant social situations.

75. While human-animal interaction researchers have acknowledged the long-standing technical existence of a multispecies family across large swaths of human history, in which dogs, cats, and people coexisted together (for example, see Charles 2014; Irvine and Cilia 2017; Morey 2014), scholars have also written about the emergence of the family animal as kin within the postmodern family (Charles and Davies 2008; Charles 2014, 2016). My use of "multispecies family" in this book references this modern conceptualization.

76. Grier 2006.

77. Grier 2006.

78. Smith 1993.

79. US Census Bureau 2019.

80. Simpson 2018.

81. See Harris 2008 for an extended treatment on this subject.

82. Cherlin 2009.

83. Manning 2015.

84. For more on this subject in the United Kingdom, see Charles, Davies, and Harris 2008. In the United States, see Smock and Greenland 2010.

85. Ariès 1980; Lesthaeghe 2010.

86. Cherlin 2009.

87. Inglehart 1990.

88. Zaidi and Morgan 2017.

89. Bianchi 2014; Lesthaeghe 2010.

90. Bianchi 2014.

91. Thornton 2005.

92. During this first demographic transition, marriage and childbirth remained tightly intertwined in the kinship institution (thus reinforcing the cultural definition within the United States of SNAF—married parents and their children as the sole proprietors of who "counts" as family). Contrary to the instrumental nature of marriage in the past, a companionate family emerged in which affection for both spouse and children is of central concern and the family is a place of personal dependencies and obligations (Coontz 2000). The percentage of adults ever married remained high, divorce rates were relatively low, and society became emotionally and financially centered on the child.

93. Ariès 1980:647.

94. Ariès 1980; Lesthaeghe 2010.

95. Charles 2014.

96. Van de Kaa 1987:11; Lesthaeghe 1995. Van de Kaa (1987) and Lesthaeghe (1995) have argued that a second demographic transition took place in which fertility rates in highly developed nations continued dropping to below replacement level

(2.1 children born per woman in most populations) and, in some cases, achieved a lowest low fertility (fertility rates well below replacement for the population)—denying society a fertility-mortality balance that would result in perfectly sustained population numbers. These dramatic drops in childbirth were produced by new ideational motivations that lay in self-fulfillment and self-realization (Lesthaeghe 2010) and resulted in a growing diversity of family structures within American society. For example, between 1955 and 1970, the rate of divorce increased, age at first marriage became increasingly delayed, and fertility dropped below replacement (Lesthaeghe 1995). Lesthaeghe (1995) notes that, by the late 1970s, cohabitation before marriage began to rise, as did births to unmarried mothers. While divorce rates stabilized in the mid-1980s, rather than remarrying as in the past, people increasingly just cohabited with newfound mates after divorce (and widowhood).

97. Cherlin 2009.
98. Charles 2014.
99. Lesthaeghe and Neidert 2006.
100. Cherlin 2009:31.
101. Giddens 1992:75.
102. Giddens 1992:75.
103. Giddens 1992:90.
104. Giddens 1992:58.
105. Of course, when individuals are focused on a "pure relationship," the existence of which is contingent on self-satisfaction and happiness, relationship dynamics rest on the assumption that the entire bond is temporary. There is no macro-level demand that relationships be permanent in their existence. The emergence of the pure relationship contributes to understanding why it is that divorce, cohabitation, and even a decrease in marital rates occur in the postmodern period. Giddens's concept of the pure relationship also informs who counts as family. Indeed, the continued existence of the family unit itself becomes contingent on the self-satisfaction for which both partners constantly monitor. Thus, neither partner nor children take precedence over the self and the pursuit of ontological security (Giddens 1992). If one partner is no longer happy, there is nothing culturally or socially that demands that the relationship remain intact.
106. Blackstone 2014, 2019.
107. Blackstone 2019; Greenebaum 2004; Laurent-Simpson 2017b; Owens and Grauerholz 2019; Walsh 2009.
108. Bianchi 2014; Cherlin 2009.
109. Bianchi 2014.
110. Cherlin 2009.
111. Powell et al. 2010.
112. Mary did not share her cat's name with me.
113. Blouin 2013; Charles 2016; Power 2008.
114. Shir-Vertesh 2012.

115. Irvine and Cilia 2017.
116. Shir-Vertesh 2012.
117. Irvine and Cilia 2017; Power 2008.
118. Haraway 2008; Beverland, Farrelly, and Lim 2008.
119. Greenebaum 2009; Haraway 2008.
120. The Humane Society of the United States (2020) estimates that, of the six to eight million animals that wind up in a shelter each year, about a quarter are labeled purebreds. The practice of surrendering animals who have cost so much to acquire in the first place is prevalent enough that hundreds of breed-specific rescue groups—organizations focused on finding homes for only one or a few specific breeds of dog or cat—have formed across the United States. The American Society for the Prevention of Cruelty to Animals (2020) estimates that 47 percent of surrendered dogs and 42 percent of surrendered cats are given up because of "pet problems" that include health issues, behavioral problems, animals who became larger than expected, and aggressiveness.
121. It is important to note that the multispecies family as a unique family form may not be considered a family form at all by family researchers in sociology because of its "nonhumanness." While its appearance as a diverse family form, at least in the form that is present in the United States today, probably required the conditions set in motion by the SDT, the multispecies family may or may not be a permanent state for human families. Of course, this is no different from the married nuclear family, which ended in divorce at a rate of 3.2 divorces per 1,000 marriages in 2016 (Statista 2019a). Indeed, one in five children under the age of nine and born with married parents experience divorce of their biological parents while they are still at home. Nor is this potentially fleeting state different from the increased likelihood of divorce for stepfamilies, within which previously divorced individuals "probably have different attitudes about divorce . . . than do never-divorced individuals. . . . Divorce holds less fear for them, and they see fewer barriers to ending a marriage" (Coleman and Ganong 2015:353). Children born into cohabiting parent families have a one-in-two chance of experiencing divorce before the age of nine (Livingston 2018a). These varying familial arrangements indeed suggest that there is a fleeting state of family form for "only-human" families in the United States as well.
122. AVMA 2018.
123. Grimm 2014:148.
124. Grimm 2014:147.

2. "SHE LOVES TO BE READ TO"
1. All names are anonymized to protect the identity of participants.
2. Burke and Stets 2009.
3. Stryker 1980:54; Stryker and Burke 2000.
4. Stryker 1980.
5. McCall and Simmons 1978:69–70.

6. When a role identity is formed, it is in relation to another role identity, such as parent-child or teacher-student, as a means of telling us how we should behave (Burke 1980; McCall and Simmons 1978; Stryker 1980). Counteridentities are an important component of interaction because without their presence, the role identity cannot successfully be performed (Burke 1980). Rather, these identities and their corresponding performances are negotiated with other people in an effort to agree on how they will successfully interconnect with one another (Burke and Stets 2009; Stets and Burke 2003; McCall and Simmons 1978). When an identity is formed, it emerges counter to another meaningful identity to create an identity pairing, such as parent-child or teacher-student. These pairings are an important component of interaction because without their presence, we would struggle to understand how to behave in relation to other actors. As a result, these identities and their corresponding performances are negotiated with other people in an effort to agree on how they will successfully interconnect with one another. Using the parent-child pairing as an example, an actor's perception of themselves as a parent means that they have also defined the child as occupying that counterstatus. The person's expectation of how a child should act drives their own behavior as a parent. The same is true for the child's interpretation of how the parent should act. A person who performs the parent identity can, presumably, only effectively do so in the presence of another actor who is perceived as child. For example, imagine a couple out on a date. If one of the two enacts the parent identity as a counter to romantic partner, things get really weird and inappropriate, really fast. The expectations associated with these two identities do not counter each other properly, resulting in confusion, aggravation, and ultimately the dissolution of interaction (assuming that a more appropriate set of identity pairings is not negotiated between the actors first).

7. Burke and Stets 2009; Stets 2006; Stryker and Burke 2000; Stryker 1980. Sheldon Stryker (1980:57), a pioneer of both structural symbolic interaction and identity theory, noted that these statuses, or positions, are "symbols for the kinds of persons it is possible to be in society" and "like other symbolic categories . . . serve to cue behavior and [predict] behavior of persons who are placed into a category." While Stryker's (1980:59) elaboration on the definition of self as being dependent on "socially recognized categories and corresponding roles" of other human social actors is implied, the focus on symbolic systems as spheres of meaning making makes the focus on human interaction explicit. In identity theory, the meaning that comes from shared language allows a human interpretation of the social environment. That is, people see the physical world through the symbolic lens of language that only the human can develop. Ultimately, this is all predicated on the uniqueness of human-to-human interaction. Of course, this reflects the traditional interactionist stance on animals as incapable of symbolic interaction because they lack the language inherent in human culture to do so (Mead 1967). It also draws from Blumer's (1969:10) position that animals are in the same human-derived category as "physical objects, such as chairs, trees, or bicycles" while

humans are in the privileged category of "social objects, such as students, priests, a president, a mother, or a friend." Animals, then, continue to occupy a position of irrelevance in the meaning-making activities of the human realm not only for identity theory but also for structural symbolic interaction as a whole. That is, they are insignificant beyond the presence of yet another physical object with which humans pragmatically determine use in social context. For the importance of using sociological analyses to examine human-to-nonhuman animal interaction, see Cerulo 2009; Owens 2007.

8. Alger and Alger 2003b; Flynn 2000a; Irvine 2004, 2013; Sanders 1993, 2000, 2003; Young 2013.

9. Mead 1967.

10. Sanders 1993. Irvine (2004:124) has pointed out that the "overemphasis on language eliminates a considerable amount of interaction as a source of information that contributes to selfhood." Facial expressions, body language, and the "look" on one's face are all forms of alingual communication used by humans (and nonhuman animals) that relay important information about the "other" in interaction. Irvine opposes the Blumerian notion that the animal is the same as any other inanimate object that people may interact with and subscribe meaning to (Blumer 1969). Instead, she argues that there is something distinctive about nonhuman animal interaction that is similar to that of human interaction, and this draws human attention to the fact that nonhuman animals represent a subjective other with which to engage. That is, people see the animal as having a mind, intention, and desire in much the same way that the human does. Indeed, I argue that it is this sense of the subjective presence of other that would facilitate clear-cut identity formation (e.g., parent) related to human-animal interaction, even when culturally approved counterstatuses (e.g., human child) are not present.

11. Gubrium 1986; Goode 1992; Stern 1985; Sanders 2007.

12. Sanders 2007:323.

13. Arluke and Sanders 1996.

14. Owens 2007.

15. Jerolmack 2009. This approach depends heavily on Goffman's "useable others" (1986:43) to explain how the appearance of play between humans and animals is really a result of human capacity for assuming that a mutuality (or shared definition of the situation) exists between themselves and their animals. Indeed, Jerolmack argues that debating whether humans and animals have a shared understanding of social situations is moot, as empirical evidence of the animal self is probably impossible to ascertain. Furthermore, he notes that, in keeping with Goffman's (1986) con artist, it is far more possible that the perception of play in a situation by one actor is understood as something totally different by another—suggesting that just because there is interaction between human and animal, this does not automatically imply that a shared meaning of the situation between actors exists.

16. Jerolmack 2009:380.

17. Identity theory does leave room for this position by asserting that role identity has two dimensions, conventional and idiosyncratic (McCall and Simmons 1978). The conventional dimension is reflected in the meanings that people derive from cultural expectations. But role identity is also informed by an idiosyncratic component that allows each person their own interpretation, within certain identity boundaries, once internalized (Burke 1980; McCall and Simmons 1978). Differences between people can result in how identities are performed—one may interpret "student" as being academically rigorous, while another interprets it as being sociable and going out with friends (Burke and Stets 2009). Likewise, one may define "sibling" as "a playful, aggravating, but loving human of the same generation who has grown up with me in the same family with the same parent(s)," while another may see the sibling as a "playful, loving, protective dog who has grown up alongside me and juxtaposed against my parents."

18. The data discussed in the chapter traverses two types of families in which human children are not present—childfree and childless families. The distinction that I and other scholars draw between these two groups rests on two different variables: choice and fertility status. The term "childfree" refers to a single person or couple who have voluntarily chosen to either completely opt out of or intentionally delay having human children until a later time in their life course. They are physiologically capable of having children but choose not to. Alternatively, the term "childless" here refers to persons who desire to have human children, either now or in the future, but are unable to due to either their own or their partner's infertility (in some cases, both may be unable to conceive).

19. Burke and Stets 2009:49.

20. This is probably due to a connectedness that arises between human and companion animal because of in-depth interactions in which humans attribute agency to the animal (Charles 2014; Irvine 2004). Furthermore, I use Sanders's (1993:207) proposition that "doing mind" arises from shared experience and the development of meaning structure between the lingual human and alingual nonhuman animal. I assume that a recognizable parent identity will develop in the human actor as a result of this practice. The characteristics of this role identity are rooted in the parent identity literature (Alvy 1987; Maurer, Pleck, and Rane 2001; Pleck and Stueve 2004; Simon 1997; Small and Eastman 1991; Stueve and Pleck 2001) and motherhood literature (Bobel 2001; Hays 1998; Ruddick 1994).

21. Feeney et al. 2001.

22. Mueller and Yoder 1999; Park 2002, 2005; Scott 2009; Veevers 1980.

23. Mueller and Yoder 1999; Veevers 1980.

24. Simon 1997.

25. Mueller and Yoder 1999; Park 2002.

26. Russo 1976.

27. Blackstone 2019; Scott 2009; Veevers 1980.

28. Scott 2009.

29. Lampman and Dowling-Guyer 1995.

30. Basten 2009; Walsh 2009.
31. Albert and Bulcroft 1988; Carmichael and Whittaker 2007; Greenebaum 2004; Hirschman 1994; Veevers 1980.
32. Turner 2005.
33. Alvy 1987; Maurer, Pleck, and Rane 2001; Pleck and Stueve 2004; Simon 1997; Small and Eastman 1991; Stueve and Pleck 2001.
34. Hays 1998.
35. Bobel 2001.
36. Ruddick 1995.
37. Specifically, I interpreted the "caregiving" domain as behavior involved with physical and emotional care. Three key categories emerged here: in-depth health care, protection (both physical and emotional), and night care. For "parental relationship with the child," I considered any substantive discussion of one's animal as a child, son, or daughter, beyond the superficial labeling of the animal as such, as evidence of the parent's relationship with the child. Following Burke and Stets (2009), I assumed that participants' report of these types of behavior indicated the presence of an internalized parent identity. "Life modification" included any activity in which the participant had actively modified, or planned to modify, their own life trajectory for the sake of the animal, such as ending relationships or planning future career trajectories with the animal in mind.
38. Alvy 1987.
39. Ezzo and Bucknam 2012; Ferber 2006; Gethin and MacGregor 2011; Pantley 2002.
40. Sanders 1993.
41. Shaheen 2019.
42. Wyness 1997:304.
43. Milkie et al. 2010.
44. Franchise Chatter 2019.
45. Williams 2020.
46. Franchise Chatter 2019.
47. As Stueve and Pleck (2001) note, promoting childhood development is a key parental domain and one that is expected of the parent identity in American culture. Alvy (1987) notes that parents are expected to guide cognitive, social, moral, educational, and spiritual development in their children.
48. Chambers and Horn 2010.
49. At the writing of this book, I was able to find multiple mobile apps, targeted to a variety of dog and dog-owner playdate matching needs. For example, Dog Date Afternoon promises to match mate-seeking humans and their canine counterparts. The Bark Happy app allows dogs and their humans to find other dog owners nearby and to locate "dog friendly places and events." Meet My Dog promises to help users find canine friends for their dogs.
50. Pejar 2020.
51. *Daily Cat* 2018.
52. Strauss 1991; Flynn 1994, 1999.

53. Dadds and Tully 2019; Regalado et al. 2004; Barkin et al. 2007.

54. Regalado et al. 2004; Barkin et al. 2007.

55. Indeed, Baumrind (1967, 1971) notes four styles of parenting used with human children: *authoritarian*, marked by strict boundaries with little explanation for violation of those boundaries and marked by physical punishment; *authoritative*, a mixture of firm but loving boundary setting and explanation of infractions followed with consequences appropriate for the violation; *permissive*, a loving environment in which few boundaries are set and consequences are minimal; and *uninvolved*, an environment in which there are no boundaries set and a loving relationship is not present. With regard to parenting styles related to the multispecies family, Volsche and Gray (2016) have also identified parallels between varying parenting styles and modes of dog training. A very recent study (van Herwijnen et al. 2018) based on Dutch dog-owning parents found that similar styles of parenting exist within owner-dog relationships. While the authors note that they only identified authoritarian and authoritative styles in their sample, they also note that these "dog-directed" styles were due to a population composed of devoted dog owners. While this is not the focus of this book, considering what Lynn notes here, I would suggest that examining discipline, or the lack thereof, within the human–companion animal relationship may open up better identification of permissive styles among animal parents.

56. Newman 2016.

57. Chicone 2015; Yin 2010.

58. Both marriage and children are key qualifiers for being considered family, as is heterosexuality. For example, an unmarried man and woman with children are considered family by 83 percent of people in the United States. However, remove children from the equation, and the percentage of people who agree that this unmarried couple constitutes a family drops to 40 percent. Likewise, a lesbian couple with children is recognized as family by 66 percent of people, while their gay counterparts are accorded this same status by only 64 percent (Powell et al. 2010).

59. McReynolds 2018.

60. STARelief 2020.

61. Owens and Grauerholz 2019.

3. "PHIL'S CALLING GRANDMA"

1. The vet techs and I had agreed that they would let me know when a client was waiting in an exam room and available to consider participation in my research. This typically meant that clients were there for services that would take longer than shots, nail clipping, or ear cleaning. The techs were not supposed to alert me if they simply thought I might find a client interesting, as I felt that this would introduce a form of bias into the fieldwork. But this particular day, the tech did so anyway.

2. Single mothers: Bock 2000; Nelson 2006. Gay and lesbian adoptive families: Bos et al. 2008; Goldberg and Smith 2011.

3. Taylor and Signal 2005.

4. Goffman 2009:9.

5. Childfree: Park 2002; Scott 2009. Pet parent: Greenebaum 2004; Irvine and Cilia 2017.

6. Goffman 2009:9.

7. Scott and Lyman 1968.

8. Kelly 1996; Coontz 1992.

9. L. Stone 2017.

10. Blackstone 2019; Ashburn-Nardo 2017; Veevers 1973; Livingston 2018b.

11. Ashburn-Nardo 2017; Blackstone 2019; Scott 2009.

12. Park 2002.

13. Ulrich and Weatherall 2000; Nachtigall, Becker, and Wozny 1992.

14. Ashburn-Nardo 2017; Park 2002; Veevers 1973.

15. Owens and Grauerholz 2019.

16. Greenebaum 2004.

17. Burke and Reitzes 1991.

18. Alexander and Lauderdale 1977.

19. Burke and Stets 2009; Burke and Reitzes 1991.

20. Cooley 1902.

21. Kinch 1963.

22. Alexander and Lauderdale 1977.

23. G. Stone 1990:143.

24. The issue of *perceived* interspecies intersubjectivity appears to be of concern based on this foundational tenet of identity theory because of the necessity of identity acknowledgment by other social actors present in the situation. However, if we accept that a person can "do mind" for other actors who have no lingual capacity (Owens 2007; Sanders 1993), such as human infants or nonhuman animals, the problem of proof of interspecies intersubjectivity is not as crucial to the placement of an actor as a social object by the counteractor as it might seem. That is, because a person can "do mind" for a nonhuman animal, effectively translating the emotions, intentions, and desires of that animal into language (Sanders 1993), the actor can also *perceive* an animal's acknowledgment of a claimed role identity such as parent in interaction with the nonhuman animal actor.

25. Burke and Stets 2009.

26. Burke and Reitzes 1991.

27. Burke and Stets 2009.

28. McCall and Simmons 1978; Stryker 1980; Burke and Reitzes 1991.

29. Indeed, the relative prominence of an identity in a social situation depends not just on an actor's self-support in that role performance but also on "the degree to which one's view of self has been supported by *relevant* [actors], . . . people whose evaluations and appraisals could be expected to count" (McCall and Simmons 1978:75, emphasis added).

30. Burke and Reitzes 1991; Burke and Stets 2009; McCall and Simmons 1978; Stryker 1980.

31. Charles, Davies, and Harris 2008.

32. See, for example, Reitzes and Mutran 2004; Cherlin and Furstenberg 1985; Troll 1985; Hayslip, Henderson, and Shore 2003; Chapman et al. 2016; Leopold and Skopek 2015.

33. Hayslip, Henderson, and Shore 2003:1.

34. Hank et al. 2018.

35. McCall and Simmons 1978:139.

36. McCall and Simmons 1978.

37. Hank et al. 2018.

38. While only four of the seven empty-nester participants interviewed noted that their adult children both had animals present in their own homes and had developed a parent-child identity pairing related to their animal(s), I mention these four as a means of demonstrating both the influence of grandparental support for the "parent" identity and the reflection of behavior that may signify the presence of a "grandparent" identity in these participants.

39. Burke and Stets 2009:51.

40. Cast 2004.

41. Stryker 1980.

42. McCall and Simmons 1978; Stryker 1987; Burke and Stets 2009.

43. McCall and Simmons 1978.

44. Stryker 1980.

45. Burke and Stets 2009.

46. Burke and Stets 2009.

47. Cast 2004:57.

4. "THEY CALL ME HIS MOMMY"

1. The AVMA provides descriptive statistics on household size (numbers of people living in the household) and household designation. Household designation is either "family" households or "non-family" households. "Family" households are defined as (1) husband and wife with or without children; (2) male householder, no wife, with children or other relative; or (3) female, no husband, with children or other relative. "Non-family" households are defined as (1) male living alone; (2) female living alone; (3) male living with nonrelative; or (4) female householder living with nonrelative. Unfortunately, the survey does not refine the "family" household designation of husband and wife with or without children to further explicate what percentage of married, pet-owning respondents are parents versus those who are not.

2. US Census Bureau 2018a.

3. AVMA 2018.

4. Rowan 2018.

5. Melson 2001; Jacobson and Chang 2018; Walsh 2009.

6. This is a significant point to make based on the widespread nature of this claim about only children and pets. Rowan's (2018) estimation based on the AHS is drawn from family households with children *between the ages of five and seventeen.* This is not a detail to gloss over, as families with children under the age of five (regardless of the number of children) are less likely to be pet owners due to the challenges of navigating having toddlers and companion animals together. The demographic survey data drawn from the CPS on single- and multiple-child families consider all households with children under the age of eighteen. To further complicate the issue, AVMA methodology operationalizes the variable "family households" as households with two spouses present, with or without children. This creates an issue in and of itself, as childfree and childless households are qualitatively different from households with children present. It also may overlook single-parent households.

7. Parker, Horowitz, and Rohal 2015.

8. Melson 2001.

9. US Census Bureau 2018b.

10. AVMA 2018.

11. Henderson 2013.

12. Another statistical issue arises with even this claim (and the sibling claim earlier), however. Readers here may have noticed that varying sources of data (from the AVMA to the APPA to the AHS to the Harris Poll and Pew Research Center) appear to report different rates of ownership and inclusion as family members. Brulliard and Clement (2019) have compared four distinct data sources (AVMA, APPA, Simmons National Consumer Survey, and AHS) to explain why this is the case. Of course, the answer lies in distinct (and disparate) statistical and methodological designs. For example, both the AVMA and APPA surveys are online, which presents both a self-selection bias in the data and a problem with accessing a representative population for analysis. Indeed, accessing a distinct, digitally present population may well mean sacrificing data from respondents in the lower strata of socioeconomic status (read: poorer households may not be adequately represented or statistically weighted for in analysis). In contrast, the Simmons survey contacts people by phone and mail via a randomly generated list taken from a database of addresses from the US Postal Service. Alternatively, the AHS sends US Census Bureau field representatives out to interview a nationally representative sample of respondents in person (or over the phone) about the housing units in which they live. The survey is both cohort and longitudinal in nature, meaning that data are collected from the same geographic location (the housing unit) every two years in order to follow trends in housing changes. What all of these methodological differences add up to is the inability to make statistical claims that go beyond comparing apples and oranges (such as total families with two parents present and total families with two parents present that also own a pet).

13. Endenburg 1995; Fifield and Forsyth 1999.
14. Albert and Bulcroft 1988; Maharaj and Haney 2015; Walsh 2009.
15. Melson 2001; Walsh 2009.
16. Solomon 2010.
17. Paul and Serpell 1993.
18. Melson 2001.
19. Hacker 2003; Livingston 2019.
20. Lareau 2003.
21. Melson 2001.
22. Rost and Hartmann 1994.
23. Melson 2001.
24. Jacobson and Chang 2018.
25. Daly and Morton 2003.
26. Daly and Morton 2006.
27. Jacobson and Chang 2018.
28. Daly and Morton 2009. The Empathy Quotient is a psychological inventory containing sixty items that has been designed to measure empathy in adults. One of its many uses is to aid in diagnoses of autism—a disorder marked by impairment of empathy.
29. Taylor and Signal 2005.
30. McNicholas and Collis 2002; Melson 2001.
31. Cassels et al. 2017.
32. Melson 2001:49.
33. McNicholas and Collis 2002.
34. Turner 2005.
35. Gadomski et al. 2015; Black 2012.
36. Poresky and Hendrix 1989; Paul and Serpell 1996.
37. Jacobson and Chang 2018.
38. Bureau of Labor Statistics 2017a.
39. Walsh 2009:482.
40. Rew 2000.
41. AVMA 2018.
42. I did not find the lack of insurance unusual given that, in 2018, only 2.3 percent of dogs and 0.4 percent of cats in the United States had owners who have taken out these sort of health policies for them (North American Pet Health Insurance Association 2019).
43. Thorne 1993.
44. Shir-Vertesh 2012.
45. Owens and Grauerholz 2019.
46. Bureau of Labor Statistics 2017b.
47. As an exception, one empty nester shared that, when her now-grown daughter was younger, they paid $4,000 for knee-replacement surgery twice on one of their dogs who had since passed.

48. It is regretful that neither the BLS data nor the AVMA data break down specific spending on veterinarian visits by family type. As noted earlier, the BLS does offer average *household* spending on veterinarian visits. The AVMA offers more specific spending and visit information, such as total veterinarian visits by species, reasons for bringing the pet to the veterinarian, reasons for not taking the animal to the veterinarian, average amount spent, and euthanasia and sterilization visits, but does not break down any of this by household composition.

49. Henderson 2013.

50. The other half of empty nesters in my data appeared to be willing to spend larger amounts of money on their family animals regardless of the presence of children at home. It is important to note that all of the empty nesters with whom I spoke were well educated, were married to their original spouses, and could be classified as upper middle class. This suggests that those who were willing to spend large amounts of money—regardless of the presence of their children—did so because their disposable income allowed for it.

51. Henderson 2013.

52. For members of this group, who often appear to have little reservation about blurring the line between child and companion animal, spending averages $698 per year.

53. McNicholas and Collis 2002.

54. Tipper 2011. In a study comparing two groups of British adults, men and women over the age of sixty and men and women under the age of forty, Charles (2014) found that those respondents in the over-sixty group were far more likely to view their animals in a utilitarian fashion. Older participants remembered animals as "sources of food, working animals, and sometimes they were pets" (720). The distinction between this older group and the younger group, who were far more likely to discuss their childhood pets in terms of kinship, is clearly postmodern in nature, especially with regard to increased awareness of animals as sentient (Irvine 2004). It is also a result, as I argue in chapter 1, of a continued diversification of family in which the multispecies family has thrived in a demographic climate of decreasing fertility rates, decreasing marital rates, and increasing cohabitation that has seen paradigmatic shifts in who counts as family.

55. Charles 2014; Irvine and Cilia 2017; Power 2008.

56. Cultural and social educator and caretaker: Reynolds, Dorner, and Orellana 2010; Ochs 2002. Nonparental social support and companionship: Bryant 1994. Playmate: McHale and Crouter 1996.

57. Charles 2014; Endenburg 1995; McNicholas and Collis 2001; Tipper 2011.

58. Gennifer, a fifty-two-year-old empty nester, recalled how her only child, Holly, instantly attached to their rescue dog, Sola. She noted, "Yeah, they were really tight. [Sola] really loves Holly, and Holly really loves Sola. . . . She [Holly] always considered herself Sola's mom, and she considers me Sola's grandma, which kills me—but whatever, okay?" And while this mother-child and grandmother-grandchild identity pairing only presented itself once in participants' narratives

regarding their human children, it does make me wonder if the potential for a parent-child identity pairing, as with the childfree participants in chapter 3, develops before children become adults out on their own. Likewise, it is possible that the introduction of the grandparent-grandchild identity pairing, as Holly did with Gennifer, acts as an intergenerational primer for future extended family identity formation like that discussed in chapter 3.

59. Melson 2001.

60. Interestingly, Victoria shared later in her interview that her sleeping arrangements with her pets had changed as the number of her human family members grew. "I usually had my dogs or cats in bed with me, . . . but when you have a bigger family and a different dynamic, the purpose my pets served when I was single was more of an equal. But now I have a family. I have a husband, and I have children. Everyone needs to know their place and provide a balanced atmosphere. I can't have an alpha male shoving everyone around or being bossy for that reason." Similar to Shir-Vertesh's experience (2012), Victoria's animals took a step down in status when children entered her familial picture.

61. Fleary and Heffer 2013.

62. Owens and Grauerholz 2019.

63. Bobel 2001; Hays 1988.

5. "THIS IS MY SON ROSENBERG"

1. Shorty Awards 2019.

2. Stryker 1980.

3. Burke and Stets 2009.

4. Single-mother families: Bock 2000; Goldscheider and Kaufman 2006. Single-father families: Goldscheider and Kaufman 2006; Kaufman 2013. LGBTQ families: Dozier 2015.

5. Irvine 2009.

6. Grimm 2014.

7. Arluke and Sanders 1996; Birke, Arluke, and Michael 2007.

8. Schaffer 2009.

9. For more on methods used for this chapter, see the Methods Appendix.

10. Spears, Mowen, Chakraborty 1996; Lancendorfer, Atkin, and Reece 2008.

11. APPA 2020.

12. APPA 2020.

13. Grimm 2014.

14. Grier (2006) notes that birds were the first household pet for whom toys and cages became part of a consumer product lineup. She also points out that the market for these products first began to grow tremendously for dogs during the early twentieth century and was later followed by cat products lining the shelves of pet stores (2006:304).

15. Hirschman and Sanders 1997.

16. McCrindle and Odendaal 1994; Serpell 1996.

17. Grazian 2017.
18. Hirschman and Sanders 1997.
19. Daston and Mitman 2005.
20. See, for example, Hirschman and Sanders 1997; Arluke 1994; Irvine and Arluke 2017; Kennedy and McGarvey 2008; Lerner and Kalof 1999; Spears and Germaine 2007; Spears, Mowen, Chakraborty 1996.
21. Gender and racial boundaries: Arluke 1994; Hirschman and Sanders 1997; Irvine and Arluke 2017; Lerner and Kalof 1999. Building social relationships: Spears and Germaine 2007. Importance of family formation and reproduction: Hirschman and Sanders 1997; Spears and Germaine 2007.
22. Haraway 2008.
23. Berger 2015.
24. I am not suggesting that advertisers have stopped metaphorically anthropomorphizing companion animals in exchange for literal assignments of human identity. The Barkleys ad for Subaru mentioned earlier makes this apparent. For example, Lancendorfer, Atkin, and Reece (2008) make it clear that merely adding an animal to the image increases the chance that the consumer will have a positive reaction to the ad. Rather, I am suggesting that a new category of anthropomorphism has arisen in advertising that assigns literal familial identities to dogs and cats in a way that no longer simply makes the animal a stand-in for humans. Instead, the ads that I explore here depict these animals as legitimately "claiming" these positions within the family.
25. Bobel 2001; Hays 1998; Lynch 2005.
26. Irvine 2004.
27. Hays 1998:8.
28. Ruddick 1995.
29. Lynch 2005:50.
30. Laat and Baumann 2016.
31. The number of advertisements refers to the actual number of ads coded within the sample. "Number of representations" refers to distinct representations of identity within each ad. One ad from PetSmart in my sample contained seven *representations* of mother, resulting in thirty-three representations of the mother identity in twenty-eight ads.
32. Kennedy and McGarvey 2008.
33. Hays 1998; Lynch 2005.
34. Hook and Wolfe 2011; Levant and Wimer 2009; Rossi 1984.
35. Atkinson and Blackwelder 1993; Humberd, Ladge, and Harrington 2015; McGill 2014.
36. Allan and Coltrane 1996; Day and Mackey 1986; Gentry and Harrison 2010; LaRossa 1988; McGill 2014; Pleck 1987; Wall and Arnold 2007.
37. There were five representations of fathers in one PetSmart ad, resulting in fifteen representations in twelve ads.
38. Atkinson and Blackwelder 1993; Humphreys 2016; McGill 2014.

39. Berger 2015.
40. This "cross-coding" is to be expected because an identity never exists in and of itself. Rather, an identity always has a complement. Indeed, this is one of the ways that social actors are able to distinguish appropriate behavior toward other social actors within a situation. When an actor internalizes one identity (e.g., mother or father), there will always be a counter identity used to guide the actor's behavior as well as behavioral expectations for the other actor's identity in the situation. Both the identity and counter identity (which constitute the identity pairing) will always be used to access culturally assigned roles (expected behaviors for that status) in order to guide behavioral output (Burke 1980; McCall and Simmons 1978; Stryker 1980). As a result, it is reasonable to expect a large amount of cross-coding between parental and child identities in ads that directly convey these relationships (meaning both pet and person are present in the image).
41. Lareau 2003.
42. Bornstein 2012; Lareau 2003.
43. Spears, Mowen, and Chakraborty 1996.
44. Kennedy and McGarvey 2008.
45. Leashes are infrequently used on dogs in these ads, with the only exception being if the pair is in a public place such as a running trail or park. Even then, a leash only appears about half of the time. Collars for dogs are present about half the time, while cats rarely have a visible collar on at all. This reflects Kennedy and McGarvey's (2008) findings that leashing dogs in advertising began disappearing in the 1980s because dogs were increasingly being portrayed as generalized family members (without specific identities at that point).
46. The other seventeen ads were coded "friend" rather than "family"—these ads, while depicting a close relationship between pet and owner, convey imagery that suggests friendship. For example, one ad for VetriScience shows a man and a dog in a field dancing with each other, referring to the dog as a "dance partner" in the copy. Another ad, for Ruff Haus Pets, uses copy to refer to a Chihuahua as "best friend." In these cases, I chose to code ads as "friend" most often because the copy either directly labels the animal "friend" or presents a scenario that would typically be reserved for friends (e.g., an ad for Shiner Bock beer that shows a dog lying on a porch next to a bottle of the beer, with copy that says, "Never drink alone.")
47. Taylor, Funk, and Craighill 2006.
48. Shannon-Missal 2015.
49. Cohen 2002; Kidd and Kidd 1989; Martens, Enders-Slegers, and Walker 2016.
50. Shannon-Missal 2015.
51. Shannon-Missal 2015.
52. Lane 2018.
53. Blazina and Kogan 2019.
54. Gentry and Harrison 2010; Wall and Arnold 2007.
55. Sunderland 2006; Tsai and Shumow 2011.

56. Ads coded as "White" included those people whom I visually perceived as either non-Hispanic White or White Hispanic. I discuss methodological implications of visually assigning "race" categories like this in the Methods Appendix.
57. Brown 2002:455.
58. Applebaum, Peek, and Zsembik 2020.
59. Applebaum, Peek, and Zsembik 2020.
60. Elder, Wolch, and Emel 2009:26.
61. Wall 2014.
62. Mayorga-Gallo 2018.
63. Tissot 2011.
64. Drew 2012.
65. Mayorga-Gallo 2018.
66. Parker 2019.
67. Shannon-Missal 2015.
68. AVMA 2018.
69. Shannon-Missal 2015.
70. Volsche 2018:369; Siegel 1993.
71. Siegel 1993; Coren 2013; Greenebaum 2004.
72. Lou 2016.
73. Zasloff 1996; Castelli, Hart, and Zasloff 2001.
74. Albert and Bulcroft 1988; Kidd and Kidd 1989; Kurdek 2009a.
75. Potter and Mills 2015; Mariti et al. 2013; Rehn and Keeling 2016.
76. Taylor, Funk, and Craighill 2006.
77. Shannon-Missal 2015.
78. Andics et al. 2016; Kujala et al. 2017.

CONCLUSION

1. Animal League America 2019.
2. International Street Dog Foundation 2019.
3. Sato Project 2019.
4. Farrell, VandeVusse, and Ocobock 2012.
5. Cherlin 2009; Coontz 2000; Bianchi 2014; Livingston 2018a; Olson 2015; Lesthaeghe 1995, 2010; Lesthaeghe and Neidert 2006; van de Kaa 1987.
6. Franklin 1999; Irvine 2004.
7. Farrell, VandeVusse, and Ocobock 2012.
8. Livingston 2019.
9. Bianchi 2014.
10. Laurent-Simpson 2017b.
11. Smith et al. 2018. While the AVMA and the APPA have been producing nationally representative data sets since 1981 and 1988, respectively, they have not allowed researchers external to their organizations access to the raw data.
12. AVMA 2018; Bureau of Labor Statistics 2017a.
13. Smith et al. 2018.

14. Lesthaeghe 2010, 2014. Others have criticized the SDT perspective, arguing that these demographic trends are isolated to specific regions of the world (Lesthaeghe 2014), that some of the diversification in family was already underway before the purported SDT(Coleman 2004), and that conclusions from the SDT are reliant on cross-sectional rather than longitudinal data (Zaidi and Morgan 2017).

15. Franklin 1999.

16. van de Kaa 1987.

17. McRobbie 2017.

18. Maguire Family Law 2019; *Sky News* 2013.

19. Veldkamp 2009.

20. Evans and Buerk 2012.

21. Animal Medicines Australia 2019.

22. United States: AVMA 2018; Shannon-Missal 2015. United Kingdom: Charles 2014, 2016. Australia: Animal Medicines Australia 2019.

23. Stryker 1980.

24. Stets 2006; Stryker 1980.

25. Sanders 1993.

26. Brewster and Puddephatt 2016.

27. Burke and Stets 2009.

28. McCall and Simmons 1978:102 (emphasis in original).

29. Burke and Stets 2009.

30. Ham 2018.

31. Meijer 2019.

32. Moore 2018.

33. Gottschalk 2010; Martínez 2011; Martey and Consalvo 2011.

34. Martínez 2011.

35. Gottschalk 2010.

36. Wohlleben 2016.

37. Eckerd, Barnett, and Jett-Dias 2016; Lavorgna and Hutton 2019; Redmalm 2015.

METHODS APPENDIX

1. Arluke and Sanders 1996.

2. Jorgenson 1989:13.

3. Jorgenson 1989.

4. Becker 1958.

5. Charmaz 2006:15.

6. One of these veterinarian clinics was the one in which I was also observing exams. Two participants who had agreed to participate in the participant observation also volunteered to participate in an in-depth interview.

7. Albert and Bulcroft 1988; Taylor, Funk, and Craighill 2006.

8. Rubin and Rubin 2011.

9. Rubin and Rubin 2011.

10. Charmaz 2006.

11. Charmaz 2006.
12. Charmaz 2006.
13. Lerner and Kalof 1999.
14. Shannon-Missal 2015; Taylor, Funk, and Craighill 2006.
15. Spears and Germaine 2007; Spears, Mowen, and Chakraborty 1996.
16. Mayo, Mayo, and Helms 2009.
17. Generally: Franklin 1999; Irvine 2004; Grier 2006; Shannon-Missal 2015. Mass-media platforms: Grier 2006; Hirschman and Sanders 1997; Lerner and Kalof 1999.
18. Denton and Deane 2010.

REFERENCES

Albert, Alexa and Kris Bulcroft. 1988. "Pets, Families, and the Life Course." *Journal of Marriage and Family* 50(2):543–52.

Alexander, C. Norman and Pat Lauderdale. 1977. "Situated Identities and Social Influence." *Sociometry* 40(3):225–33.

Alger, Janet M. and Steven F. Alger. 2003a. *Cat Culture: The Social World of a Cat Shelter*. Philadelphia: Temple University Press.

Alger, Janet M. and Steven F. Alger. 2003b. "Drawing the Line between Humans and Animals: An Examination of Introductory Sociology Textbooks." *International Journal of Sociology and Social Policy* 23(3):69–93.

Allan, Kenneth and Scott Coltrane. 1996. "Gender Displaying Television Commercials: A Comparative Study of Television Commercials in the 1950s and 1980s." *Sex Roles* 35(3):185–203.

Alvy, Kerby T. 1987. *Parent Training: A Social Necessity*. Studio City, CA: Center for the Improvement of Child Caring.

American Society for the Prevention of Cruelty to Animals. 2020. "Pet Statistics." Retrieved April 21, 2020 (www.aspca.org).

Andics, Atila, Anna Gábor, Márta Gácsi, Tamás Faragó, Dóra Szabó, and Ádám Miklósi. 2016. "Neural Mechanisms for Lexical Processing in Dogs." *Science* 353(6303):1030–32.

Animal League America. 2019. "International Pet Rescue | Rescue." Retrieved December 2, 2019 (www.animalleague.org).

Animal Medicines Australia. 2019. *Pets in Australia: A National Survey of Pets and People*. Barton: Animal Medicines Australia.

APPA (American Pet Products Association). 2020. "Pet Industry Market Size & Ownership Statistics." Retrieved October 28, 2020 (www.americanpetproducts .org).

Applebaum, Jennifer W., Chuck W. Peek, and Barbara A. Zsembik. 2020. "Examining U.S. Pet Ownership Using the General Social Survey." *The Social Science Journal* March: 1–10.

Ariès, Philippe. 1980. "Two Successive Motivations for the Declining Birth Rate in the West." *Population and Development Review* 6(4):645–50.

Arluke, Arnold. 1994. "'We Build a Better Beagle': Fantastic Creatures in Lab Animal Ads." *Qualitative Sociology* 17(2):143–58.

Arluke, Arnold, Jack Levin, Carter Luke, and Frank Ascione. 1999. "The Relationship of Animal Abuse to Violence and Other Forms of Antisocial Behavior." *Journal of Interpersonal Violence* 14(9):963–75.

Arluke, Arnold and Clinton R. Sanders. 1996. *Regarding Animals*. Philadelphia: Temple University Press.

Ashburn-Nardo, Leslie. 2017. "Parenthood as a Moral Imperative? Moral Outrage and the Stigmatization of Voluntarily Childfree Women and Men." *Sex Roles* 76(5–6):393–401.

Atkinson, Maxine P. and Stephen P. Blackwelder. 1993. "Fathering in the 20th Century." *Journal of Marriage and Family* 55(4):975–86.

AVMA (American Veterinary Medical Association). 2018. *AVMA Pet Ownership and Demographics Sourcebook: 2017–2018 Edition*. Schaumburg, IL: AVMA, Veterinary Economics Division.

AVMA (American Veterinary Medical Association). 2019. "Ownership vs Guardianship." Retrieved November 23, 2019 (www.avma.org).

Barkin, Shari, Benjamin Scheindlin, Edward H. Ip, Irma Richardson, and Stacia Finch. 2007. "Determinants of Parental Discipline Practices: A National Sample from Primary Care Practices." *Clinical Pediatrics* 46(1):64–69.

Basten, Stuart. 2009. "Voluntary Childlessness and Being Childfree." Working paper, University of Oxford, UK.

Baumrind, Diana. 1967. "Child Care Practices Anteceding Three Patterns of Preschool Behavior." *Genetic Psychology Monographs* 75(1):43–88.

Baumrind, Diana. 1971. "Current Patterns of Parental Authority." *Developmental Psychology* 4(1, pt. 2):1–103.

Becker, Howard S. 1958. "Problems of Inference and Proof in Participant Observation." *American Sociological Review* 23(6):652–60.

Berger, Arthur Asa. 2015. *Ads, Fads, and Consumer Culture: Advertising's Impact on American Character and Society*. Lanham, MD: Rowman and Littlefield.

Beverland, Michael B., Francis Farrelly, and Elison Ai Ching Lim. 2008. "Exploring the Dark Side of Pet Ownership: Status- and Control-Based Pet Consumption." *Journal of Business Research* 61(5):490–96.

Bianchi, Suzanne M. 2014. "A Demographic Perspective on Family Change." *Journal of Family Theory & Review* 6(1):35–44.

Birke, Lynda, Arnold Arluke, and Mike Michael. 2007. *The Sacrifice: How Scientific Experiments Transform Animals and People*. West Lafayette, IN: Purdue University Press.

Black, Keri. 2012. "The Relationship between Companion Animals and Loneliness among Rural Adolescents." *Journal of Pediatric Nursing* 27(2):103–12.

Blackstone, Amy. 2014. "Childless . . . or Childfree?" *Contexts* 13(4):68–70.

Blackstone, Amy. 2019. *Childfree by Choice: The Movement Redefining Family and Creating a New Age of Independence*. New York: Dutton.

Blackstone, Amy and Mahala Dyer Stewart. 2012. "Choosing to Be Childfree: Research on the Decision Not to Parent." *Sociology Compass* 6(9):718–27.

Blazina, Chris and Lori Kogan. 2019. "Do Men Underreport and Mask Their Emotional Attachment to Animal Companions? The Influence of Precarious Masculinity on Men's Bonds with Their Dogs." *Anthrozoös* 32(1):51–64.

Blouin, David D. 2013. "Are Dogs Children, Companions, or Just Animals? Understanding Variations in People's Orientations toward Animals." *Anthrozoös* 26(2):279–94.

Blumer, Herbert. 1969. *Symbolic Interactionism: Perspective and Method.* Berkeley: University of California Press.

Bobel, Christina G. 2001. "Bounded Liberation: A Focused Study of La Leche League International." *Gender & Society* 15(1):130–51.

Bock, Jane D. 2000. "Doing the Right Thing? Single Mothers by Choice and the Struggle for Legitimacy." *Gender & Society* 14(1):62–86.

Bornstein, Marc H. 2012. "Cultural Approaches to Parenting." *Parenting, Science and Practice* 12(2–3):212–21.

Bos, Henny M. W., Nanette K. Gartrell, Heidi Peyser, and Frank van Balen. 2008. "The USA National Longitudinal Lesbian Family Study (NLLFS): Homophobia, Psychological Adjustment, and Protective Factors." *Journal of Lesbian Studies* 12(4):455–71.

Brandes, Stanley. 2010. "The Meaning of American Pet Cemetery Gravestones." *Ethnology: An International Journal of Cultural and Social Anthropology* 48(2):99–118.

Brewster, Bradley H. and Antony J. Puddephatt. 2016. "George Herbert Mead as a Socio-Environmental Thinker." Pp. 144–46 in *The Timeliness of George Herbert Mead*, edited by H. Joas and D. R. Huebner. Chicago: University of Chicago Press.

Brown, Sue-Ellen. 2002. "Ethnic Variations in Pet Attachment among Students at an American School of Veterinary Medicine." *Society & Animals* 10(4):455–56.

Brulliard, Karin and Scott Clement. 2019. "How Many Americans Have Pets? An Investigation of Fuzzy Statistics." *Washington Post*, January 31.

Bryant, Brenda. 1994. "How Does Social Support Function in Childhood?" Pp. 23–36 in *Social Networks and Social Support in Childhood and Adolescence*. New York: Walter de Gruyter.

Bryant, Clifton D. 1979. "The Zoological Connection: Animal-Related Human Behavior." *Social Forces* 58(2):399–421.

Bureau of Labor Statistics. 2017a. "Employment in Families with Children in 2016: The Economics Daily: U.S. Bureau of Labor Statistics." Retrieved August 20, 2019 (www.bls.gov).

Bureau of Labor Statistics. 2017b. *Households Spent an Average of $528 on Pets in 2015.* Washington, DC: Bureau of Labor Statistics.

Burke, Peter J. 1980. "The Self: Measurement Requirements from an Interactionist Perspective." *Social Psychology Quarterly* 43(1):18–29.

Burke, Peter J. and Donald C. Reitzes. 1991. "An Identity Theory Approach to Commitment." *Social Psychology Quarterly* 54(3):239–51.

Burke, Peter J. and Jan E. Stets. 2009. *Identity Theory.* Oxford: Oxford University Press.

Cain, Ann Ottney. 1985. "Pets as Family Members." Pp. 5–10 in *Pets and the Family*, edited by M. Sussman. New York: Haworth.

CareCredit. 2019. "What Is CareCredit?" Retrieved October 25, 2019 (www.carecredit
.com).

Carmichael, Gordon A. and Andrea Whittaker. 2007. "Choice and Circumstance:
Qualitative Insights into Contemporary Childlessness in Australia." *European Journal of Population / Revue Européenne de Démographie* 23(2):111–43.

Carson, Rachel. 1962. *Silent Spring*. Boston: Houghton Mifflin Harcourt.

Carter, Bob and Nickie Charles. 2018. "The Animal Challenge to Sociology." *European
Journal of Social Theory* 21(1):79–97.

Cassels, Matthew T., Naomi White, Nancy Gee, and Claire Hughes. 2017. "One of the
Family? Measuring Young Adolescents' Relationships with Pets and Siblings." *Journal of Applied Developmental Psychology* 49:12–20.

Cast, Alicia D. 2004. "Well-Being and the Transition to Parenthood: An Identity
Theory Approach." *Sociological Perspectives* 47(1):55–78.

Castelli, Paolo, Lynette Hart, and R. Lee Zasloff. 2001. "Companion Cats and the Social
Support Systems of Men with Aids." *Psychological Reports* 89(1):177–87.

CDC (Centers for Disease Control and Prevention). 2019. "Adult Obesity Facts: Over-
weight & Obesity." Retrieved October 25, 2019 (www.cdc.gov).

CDC (Centers for Disease Control and Prevention). 2020. "FastStats." Retrieved
May 28, 2020 (www.cdc.gov).

Cerulo, Karen A. 2009. "Nonhumans in Social Interaction." *Annual Review of Sociology*
35(1):531–52.

Chambers, Cynthia R. and Eva M. Horn. 2010. "Strategies for Family Facilitation of
Play Dates." *Young Exceptional Children* 13(3):2–14.

Chapman, Ashton, Caroline Sanner, Lawrence Ganong, Marilyn Coleman, Luke
Russell, Youngjin Kang, and Sarah Mitchell. 2016. "Exploring the Complexity of
Stepgrandparent-Stepgrandchild Relationships." Pp. 101–30 in *Divorce, Separation,
and Remarriage: The Transformation of Family*, Contemporary Perspectives in
Family Research 10. Bingley, UK: Emerald Group.

Charles, Nickie. 2014. "'Animals Just Love You as You Are': Experiencing Kinship
across the Species Barrier." *Sociology* 48(4):715–30.

Charles, Nickie. 2016. "Post-Human Families? Dog-Human Relations in the Domestic
Sphere." *Sociological Research Online* 21(3):1–12.

Charles, Nickie and Charlotte Aull Davies. 2008. "My Family and Other Animals: Pets
as Kin." *Sociological Research Online* 13(5):1–14.

Charles, Nickie, Charlotte Aull Davies, and Christopher Charles Harris. 2008. *Families
in Transition: Social Change, Family Formation and Kin Relationships*. Bristol, UK:
Policy.

Charmaz, Kathy. 2006. *Constructing Grounded Theory*. Thousand Oaks, CA: Sage.

Cherlin, Andrew J. 2009. *The Marriage-Go-Round: The State of Marriage and the Family in America Today*. New York: Vintage Books.

Cherlin, Andrew J. and Frank F. Furstenberg. 1985. "Styles and Strategies of Grandparenting." Pp. 97–116 in *Grandparenthood*, edited by V. Bengston and J. Robertson.
London: Sage.

Chicone, Donna. 2015. *Being a Super Pet Parent: Everything You Need to Know to Foster a Long, Loving Relationship with Your Dog.* N.p.: Dancing Paws.

Cohen, Susan Phillips. 2002. "Can Pets Function as Family Members?" *Western Journal of Nursing Research* 24(6):621–38.

Coleman, David. 2004. "Why We Don't Have to Believe without Doubting in the 'Second Demographic Transition'—Some Agnostic Comments." *Vienna Yearbook of Population Research* 2:11–24.

Coleman, Marilyn and Lawrence Ganong. 2015. "Stepfamilies as They Really Are: Neither Cinderella nor the Brady Bunch." Pp. 343–57 in *Families as They Really Are*, edited by B. J. Risman and V. Rutter. New York: Norton.

Cooley, Charles Horton. 1902. *Human Nature and the Social Order.* New York York: Scribner.

Coontz, Stephanie. 1992. *The Way We Never Were: American Families and the Nostalgia Trap.* New York: Basic Books.

Coontz, Stephanie. 1997. *The Way We Really Are: Coming to Terms with America's Changing Families.* New York: Basic Books.

Coontz, Stephanie. 2000. "Historical Perspectives on Family Studies." *Journal of Marriage and Family* 62(2):283–97.

Coren, Stanley. 2013. "The Truth about Cats and Dogs—by the Numbers." *Psychology Today*, May 14. Retrieved July 19, 2019 (www.psychologytoday.com).

Cowan, Sharon and Jacqueline Hodgson. 2016. "Violence in a Family Context: The Criminal Law's Response to Domestic Violence." Pp. 43–60 in *Family Life and the Law: Under One Roof*, edited by R. Probert. Aldershot, UK: Ashgate.

Dadds, Mark R. and Lucy A. Tully. 2019. "What Is It to Discipline a Child? What Should It Be? A Reanalysis of Time-Out from the Perspective of Child Mental Health, Attachment, and Trauma." *American Psychologist* 74(7):794–808.

Daily Cat. 2018. "Host a Cat Playdate." July 1. Retrieved June 1, 2020 (https://thedailycat .com).

Daly, Beth and L. L. Morton. 2003. "Children with Pets Do Not Show Higher Empathy: A Challenge to Current Views." *Anthrozoös* 16(4):298–314.

Daly, Beth and L. L. Morton. 2006. "An Investigation of Human-Animal Interactions and Empathy as Related to Pet Preference, Ownership, Attachment, and Attitudes in Children." *Anthrozoös* 19(2):113–27.

Daly, Beth and L. L. Morton. 2009. "Empathic Differences in Adults as a Function of Childhood and Adult Pet Ownership and Pet Type." *Anthrozoös* 22(4):371–82.

Daston, Lorraine and Gregg Mitman. 2005. *Thinking with Animals: New Perspectives on Anthropomorphism.* New York: Columbia University Press.

Day, Randal D. and Wade C. Mackey. 1986. "The Role Image of the American Father: An Examination of a Media Myth." *Journal of Comparative Family Studies* 17(3):371–88.

Denton, Nancy and Glenn Deane. 2010. "Researching Race and Ethnicity: Methodological Issues." Pp. 67–89 in *The Sage Handbook of Race and Ethnic Studies*, edited by P. H. Collins and J. Solomos. London: Sage.

Dewey, Caitlin. 2018. "The Surprising Argument for Extending Food Stamps to Pets." *Washington Post*, January 23. Retrieved November 25, 2019 (www.washingtonpost .com).

Dozier, Raine. 2015. "The Power of Queer: How 'Guy Moms' Challenge Heteronormative Assumptions about Mothering and Family." Pp. 458–74 in *Families as They Really Are*, edited by B. J. Risman and V. Rutter. New York: Norton.

Drew, Emily M. 2012. "'Listening Through White Ears': Cross-Racial Dialogues as a Strategy to Address the Racial Effects of Gentrification." *Journal of Urban Affairs* 34(1):99–115.

Duffin, Erin. 2019. "U.S.: Number of Households 1960–2018." Statista. Retrieved October 21, 2019 (www.statista.com).

Durkheim, Émile. 2005. "The Dualism of Human Nature and Its Social Conditions." *Durkheimian Studies* 11(1):35–45.

Dye, Jane Lawler. 2010. *Fertility of American Women: 2008*. P20-563. Washington, DC: US Census Bureau.

Eckerd, Lizabeth M., James E. Barnett, and Latishia Jett-Dias. 2016. "Grief Following Pet and Human Loss: Closeness Is Key." *Death Studies* 40(5):275–82.

Ehrlich, Paul R. 1978. *The Population Bomb*. New York: Ballantine.

Elder, Glen, Jennifer Wolch, and Jody Emel. 2009. "Race, Place, and the Human-Animal Divide." Pp. 21–33 in *Between the Species: Readings in Human-Animal Relations*, edited by A. Arluke and C. R. Sanders. Boston: Allyn Bacon.

Endenburg, Nienke. 1995. "The Attachment of People to Companion Animals." *Anthrozoös* 8(2):83–89.

Evans, Ruth and Roland Buerk. 2012. "Why Japan Prefers Pets to Parenthood." *The Guardian*, June 8.

Ezzo, Gary and Robert Bucknam. 2012. *On Becoming Babywise*. Mount Pleasant, SC: Parentwise Solutions.

Farrell, Betty, Alicia VandeVusse, and Abigail Ocobock. 2012. "Family Change and the State of Family Sociology." *Current Sociology* 60(3):283–301.

Feeney, Judith A., Lydia Hohaus, Patricia Noller, and Richard P. Alexander. 2001. *Becoming Parents: Exploring the Bonds Between Mothers, Fathers, and Their Infants*. Cambridge: Cambridge University Press.

Ferber, Richard. 2006. *Solve Your Child's Sleep Problems: New, Revised, and Expanded Edition*. New York: Simon and Schuster.

Fifield, Sarah J. and Darryl K. Forsyth. 1999. "A Pet for the Children: Factors Related to Family Pet Ownership." *Anthrozoös* 12(1):24–32.

Fleary, Sasha A. and Robert W. Heffer. 2013. "Impact of Growing Up with a Chronically Ill Sibling on Well Siblings' Late Adolescent Functioning." *International Scholarly Research Notes: Family Medicine*, January 28.

Flynn, Clifton P. 1994. "Regional Differences in Attitudes toward Corporal Punishment." *Journal of Marriage and Family* 56(2):314–24.

Flynn, Clifton P. 1999. "Exploring the Link between Corporal Punishment and Children's Cruelty to Animals." *Journal of Marriage and Family* 61(4):971–81.

Flynn, Clifton P. 2000a. "Battered Women and Their Animal Companions: Symbolic Interaction Between Human and Nonhuman Animals." *Society and Animals* 8(2):99–127.

Flynn, Clifton P. 2000b. "Woman's Best Friend: Pet Abuse and the Role of Companion Animals in the Lives of Battered Women." *Violence Against Women* 6(2):162–77.

Franchise Chatter. 2018. "Dogtopia—Average Sales, Cost of Goods Sold, Payroll, Rent, Other Expenses, Operating Profits (2017 FDD)." Retrieved October 23, 2019 (www.franchisechatter.com).

Franchise Chatter. 2019. "13 Best Pet Franchises of 2020 (UPDATED RANKINGS)." Retrieved June 1, 2020 (www.franchisechatter.com).

Francione, Gary L. 2000. *Introduction to Animal Rights: Your Child or the Dog.* Philadelphia: Temple University Press.

Franklin, Adrian. 1999. *Animals and Modern Cultures: A Sociology of Human-Animal Relations in Modernity.* London: Sage.

Gadomski, Anne M., Melissa B. Scribani, Nicole Krupa, Paul Jenkins, Zsolt Nagykaldi, and Ardis L. Olson. 2015. "Pet Dogs and Children's Health: Opportunities for Chronic Disease Prevention?" *Preventing Chronic Disease* 12.

Gauthier, Anne. 2002. "The Role of Grandparents." *Current Sociology* 50(2):295–307.

Gentry, James and Robert Harrison. 2010. "Is Advertising a Barrier to Male Movement toward Gender Change?" *Marketing Theory* 10(1):74–96.

Gethin, Anni and Beth Macgregor. 2011. *Helping Your Baby to Sleep: Why Gentle Techniques Work Best.* Sydney: Finch.

Giddens, Anthony. 1991. *Modernity and Self-Identity: Self and Society in the Late Modern Age.* Stanford, CA: Stanford University Press.

Giddens, Anthony. 1992. *The Transformation of Intimacy: Sexuality, Love, and Eroticism in Modern Societies.* Stanford, CA: Stanford University Press.

Goffman, Erving. 1959. *The Presentation of Self in Everyday Life.* New York: Doubleday.

Goffman, Erving. 1986. *Frame Analysis: An Essay on the Organization of Experience.* Boston: Northeastern University Press.

Goffman, Erving. 2009. *Stigma: Notes on the Management of Spoiled Identity.* New York: Simon and Schuster.

Goldberg, Abbie E. and JuliAnna Z. Smith. 2011. "Stigma, Social Context, and Mental Health: Lesbian and Gay Couples Across the Transition to Adoptive Parenthood." *Journal of Counseling Psychology* 58(1):139–50.

Goldscheider, Frances and Gayle Kaufman. 2006. "Single Parenthood and the Double Standard." *Fathering: A Journal of Theory, Research, and Practice about Men as Fathers* 4(2):191–208.

Goode, David A. 1992. "Who Is Bobby? Ideology and Method in the Discovery of a Down Syndrome Person's Competence." Pp. 197–212 in *Interpreting Disability: A Qualitative Reader*, edited by P. Ferguson, D. Ferguson, and S. Taylor. New York: Teachers College Press.

Gottschalk, Simon. 2010. "The Presentation of Avatars in Second Life: Self and Interaction in Social Virtual Spaces." *Symbolic Interaction* 33(4):501–25.

Gray, Peter B., Shelly L. Volsche, Justin R. Garcia, and Helen E. Fisher. 2015. "The Roles of Pet Dogs and Cats in Human Courtship and Dating." *Anthrozoös* 28(4):673–83.

Gray, Peter B. and Sharon M. Young. 2011. "Human-Pet Dynamics in Cross-Cultural Perspective." *Anthrozoös* 24(1):17–30.

Grazian, David. 2017. *American Zoo: A Sociological Safari*. Princeton, NJ: Princeton University Press.

Greenebaum, Jessica. 2004. "It's a Dog's Life: Elevating Status from Pet to 'Fur Baby' at Yappy Hour." *Society & Animals* 12(2):117–35.

Greenebaum, Jessica. 2009. "'I'm Not an Activist!': Animal Rights vs. Animal Welfare in the Purebred Dog Rescue Movement." *Society & Animals* 17(4):289–304.

Grier, Katherine C. 2006. *Pets in America: A History*. Chapel Hill: University of North Carolina Press Books.

Grimm, David. 2014. *Citizen Canine: Our Evolving Relationship with Cats and Dogs*. New York: PublicAffairs.

Gubrium, Jaber F. 1986. "The Social Preservation of Mind: The Alzheimer's Disease Experience." *Symbolic Interaction* 9(1):37–51.

Hacker, J. David. 2003. "Rethinking the 'Early' Decline of Marital Fertility in the United States." *Demography* 40(4):605–20.

Ham, Becky. 2018. "Personalized 'Deep Learning' Equips Robots for Autism Therapy." *MIT News*, June 27. Retrieved November 26, 2019 (http://news.mit.edu).

Hank, Karsten, Giulia Cavrini, Giorgio Di Gessa, and Cecilia Tomassini. 2018. "What Do We Know about Grandparents? Insights from Current Quantitative Data and Identification of Future Data Needs." *European Journal of Ageing* 15(3):225–35.

Hankin, Susan J. 2009. "Making Decisions About Our Animals' Health Care: Does It Matter Whether We Are Owners or Guardians?" *Stanford Journal of Animal Law and Policy* 2:1–51.

Haraway, Donna J. 2008. *When Species Meet*. Minneapolis: University of Minnesota Press.

Harleman, James. 2015. "The 10 Most Expensive Purebred Dogs Ever." *The Dog People*, Rover.com. Retrieved April 16, 2020 (www.rover.com).

Harris, Scott R. 2008. "What Is Family Diversity? Objective and Interpretive Approaches." *Journal of Family Issues* 29(11):1407–25.

Hays, Sharon. 1998. *The Cultural Contradictions of Motherhood*. New Haven, CT: Yale University Press.

Hayslip, Bert, Jr., Craig E. Henderson, and R. Jerald Shore. 2003. "The Structure of Grandparental Role Meaning." *Journal of Adult Development* 10(1):1–11.

Henderson, Steve. 2013. "Spending on Pets: 'Tails' from the Consumer Expenditure Survey." *Beyond the Numbers* (US Bureau of Labor Statistics) 2(16).

Herzog, Hal. 2010. *Some We Love, Some We Hate, Some We Eat*. New York: HarperCollins.

Hirschman, Elizabeth C. 1994. "Consumers and Their Animal Companions." *Journal of Consumer Research* 20(4):616–32.

Hirschman, Elizabeth C. and Clinton R. Sanders. 1997. "Motion Pictures as Metaphoric Consumption: How Animal Narratives Teach Us to Be Human." *Semiotica* 115(1–2):53–80.

Holbrook, Morris B. and Arch G. Woodside. 2008. "Animal Companions, Consumption Experiences, and the Marketing of Pets: Transcending Boundaries in the Animal-Human Distinction." *Journal of Business Research* 61(5):377–81.

Hook, Jennifer L. and Christina M. Wolfe. 2011. "Parental Involvement and Work Schedules: Time with Children in the United States, Germany, Norway and the United Kingdom." *European Sociological Review* 29(3):411–25.

Humane Society of the United States. 2020. "Adopting from an Animal Shelter or Rescue Group." Retrieved April 21, 2020 (www.humanesociety.org).

Humberd, Beth, Jamie J. Ladge, and Brad Harrington. 2015. "The 'New' Dad: Navigating Fathering Identity Within Organizational Contexts." *Journal of Business and Psychology* 30(2):249–66.

Humphreys, Kristi Rowan. 2016. "Ads and Dads: TV Commercials and Contemporary Attitudes Toward Fatherhood." Pp. 107–24 in *Pops in Pop Culture: Fatherhood, Masculinity, and the New Man*, edited by E. Podnieks. New York: Palgrave Macmillan.

In Defense of Animals USA. 2019. "Guardian Initiative." Retrieved November 23, 2019 (www.idausa.org).

Inglehart, Ronald. 1990. *Culture Shift in Advanced Industrial Society*. Princeton, NJ: Princeton University Press.

International Street Dog Foundation. 2019. "Why International Adoption?" Retrieved December 2, 2019 (www.istreetdog.com).

Irvine, Leslie. 2004. *If You Tame Me: Understanding Our Connection with Animals*. Philadelphia: Temple University Press.

Irvine, Leslie. 2009. *Filling the Ark*. Philadelphia: Temple University Press.

Irvine, Leslie. 2013. *My Dog Always Eats First: Homeless People and Their Animals*. Boulder, CO: Lynne Rienner.

Irvine, Leslie and Arnold Arluke. 2017. "Flamingos and Gender Ideology." Pp. 277–95 in *Flamingos: Behavior, Biology, and Relationship with Humans*, edited by M. Anderson. Hauppauge, NY: Nova Science.

Irvine, Leslie and Laurent Cilia. 2017. "More-Than-Human Families: Pets, People, and Practices in Multispecies Households." *Sociology Compass* 11(2):e12455.

Jacobson, Kristen C. and Laura Chang. 2018. "Associations Between Pet Ownership and Attitudes Toward Pets With Youth Socioemotional Outcomes." *Frontiers in Psychology* 9(2304):1–12.

Jerolmack, Colin. 2009. "Humans, Animals, and Play: Theorizing Interaction When Intersubjectivity Is Problematic." *Sociological Theory* 27(4):371–89.

Jorgensen, Danny L. 1989. *Participant Observation: A Methodology for Human Studies*. Thousand Oaks, CA: Sage.

Kaufman, Gayle. 2013. *Superdads: How Fathers Balance Work and Family in the 21st Century*. New York: NYU Press.

Kelly, Deidre. 1996. "Stigma Stories: Four Discourses About Teen Mothers, Welfare, and Poverty." *Youth & Society* 27(4):421–49.

Kennedy, Patricia F. and Mary G. McGarvey. 2008. "Animal-Companion Depictions in Women's Magazine Advertising." *Journal of Business Research* 61(5):424–30.

Khalil, Shireen. 2018. "This Dog Earns More than You Do, Just by Posting Cute Photos." *News.com.au*. Retrieved June 10, 2019 (www.news.com.au).

Kidd, Aline and Robert Kidd. 1989. "Factors in Adults' Attitudes Toward Pets." *Psychological Reports* 65(3):903–10.

Kinch, John W. 1963. "A Formalized Theory of the Self-Concept." *American Journal of Sociology* 68(4):481–86.

Kujala, Miiamaaria V., Sanni Somppi, Markus Jokela, Outi Vainio, and Lauri Parkkonen. 2017. "Human Empathy, Personality and Experience Affect the Emotion Ratings of Dog and Human Facial Expressions." *PLoS ONE* 12(1):e0170730.

Kurdek, Lawrence A. 2009a. "Pet Dogs as Attachment Figures for Adult Owners." *Journal of Family Psychology* 23(4):439–46.

Kurdek, Lawrence A. 2009b. "Young Adults' Attachment to Pet Dogs: Findings from Open-Ended Methods." *Anthrozoös* 22(4):359–69.

Laat, Kim de and Shyon Baumann. 2016. "Caring Consumption as Marketing Schema: Representations of Motherhood in an Era of Hyperconsumption." *Journal of Gender Studies* 25(2):183–99.

Lampman, Claudia and Seana Dowling-Guyer. 1995. "Attitudes Toward Voluntary and Involuntary Childlessness." *Basic and Applied Social Psychology* 17(1–2):213–22.

Lancendorfer, Karen M., JoAnn L. Atkin, and Bonnie B. Reece. 2008. "Animals in Advertising: Love Dogs? Love the Ad!" *Journal of Business Research* 61(5):384–91.

Lane, Lea. 2018. "Just Out: New Report on American Attitudes About Pets & Their Safety in Cars." *Forbes*, March 23. Retrieved July 17, 2019 (www.forbes.com).

Lareau, Annette. 2003. *Unequal Childhoods: Class, Race, and Family Life*. Berkeley: University of California Press.

LaRossa, Ralph. 1988. "Fatherhood and Social Change." *Family Relations* 37(4):451–57.

Laurent-Simpson, Andrea. 2017a. "Considering Alternate Sources of Role Identity: Childless Parents and Their Animal 'Kids.'" *Sociological Forum* 32(3):610–34.

Laurent-Simpson, Andrea. 2017b. "'They Make Me Not Wanna Have a Child': Effects of Companion Animals on Fertility Intentions of the Childfree." *Sociological Inquiry* 87(4):586–607.

Lavorgna, Bianca F. and Vicki E. Hutton. 2019. "Grief Severity: A Comparison between Human and Companion Animal Death." *Death Studies* 43(8):521–26.

Leopold, Thomas and Jan Skopek. 2015. "The Demography of Grandparenthood: An International Profile." *Social Forces* 94(2):801–32.

Lerner, Jennifer E. and Linda Kalof. 1999. "The Animal Text: Messaging and Meaning in Television Advertisements." *Sociological Quarterly* 40(4):565–86.

Lesthaeghe, Ron J. 1995. "The Second Demographic Transition in Western Countries: An Interpretation." Pp. 17–62 in *Gender and Family Change in Industrialized Countries*, edited by K. O. Mason and A.-M. Jensen. Oxford, UK: Clarendon.

Lesthaeghe, Ron J. 2010. "The Unfolding Story of the Second Demographic Transition." *Population and Development Review* 36(2):211–51.

Lesthaeghe, Ron J. 2014. "The Second Demographic Transition: A Concise Overview of Its Development." *Proceedings of the National Academy of Sciences* 111(51):18112–15.

Lesthaeghe, Ron J. and Lisa Neidert. 2006. "The Second Demographic Transition in the United States: Exception or Textbook Example?" *Population and Development Review* 32(4):669–98.

Levant, Ronald and David Wimer. 2009. "The New Fathering Movement." Pp. 41–60 in *Counseling Fathers*, edited by C. Oren and D. Oren. New York: Routledge.

Linzey, Andrew and Priscilla N. Cohn. 2011. "Terms of Discourse." *Journal of Animal Ethics* 1(1):vii–ix.

Livingston, Gretchen. 2018a. "About One-Third of U.S. Children Are Living with an Unmarried Parent." *Fact Tank* (Pew Research Center), April 27.

Livingston, Gretchen. 2018b. *They're Waiting Longer, but U.S. Women Today More Likely to Have Children than a Decade Ago.* Washington, DC: Pew Research Center.

Livingston, Gretchen. 2019. "Is U.S. Fertility at an All-Time Low? Two of Three Measures Point to Yes." *Fact Tank* (Pew Research Center), May 22.

Lou, JoAnna. 2016. "Pawternity Leave." *The Bark*, April. Retrieved July 19, 2019 (https://thebark.com).

Lynch, Karen Danna. 2005. "Advertising Motherhood: Image, Ideology, and Consumption." *Berkeley Journal of Sociology* 49:32–57.

Maguire Family Law. 2018. "Animal Loving Brits Wising Up to Pet-Nups." Retrieved December 2, 2019 (www.family-law.co.uk).

Maharaj, Nandini and Colleen J. Haney. 2015. "A Qualitative Investigation of the Significance of Companion Dogs." *Western Journal of Nursing Research* 37(9):1175–93.

Mahoney, Martha R. 1991. "Legal Images of Battered Women: Redefining the Issue of Separation." *Michigan Law Review* 90(1):1–94.

Manning, Wendy D. 2015. "Cohabitation and Child Wellbeing." *Future of Children* (Center for the Future of Children, David and Lucile Packard Foundation) 25(2):51–66.

Mariti, Chiara, Eva Ricci, Beatrice Carlone, Jane L. Moore, Claudio Sighieri, and Angelo Gazzano. 2013. "Dog Attachment to Man: A Comparison between Pet and Working Dogs." *Journal of Veterinary Behavior* 8(3):135–45.

Marquand, Barbara. 2016. "Trusts for Dogs? Providing for Pets After You're Gone." *Forbes*, December 1. Retrieved February 21, 2019 (www.forbes.com).

Mars Petcare. 2016. "New Survey Shows Pets Are Social Media's Top Dogs (and Cats)." *PR Newswire*, April 27. Retrieved June 10, 2019 (www.prnewswire.com).

Martens, Pim, Marie-José Enders-Slegers, and Jessica K. Walker. 2016. "The Emotional Lives of Companion Animals: Attachment and Subjective Claims by Owners of Cats and Dogs." *Anthrozoös* 29(1):73–88.

Martey, Rosa Mikeal and Mia Consalvo. 2011. "Performing the Looking-Glass Self: Avatar Appearance and Group Identity in Second Life." *Popular Communication* 9(3):165–80.

Martínez, Nicola Marae. 2011. "Liminal Phases of Avatar Identity Formation in Virtual World Communities." Pp. 59–80 in *Reinventing Ourselves: Contemporary Concepts of Identity in Virtual Worlds*, Springer Series in Immersive Environments, edited by A. Peachey and M. Childs. London: Springer.

Matheson, Kathy. 2011. "Pet? Companion Animal? Ethicists Say Term Matters." *Phys. org*, May 4, Retrieved November 23, 2019 (https://phys.org).

Mathews, T. J. and Brady Hamilton. 2002. "National Vital Statistics Reports." Centers for Disease Control. Retrieved May 28, 2020 (www.cdc.gov).

Maurer, Trent W., Joseph H. Pleck, and Thomas R. Rane. 2001. "Parental Identity and Reflected-Appraisals: Measurement and Gender Dynamics." *Journal of Marriage and Family* 63(2):309–21.

Mayo, Charles M., Donna T. Mayo, and Marilyn M. Helms. 2009. "Pets in Print Advertising—Are We Seeing More of Rover and Fluffy? A Content Analysis of Four Popular Magazines." *Academy of Marketing Studies Journal* 13(1):45–50.

Mayorga-Gallo, Sarah. 2018. "Whose Best Friend? Dogs and Racial Boundary Maintenance in a Multiracial Neighborhood." *Sociological Forum* 33(2):505–28.

McCall, George J. and Jerry Laird Simmons. 1978. *Identities and Interactions: An Examination of Human Associations in Everyday Life*. New York: Free Press.

McCrindle, Cheryl M. E. and Johannes S. J. Odendaal. 1994. "Animals in Books Used for Preschool Children." *Anthrozoös* 7(2):135–46.

McGill, Brittany S. 2014. "Navigating New Norms of Involved Fatherhood: Employment, Fathering Attitudes, and Father Involvement." *Journal of Family Issues* 35(8):1089–1106.

McHale, Susan M. and Ann C. Crouter. 1996. "The Family Contexts of Children's Sibling Relationships." Pp. 173–95 in *Sibling Relationships: Their Causes and Consequences*, Advances in Applied Developmental Psychology 10. Westport, CT: Ablex.

McKinney, Maureen. 2018. "Pet Cloning: Where We Are Today." *American Veterinarian* November 11, p. 1. Retrieved October 23, 2019 (www.americanveterinarian.com).

McNicholas, June and Glyn Collis. 2002. "Children's Representations of Pets in Their Social Networks." *Child: Care, Health and Development* 27(3):279–94.

McReynolds, Tony. 2018. "Food Stamps for Pets?" American Animal Hospital Association, January 24. Retrieved June 1, 2020 (www.aaha.org).

McRobbie, Linda Rodriguez. 2017. "Should We Stop Keeping Pets? Why More and More Ethicists Say Yes." *The Guardian*, August 1.

Mead, George Herbert. 1967. *Mind, Self, and Society from the Standpoint of a Social Behaviorist*. Edited by C. W. Morris. Chicago: University of Chicago Press.

Mediakix. 2018. "Pet Influencers: Top 15 Animals on Instagram Making Social Media Noise." Retrieved June 10, 2019 (https://mediakix.com).

Meijer, Eva. 2019. *When Animals Speak: Toward an Interspecies Democracy*. New York: NYU Press.

Melson, Gail F. 2001. *Why the Wild Things Are*. Cambridge, MA: Harvard University Press.

Milkie, Melissa A., Sarah M. Kendig, Kei M. Nomaguchi, and Kathleen E. Denny. 2010. "Time with Children, Children's Well-Being, and Work-Family Balance among Employed Parents." *Journal of Marriage and Family* 72(5):1329–43.

Moore, Lisa Jean. 2017. *Catch and Release: The Enduring yet Vulnerable Horseshoe Crab*. New York: NYU Press.

Morey, Darcy F. 2014. "In Search of Paleolithic Dogs: A Quest with Mixed Results." *Journal of Archaeological Science* 52:300–307.

Murphy, Raymond. 1995. "Sociology as If Nature Did Not Matter: An Ecological Critique." *British Journal of Sociology* 46(4):688–707.

Mueller, Karla A. and Janice D. Yoder. 1999. "Stigmatization of Non-Normative Family Size Status." *Sex Roles* 41(11):901–19.

Nachtigall, Robert D., Gay Becker, and Mark Wozny. 1992. "The Effects of Gender-Specific Diagnosis on Men's and Women's Response to Infertility." *Fertility and Sterility* 57(1):113–21.

Nelson, Margaret K. 2006. "Single Mothers 'Do' Family." *Journal of Marriage and Family* 68(4):781–95.

Newman, Judith. 2016. "New Self-Help Books for Pet Parents." *New York Times*, September 7.

North American Pet Health Insurance Association. 2019. "Pet Insurance in North America." Retrieved September 13, 2019 (https://naphia.org/).

Ochs, Elinor. 2002. "Becoming a Speaker of Culture." Pp. 99–120 in *Language Acquisition and Language Socialization: Ecological Perspectives*, edited by C. Kramsch. New York: Continuum.

Olick, Diana. 2018. "Millennials Put Pets First When Buying a Home." *CNBC*, August 31. Retrieved June 2, 2020 (www.cnbc.com).

Olson, Randal. 2015. "144 Years of Marriage and Divorce in 1 Chart." Randal Olson's website, June 15. Retrieved March 14, 2019 (www.randalolson.com).

Orwell, George. 1946. "Politics and the English Language." Orwell Foundation. Retrieved June 1, 2020 (www.orwellfoundation.com).

Owens, Erica. 2007. "Nonbiologic Objects as Actors." *Symbolic Interaction* 30(4):567–84.

Owens, Nicole and Liz Grauerholz. 2019. "Interspecies Parenting: How Pet Parents Construct Their Roles." *Humanity & Society* 43(2):96–119.

Pantley, Elizabeth. 2002. *The No-Cry Sleep Solution: Gentle Ways to Help Your Baby Sleep Through the Night*. New York: McGraw-Hill.

Park, Kristin. 2002. "Stigma Management among the Voluntarily Childless." *Sociological Perspectives* 45(1):21–45.

Park, Kristin. 2005. "Choosing Childlessness: Weber's Typology of Action and Motives of the Voluntarily Childless." *Sociological Inquiry* 75(3):372–402.

Parker, Kim, Juliana Menasce Horowitz, and Molly Rohal. 2015. *Parenting in America: Outlook, Worries, Aspirations Are Strongly Linked to Financial Situation*. Washington, DC: Pew Research Center.

Parker, Lynette. 2019. "Who Let the Dogs In? Antiblackness, Social Exclusion, and the Question of Who Is Human." *Journal of Black Studies* 50(4):367–87.

Parsons, Talcott. 1937. *The Structure of Social Action*. New York: Free Press.

Paul, Elizabeth and James A. Serpell. 1993. "Childhood Pet Keeping and Humane Attitudes in Young Adulthood." *Animal Welfare* 2(4):321–37.

Paul, Elizabeth and James A. Serpell. 1996. "Obtaining a New Pet Dog: Effects on Middle Childhood Children and Their Families." *Applied Animal Behaviour Science* 47(1):17–29.

Pejar, Nicole. 2020. "8 Ways to Host the Best Dog Playdate." *PawCulture*. Retrieved June 1, 2020 (www.pawculture.com).

Peterson, Helen and Kristina Engwall. 2019. "'Why Would You Want a Baby When You Could Have a Dog?': Voluntarily Childless Women's 'Peternal' Feelings, Longing and Ambivalence." *Social Sciences* 8(4):126.

Pew Research Center. 2019. "Demographics of Social Media Users and Adoption in the United States." June 12.

Pleck, Joseph H. 1987. "American Fathering in Historical Perspective." Pp. 83–97 in *Changing Men: New Directions in Research on Men and Masculinities*, edited by M. Kimmel. Beverly Hills, CA: Sage.

Pleck, Joseph H. and Jeffrey Stueve. 2004. "A Narrative Approach to Paternal Identity: The Importance of Parental Identity 'Conjointness.'" Pp. 72–92 in *Conceptualizing and Measuring Father Involvement*, edited by R. D. Day and M. E. Lamb. New York: Routledge.

Poresky, Robert H. and Charles Hendrix. 1989. "Companion Animal Bonding, Children's Home Environments, and Young Children's Social Development." Paper presented at the National Biennial Meeting of the Society for Research in Child Development, April 27–30.

Potter, Alice and Daniel Mills. 2015. "Domestic Cats (Felis Silvestris Catus) Do Not Show Signs of Secure Attachment to Their Owners." *PLoS ONE* 10(9):e0135109.

Powell, Brian, Catherine Blozendahl, Claudia Geist, and Lala Carr Steelman. 2010. *Counted Out: Same-Sex Relations and Americans' Definitions of Family*. New York: Russell Sage Foundation.

Power, Emma. 2008. "Furry Families: Making a Human-Dog Family through Home." *Social and Cultural Geography* 9(5):535–55.

Redmalm, David. 2015. "Pet Grief: When Is Non-Human Life Grievable?" *Sociological Review* 63(1):19–35.

Regalado, Michael, Harvinder Sareen, Moira Inkelas, Lawrence S. Wissow, and Neal Halfon. 2004. "Parents' Discipline of Young Children: Results from the National Survey of Early Childhood Health." *Pediatrics* 113(Supp. 5):1952–58.

Rehn, Therese and Linda J. Keeling. 2016. "Measuring Dog-Owner Relationships: Crossing Boundaries between Animal Behaviour and Human Psychology." *Applied Animal Behaviour Science* 183:1–9.

Reitzes, Donald C. and Elizabeth J. Mutran. 2004. "Grandparent Identity, Intergenerational Family Identity, and Well-Being." *Journals of Gerontology: Series B* 59(4):S213–19.

Rew, Lynn. 2000. "Friends and Pets as Companions: Strategies for Coping with Loneliness among Homeless Youth." *Journal of Child and Adolescent Psychiatric Nursing* 13(3):125–32.

Reynolds, Jennifer F., Lisa M. Dorner, and Marjorie Faulstich Orellana. 2010. "Siblings as Cultural Educators and Socializing Agents." Pp. 107–21 in *Sibling Development: Implications for Mental Health Practitioners*, edited by J. Caspi. London: Springer.

Ritvo, Harriet. 1987. *The Animal Estate: The English and Other Creatures in the Victorian Age*. Cambridge, MA: Harvard University Press.

Rogers, John. 2018. "California Divorce Courts Go to Dogs as Pets Gain Status." *AP News*, September 28. Retrieved February 19, 2019 (https://apnews.com).

Rossi, Alice S. 1984. "Gender and Parenthood." *American Sociological Review* 49(1):1–19.

Rost, Detlef H. and Anette H. Hartmann. 1994. "Children and Their Pets." *Anthrozoös* 7(4):242–54.

Rowan, Andrew N. 2018. *Companion Animal Statistics in the USA*. Washington, DC: Humane Society Institute for Science and Policy.

Rubin, Herbert J. and Irene S. Rubin. 2011. *Qualitative Interviewing: The Art of Hearing Data*. Thousand Oaks, CA: Sage.

Ruddick, Sara. 1994. "Thinking Mothers / Conceiving Birth." Pp. 29–45 in *Representations of motherhood*, edited by D. Bassin, M. Honey, and M. M. Kaplan. New Haven, CT: Yale University Press.

Ruddick, Sara. 1995. *Maternal Thinking: Toward a Politics of Peace*. Boston: Beacon.

Russo, Nancy Felipe. 1976. "The Motherhood Mandate." *Journal of Social Issues* 32(3):143–53.

Sanders, Clinton R. 1993. "Understanding Dogs: Caretakers' Attributions of Mindedness in Canine-Human Relationships." *Journal of Contemporary Ethnography* 22(2):205–26.

Sanders, Clinton R. 2000. "The Impact of Guide Dogs on the Identity of People with Visual Impairments." *Anthrozoös* 13(3):131–39.

Sanders, Clinton R. 2003. "Actions Speak Louder than Words: Close Relationships between Humans and Nonhuman Animals." *Symbolic Interaction* 26(3):405–26.

Sanders, Clinton R. 2007. "Mind, Self, and Human-Animal Joint Action." *Sociological Focus* 40(3):320–36.

Sato Project. 2019. Home page. Retrieved December 2, 2019 (www.thesatoproject.org).

Schaffer, Michael. 2009. *One Nation Under Dog: Adventures in the New World of Prozac-Popping Puppies, Dog-Park Politics, and Organic Pet Food*. New York: Holt.

Scott, Laura S. 2009. *Two Is Enough: A Couple's Guide to Living Childless by Choice*. New York: Basic Books.

Scott, Marvin B. and Stanford M. Lyman. 1968. "Accounts." *American Sociological Review* 33(1):46–62.

Selman, Colin, Daniel H. Nussey, and Pat Monaghan. 2013. "Aging: It's a Dog's Life." *Current Biology* 23(10):R451–53.

Semple, Jennifer. 2018. "State of the US Pet Food and Treat Industry." *Pet Food Processing*, December 28. Retrieved October 23, 2019 (www.petfoodprocessing.net).

Serpell, James A. 1996. *In the Company of Animals: A Study of Human-Animal Relationships*. Cambridge: Cambridge University Press.

Serpell, James A. 2005. "People in Disguise: Anthropomorphism and the Human-Pet Relationship." Pp. 121–36 in *Thinking with Animals: New Perspectives on Anthropomorphism*, edited by L. Daston and G. Mitman. New York: Columbia University Press.

Shaheen, Jennifer. 2019. "Building Trust with Pet Parents through Digital Marketing." *Veterinary Practice News*, February 5. Retrieved June 1, 2020 (www.veterinarypracticenews.com).

Shannon-Missal, Larry. 2015. "More than Ever, Pets Are Members of the Family." Harris Poll, July 16. Retrieved January 28, 2020 (https://theharrispoll.com).

Shir-Vertesh, Dafna. 2012. "'Flexible Personhood': Loving Animals as Family Members in Israel." *American Anthropologist* 114(3):420–32.

Shorty Awards. 2019. "Friends Are Waiting—The Shorty Awards." Retrieved June 11, 2019 (http://shortyawards.com).

Siegel, Judith M. 1993. "Companion Animals: In Sickness and in Health." *Journal of Social Issues* 49(1):157–67.

Siegel, Judith M. 1995. "Pet Ownership and the Importance of Pets among Adolescents." *Anthrozoös* 8(4):217–23.

Simon, Robin W. 1997. "The Meanings Individuals Attach to Role Identities and Their Implications for Mental Health." *Journal of Health and Social Behavior* 38:256–74.

Simpson, Ian. 2018. "Kansas Lawmakers Pass Adoption Bill Critics Say Biased against Gay Couples." *Reuters*, May 4.

Sky News. 2013. "Pets Considered Part of the Family, Census Shows." August 25. Retrieved December 2, 2019 (https://news.sky.com).

Small, Stephen A. and Gay Eastman. 1991. "Rearing Adolescents in Contemporary Society: A Conceptual Framework for Understanding the Responsibilities and Needs of Parents." *Family Relations* 40(4):455–62.

Smith, Dorothy. 1993. "The Standard North American Family: SNAF as an Ideological Code." *Journal of Family Issues* 14(1):50–65.

Smith, Tom W., Michael Davern, Jeremy Freese, and Stephen Morgan. 2018. *General Social Surveys, 1972–2018* [machine-readable data file]. Chicago: National Opinion Research Center (NORC) at the University of Chicago (https://gss.norc.org).

Smock, Pamela J. and Fiona Rose Greenland. 2010. "Diversity in Pathways to Parenthood: Patterns, Implications, and Emerging Research Directions." *Journal of Marriage and Family* 72(3):576–93.

Solomon, Olga. 2010. "What a Dog Can Do: Children with Autism and Therapy Dogs in Social Interaction." *Ethos* 38(1):143–66.

Spears, Nancy E. and Richard Germaine. 2007. "1900–2000 in Review: The Shifting Role and Face of Animals in Print Advertisements in the Twentieth Century." *Journal of Advertising* 36(3):19–33.

Spears, Nancy E., John C. Mowen, and Goutam Chakraborty. 1996. "Symbolic Role of Animals in Print Advertising: Content Analysis and Conceptual Development." *Journal of Business Research* 37(2):87–95.

Springer, Julie. 2019. *The 2017–2018 APPA National Pet Owners Survey Debut*. Greenwich, CT: American Pet Products.

STARelief. 2020. "Pet Food Pantry Application | STARelief." Retrieved June 1, 2020 (https://starelief.org).

Statista. 2019a. "US—Divorce Rate 1990–2017 | Statista." Retrieved May 2, 2019 (www.statista.com).

Statista. 2019b. "U.S. Instagram Users by Age 2019 | Statista." Retrieved June 10, 2019 (www.statista.com).

Stern, Daniel. 1985. *The Interpersonal World of the Infant: A View from Psychoanalysis and Developmental Psychology*. New York: Basic Books.

Stets, Jan E. 2006. "Emotions and Sentiments." Pp. 309–35 in *Handbook of Social Psychology*, Handbooks of Sociology and Social Research, edited by J. Delamater. Boston: Springer.

Stets, Jan E. and Peter J. Burke. 2003. "A Sociological Approach to Self and Identity Thoughts on Social Structure." Pp. 128–52 in *Handbook of Self and Identity*, edited by M. R. Leary and J. P. Tangney. New York: Guilford.

Stone, Gregory. 1990. "Appearance and the Self: A Slightly Revised Version." Pp. 141–63 in *Life as Theater: A Dramaturgical Sourcebook*, edited by D. Brissett and C. Edgley. New Brunswick, NJ: Transaction.

Stone, Lyman. 2017. "Fewer Babies, More Pets? Parenthood, Marriage, and Pet Ownership in America." Institute for Family Studies, November 15. Retrieved May 20, 2020 (https://ifstudies.org).

Strand, Elizabeth B. and Catherine A. Faver. 2006. "Battered Women's Concern for Their Pets: A Closer Look." *Journal of Family Social Work* 9(4):39–58.

Strauss, Murray A. 1991. "Discipline and Deviance: Physical Punishment of Children and Violence and Other Crimes in Adulthood." *Social Problems* 38(2):133–52.

Stryker, Sheldon. 1980. *Symbolic Interactionism: A Social Structural Version*. San Francisco: Benjamin-Cummings.

Stryker, Sheldon. 1987. "Identity Theory: Developments and Extensions." Pp. 89–103 in *Self and Identity: Psychosocial Perspectives*, edited by K. Yardley and T. Honess. New York: Wiley.

Stryker, Sheldon and Peter J. Burke. 2000. "The Past, Present, and Future of an Identity Theory." *Social Psychology Quarterly* 63(4):284–97.

Stueve, Jeffrey L. and Joseph H. Pleck. 2001. "'Parenting Voices': Solo Parent Identity and Co-Parent Identities in Married Parents' Narratives of Meaningful Parenting Experiences." *Journal of Social and Personal Relationships* 18(5):691–708.

Stump, Scott. 2018. "Woman Who Fled Wildfire Returns a Month Later to Find Lost Dog Waiting for Her." *Today*, December 10. Retrieved June 8, 2020 (www.today.com).

Sunderland, Jane. 2006. "'Parenting' or 'Mothering'? The Case of Modern Childcare Magazines." *Discourse & Society* 17(4):503–28.

Taylor, Nik and T. D. Signal. 2005. "Empathy and Attitudes to Animals." *Anthrozoös* 18(1):18–27.

Taylor, Paul, Cary Funk, and Peyton Craighill. 2006. "Gauging Family Intimacy: Dogs Edge Cats (Dads Trail Both)." Pew Research Center, March 7.

Thomas, Keith. 1983. *Man and the Natural World: Changing Attitudes in England, 1500–1800*. London: Penguin.

Thorne, Barrie. 1993. *Gender Play: Girls and Boys in School*. New Brunswick, NJ: Rutgers University Press.

Thornton, Arland. 2005. *Reading History Sideways: The Fallacy and Enduring Impact of the Developmental Paradigm on Family Life*. Chicago: University of Chicago Press.

Tipper, Becky. 2011. "'A Dog Who I Know Quite Well': Everyday Relationships between Children and Animals." *Children's Geographies* 9(2):145–65.

Tissot, Sylvie. 2011. "Of Dogs and Men: The Making of Spatial Boundaries in a Gentrifying Neighborhood." *City & Community* 10(3):265–84.

Troll, Lillian E. 1985. "The Contingencies of Grandparenting." Pp. 135–49 in *Grandparenthood*, edited by J. F. Robertson and V. L. Bengtson, Sage Focus Editions 74. Thousand Oaks, CA: Sage.

Tsai, Wan-Hsiu Sunny and Moses Shumow. 2011. "Representing Fatherhood and Male Domesticity in American Advertising." *Journal of Marketing* 1(8):12.

Turner, Wendy G. 2005. "The Role of Companion Animals throughout the Family Life Cycle." *Journal of Family Social Work* 9(4):11–21.

Ulrich, Miriam and Ann Weatherall. 2000. "Motherhood and Infertility: Viewing Motherhood through the Lens of Infertility." *Feminism & Psychology* 10(3):323–36.

US Census Bureau. 2017. "American Housing Survey (AHS)." Retrieved June 3, 2020 (www.census.gov).

US Census Bureau. 2018a. "America's Families and Living Arrangements: 2018." Retrieved June 3, 2020 (www.census.gov).

US Census Bureau. 2018b. "Families and Households." Retrieved June 3, 2020 (www.census.gov).

US Census Bureau. 2019. "Subject Definitions—Family." Retrieved July 22, 2019 (www.census.gov).

van de Kaa, Dirk Jan. 1987. "Europe's Second Demographic Transition." *Population Bulletin* 42(1):1–59.

van Herwijnen, Ineke R., Joanne A. M. van der Borg, Marc Naguib, and Bonne Beerda. 2018. "The Existence of Parenting Styles in the Owner-Dog Relationship." *PLoS ONE* 13(2):e0193471.

Veevers, Jean E. 1973. "Voluntary Childlessness: A Neglected Area of Family Study." *Family Coordinator* 22(2):199–205.

Veevers, Jean E. 1980. *Childless by Choice*. Toronto: Butterworths.

Veldkamp, Elmer. 2009. "The Emergence of 'Pets as Family' and the Socio-Historical Development of Pet Funerals in Japan." *Anthrozoös* 22(4):333–46.

ViaGen Pets. 2019. Home page. Retrieved October 23, 2019 (https://viagenpets.com).

Volsche, Shelly. 2018. "Negotiated Bonds: The Practice of Childfree Pet Parenting." *Anthrozoös* 31(3):367–77.

Volsche, Shelly and Peter Gray. 2016. "'Dog Moms' Use Authoritative Parenting Styles." *Human-Animal Interaction Bulletin* 4(2):1–16.

Wall, Glenda and Stephanie Arnold. 2007. "How Involved Is Involved Fathering? An Exploration of the Contemporary Culture of Fatherhood." *Gender and Society* 21(4):508–27.

Wall, Tyler. 2014. "Legal Terror and the Police Dog." *Radical Philosophy* 188 (November–December): 2–7.

Walsh, Froma. 2009. "Human-Animal Bonds II: The Role of Pets in Family Systems and Family Therapy." *Family Process* 48(4):481–99.

Ward, Ernie. 2017. "U.S. Pets Get Fatter, Owners Disagree with Veterinarians on Nutritional Issues." Association for Pet Obesity Prevention, August 17.

Weber, Max. 1947. *The Theory of Social and Economic Organization*. New York: Free Press.

Wilkie, Rhoda and Andrew McKinnon. 2013. "George Herbert Mead on Humans and Other Animals: Social Relations after Human-Animal Studies." *Sociological Research Online* 18(4):1–13.

Williams, Mark. 2020. "Pawternity Leave: More Companies Offering Time Off When Employees Adopt a Pet." *Columbus Dispatch*, January 3. Retrieved June 1, 2020 (www.dispatch.com).

Wohlleben, Peter. 2016. *The Hidden Life of Trees: What They Feel, How They Communicate—Discoveries from a Secret World*. Vancouver: Greystone Books.

Wyness, Michael G. 1997. "Parental Responsibilities, Social Policy and the Maintenance of Boundaries." *Sociological Review* 45(2):304–24.

Yin, Sophia. 2010. *How to Behave So Your Dog Behaves*. 2nd ed. Neptune, NJ: TFH.

Young, Robert L. 2013. "Regarding Rocky: A Theoretical and Ethnographic Exploration of Interspecies Intersubjectivity." *Society & Animals* 21(3):294–313.

Zaidi, Batool and S. Philip Morgan. 2017. "The Second Demographic Transition Theory: A Review and Appraisal." *Annual Review of Sociology* 43(1):473–92.

Zasloff, R. Lee. 1996. "Measuring Attachment to Companion Animals: A Dog Is Not a Cat Is Not a Bird." *Applied Animal Behaviour Science* 47(1):43–48.

INDEX

actors. *See* social actors

AdForum, 234

adolescents: early, 40; homeless, 143

adoption, 22, 190, 191, *192*, 193; anthropomorphism and, 177; international, 203; Lynn on, 179

ads: analysis of, 232–36; BarkBox, 179, *180*; Citi credit cards, 189–90; databases for, 234; Dick van Patton's Natural Balance Limited Ingredient Diets dog food, 184, *185*; Glycoflex Plus, 182; Paws4You.org, 177, *178*; Petco, 186, *187*, 188; PetSmart, 175–77, *176*; SPCA San Francisco, 190, *191*, *192*, 193; Subaru, 170, 258n24; Wells Fargo website, 30, *30*

advertising, 171, *173*, 200, 232, 258n24, 258n31; animal involved, 31; animal themes in, 233; anthropomorphism in, 165–66, 167–73, 181, 194; cats in, 198–99; child identity in, 186–93, *187*, *189*, *191*, *192*; companion animals in, 193–94; data collection from, 201, 233–35; familial identities in, 164, 174, 176; father identity in, 181–86, *183*; friendship in, 259n46; gender roles in, 195–96, 235–36; identity pairings in, 174; mother identity in, 174–81; multispecies families and, 174, 190; parent-child relationship in, 235; parent identity in, 184; racial representations in, 196, 198, 260n56; species in, 193, 198–200

affect, positive, 105, 125–27

affection, 51

affectivity, 46

African American community, experience with dogs, 13–14, 197–98

African American veterinary students, 196–97

age, for childbirth, 22

agency, animal, 44–46

aging, 32

agreement, working, 109

AHS. *See* American Housing Survey

Alger, Janet and Steven, 12

Alicia (veterinarian), 58

alingual communication, 9, 65, 212, 243n70, 248n10

alternative treatments, 153

Amanda (child), 158, *159*

Amanda (interviewee), 90, 145

American culture, 27

American Housing Survey (AHS), 133, 254n12

American Pet Products Association (APPA), 34, 35, 254n12

American Veterinary Medical Association (AVMA), 19, 34, 35, 133, 240n5, 254n12

analysis, of ads, 232–36. *See also* data analysis

animal agency, 44–46

animal birthday, 40–41

animal boarding, 70

animal bonds, 81

animal capital, 18, 45, 47, 172–73, 189

animal car seat, 75

animal child: life modification for, 82–86, 250n37; parental relationship with, 81–82; prioritization of, 85

ABOUT THE AUTHOR

Andrea Laurent-Simpson is Lecturer in the Department of Sociology at Southern Methodist University.